Redemption, Then and Now

MENORAH

REDEMPTION, THEN AND NOW

PESAḤ HAGGADA

WITH ESSAYS AND COMMENTARY
BY
RABBI BENJAMIN BLECH

Menorah Books

Redemption, Then and Now
Pesaḥ Haggada with Essays and Commentary by Rabbi Benjamin Blech

First Edition, 2017

Menorah Books
An imprint of Koren Publishers Jerusalem Ltd.

POB 8531, New Milford, CT 06776-8531, USA
& POB 4044, Jerusalem 9104001, Israel
www.korenpub.com

© Benjamin Blech 2017

Haggada text translated by Jessica Sacks © 2013
Koren Publishers Jerusalem Ltd.

Cover Image: Jordana Klein, "Splitting of the Sea 3"

The publication of this book was made possible through
the generous support of *Torah Education in Israel.*

ISBN 978-1-940516-73-8, *hardcover*

A CIP catalogue record for this title is
available from the British Library

Printed and bound in the United States

Contents

Note to the Reader

For the full Haggada text, with translation and commentary, turn to the other end of this volume.

Preface

The Haggada is overwhelmingly the most printed book in the history of Jewish book publishing. And why, you may ask, is this book different from any of the other countless and extremely important holy works in our tradition? Many people have tried to identify the answer. Let me add mine – as well as the reason why, after more than half a century as a congregational rabbi and rebbe, teacher of thousands of students at Yeshiva University, I chose to add yet another volume to the hundreds available for your Passover table.

My love affair with the Haggada began when I was a child of three. What a remarkable feeling to suddenly become the center of attention at a religious ceremony! As the youngest of those present, I was prepared to be the star of the evening. I was told that without my role, asking four questions, nothing could proceed. My father, a rabbi, needed me! My family and all those seated round the table rejoiced at my participation because, as I later came to understand, through me they felt secure in the survival of our people. Past merged with future. Ancient history was transformed into divinely promised destiny. Our home became the synagogue. Our family and friends became contemporary versions of the twelve tribes joined by kinship, common faith, and mutual hopes and dreams.

And so I absorbed some of Judaism's most important lessons:

- Memory is the gift of the Jews to the world.
- Family is the glue for our national identity.
- Miracles are God's constant reminders of His ongoing concern and involvement.
- Gratitude makes sense of our past and creates a vision for tomorrow.
- Asking questions is key to discovering life's answers.
- And children are our most valuable national treasures – treasures who need to be inspired, to be educated, and perhaps most of all, to be loved.

On Passover night the Jewish nation was born. How fitting that in every generation, Passover and its rituals, the Seder and the Haggada, represent the ideal means to ensure continued rebirth. I became a man at my bar mitzva at the age of thirteen. I became a Jew at my first Seder at the age of three. And to this day the Seder reaffirms my commitment, my joy at being a Jew, and my ongoing gratefulness for Judaism's wisdom and teachings, which not only ennoble but also sanctify my life.

God has blessed me over the years, as a rabbi, to share with many people innovative insights into the Passover holiday as well as the Haggada text. For the longest time, I was urged to make these ideas accessible to a wider audience. The task took over a decade. What is particularly unique about the approach I have taken is the link between the story of old and the miracles of our time, between the promises of the prophets and sages of old, and the incredible fulfillment of contemporary events. The result, I hope, will engender much conversation, discussion, and exchange of ideas, as well as inspiration.

In the spirit of Passover, I dedicate this book to my family – to my wife, my children, my grandchildren, and my great-grandchildren, as well as those who will eventually follow. May they remain true to our faith and continue to celebrate our miraculous survival, as well as our ultimate messianic Redemption.

The Five Most Important Things About Passover

W hat is it about the Jews that makes us so special? Scholars have long wondered why Jews who number less than one-quarter of 1 percent of the world – as Milton Himmelfarb memorably put it, "The total population of the Jewish people is less than a statistical error in the annual birth rate of the Chinese people" – have had such a profound influence on almost every field of human endeavor.

What accounts for the remarkable fact that more than any other minority, ethnic, or cultural group, Jews have been recipients of the Nobel Prize, with almost one-fifth of all Nobel laureates being Jewish? How do we explain our success, our disproportionate contributions to civilization, and even our survival? Perhaps it all goes back to the very beginning of the birth of our people and the Passover holiday.

To my mind, in the context of this beautiful festival we imbibed five major concepts that became our mantras for how to lead successful and productive lives. They are the five most important things to know about Passover – and then to incorporate into every day of the rest of the year. Because we have absorbed them into our national psyche for the thousands of years since the Exodus, we have been privileged to fulfill in great measure our prophetically mandated role to become a "light to the nations." They are our greatest contributions to the world. They are the Passover ideas that have shaped us from the time we left Egypt to the present day. They can be summarized in five words. They are memory, optimism, faith, family, and responsibility.

THE IMPORTANCE OF MEMORY

The Irish Catholic writer Thomas Cahill was so overwhelmed by how the Jewish people literally transformed the world that he authored what proved to become an international bestseller, *The Gifts of the Jews.* One of the major gifts he credits to Jewish genius is the invention of the idea of history. "Remember that you were strangers in the land of Egypt." "Remember that the Lord took you out of the bondage of slavery." "Remember" is a biblical mandate that had never seemed important to anyone else before the Jewish people came on the scene. It was the Passover story that initiated a commitment to memory.

Henry Ford was famous for his belief that "history is bunk." The Ford Motor Company is also famous for producing the Edsel. And both were probably equally stupid blunders. History is the only way we can learn from the past. History allows us to grow by standing on the shoulders of giants. Make a mistake once, and you are human. Never learn from what happened before, and you are brainless. That is why it is so important to heed the famous words of George Santayana that "those who do not learn from the past are condemned to repeat it."

We know how horrible it can be to live without a personal memory of preceding events. For an individual, we have a name for it that fills us with terror: Alzheimer's. It is a disease we fear perhaps even more than death because it leaves us living corpses. Strangely enough, we do not have a similar word for the condition that describes ignorance of our collective past. Knowing what came before is almost as important in a historic sense as it is in a personal one. Only by being aware of our past as a people can our lives become filled with purpose and meaning. Memory links our past to our future. It turns history into destiny. Learning to treasure it was the first step in our climb up the ladder of greatness.

THE IMPORTANCE OF OPTIMISM

To study the Passover story in depth is to recognize that the most difficult task Moses had to perform was not to get the Jews out of Egypt, but to get Egypt out of the Jews. They had become so habituated to their status as slaves, they lost all hope that they could ever improve their lot. Without hope they would have been lost.

The true miracle of Passover and its relevance for the ages is the message that no difficulty is insurmountable. A tyrant like Pharaoh could be overthrown. A nation as powerful as Egypt could be defeated. Slaves could become free men. The oppressed could break the shackles of their captivity. Anything is possible – if only we dare to dream the impossible dream.

In the story of America's Great Seal, a particularly relevant chapter is the imagery suggested by Benjamin Franklin in August 1776. He chose the dramatic scene described in Exodus, where people confronted a tyrant in order to gain their freedom:

> Pharaoh sitting in an open Chariot, a Crown on his head and a Sword in his hand, passing through the divided Waters of the Red Sea in Pursuit of the Israelites: Rays from a Pillar of Fire in the Cloud, expressive of the Divine Presence and Command, beaming on Moses who stands on the shore and extending his hand over the Sea causes it to overwhelm Pharaoh.

The motto he suggested, words based on the Passover story, inspired George Washington and the founding fathers of the American colonies to rebel against their British oppressors: "Rebellion to Tyrants is Obedience to God."

It was the biblical record of the Exodus that enabled the spirit of optimism to prevail for the followers of Martin Luther King in their quest for equal rights, because they were stirred by the vision of Moses leading his people to the Promised Land. It was the hope engendered by recalling how God redeemed our ancestors that allowed Jews even when incarcerated in Auschwitz to furtively celebrate the Festival of Freedom and believe in the possibility of their own liberation.

The founders of modern-day Israel said they were guided by the philosophy that "the very difficult, we do right away, and the impossible takes just a little bit longer." That optimistic spirit, based on our own miraculous history, is the second great gift we have given to mankind and defines our identity.

THE IMPORTANCE OF FAITH

A pessimist, it has been said, is someone who has no invisible means of support. Jewish optimism is rooted in a contrary notion, a firmly held belief that we are blessed with support from above by a caring God. And that faith in a personal God gives us faith in ourselves, in our future, and in our ability to help change the world. The God of Sinai did not say, "I am the Lord your God who created the heavens and the earth." Instead, He announced, "I am the Lord your God who took you out of the land of Egypt, the house of bondage" (Ex. 20:2; Deut. 5:6). The God of Creation could theoretically have forsaken the world once He completed His task. The God of the Exodus made clear He chooses to be constantly involved in our history and has a commitment to our survival.

Thomas Cahill credits the Jews not only for monotheism but for this additional groundbreaking idea of a divine being with whom we share a personal relationship. This, he points out, is key to Western civilization's concept of personal accountability, conscience, and culpability for ourselves and the rest of the world. For the God of the Passover story, history is not happenstance. It follows a divine master plan. It has a predestined order. The word "order" in Hebrew is *seder* – and that is why the major ritual of Passover is identified by that name. Coincidence is not a Jewish concept. Coincidence is just God's way of choosing to remain anonymous. Faith gives us the certainty that whatever our present-day problems, history moves in the direction of the final messianic Redemption. That is what has always motivated us to believe in progress and to participate in *tikkun olam*, efforts to improve the world.

THE IMPORTANCE OF FAMILY

Passover taught us yet another major truth: the way to perfect the world is to begin with our own families. God built His nation by commanding not a collective gathering of hundreds of thousands in a public square but by asking Jews to turn their homes into places of family worship at a Seder devoted primarily to answering the questions of children. It seems all too obvious. Children are our future. They are the ones who most require our attention. The home is where we first form our identities and discover our values.

More even than in the synagogue, it is in our homes that we sow the seeds of the future and ensure our continuity. No wonder then that commentators point out the very first letter of the Torah is a *beit*, the letter whose meaning is house. All of the Torah follows only after we understand the primacy of family. The world may mock Jewish parents for their overprotectiveness and their child-centered way of life – but they are the ones chiefly responsible for the extraordinary achievements of their progeny. At the Seder table, the children are encouraged to be the stars, and their questions are treated with respect. And that is the first step to developing Jewish genius.

THE IMPORTANCE OF RESPONSIBILITY

One serious question begs to be asked as we celebrate our divine deliverance from the slavery of Egypt. We thank God for getting us out, but why did God allow us to become victims of such terrible mistreatment in the first place? A remarkable answer becomes evident in numerous Torah texts. We were slaves in Egypt – and so we have to have empathy for the downtrodden in every generation. We were slaves in Egypt – and so we have to be concerned with the rights of the strangers, the homeless, and the impoverished. We experienced oppression – and so we must understand more than anyone else the pain of the oppressed. The tragedy of our encounter with injustice was in no small measure meant to prepare us to serve throughout all future generations as spokesmen for those with whose pain we can personally identify. The purpose of our suffering was to turn us into a people committed to righting the wrongs of the world, to becoming partners with God in making the world worthy of final Redemption.

We begin the Seder by inviting the hungry and the homeless to join with us. We conclude the Seder by opening the door for Elijah. It is our acceptance of responsibility to others that is the key to hastening the arrival of the Messiah. From earliest childhood, every Jew identifies with these five powerful ideas that are at the heart of Passover and its message. And precisely because memory, optimism, faith, family, and responsibility have become such vital characteristics of our people, we have been able to achieve far beyond what anyone might have considered possible.

Shabbat HaGadol: History and Destiny

It is to Judaism that the world owes two revolutionary ideas about mankind's relationship to time. The first concerns the past, the second – the future. Every moment of our lives is spent in the present. It is the only tense that is real. What happened before is gone; what will be is unknown. It is not difficult to dismiss both the past and the future as meaningless and irrelevant. That is why recognition of their importance is one of the greatest breakthroughs of intellectual thought.

As Thomas Cahill perceptively pointed out in his best-selling book *The Gift of the Jews*, the very *idea* of history is a Jewish invention. Before the Hebrew Bible, the need to remember the past was unknown. More, it would have been considered a pointless and foolish extravagance. It was the Torah that turned memory into a mitzva. The first revolutionary idea is, then, that the Torah requires us to remember the past.

To this day, the Siddur includes, and some people daily recite, "The Six Remembrances" commanded by the Torah: remembrance of the Exodus from Egypt (Deut. 16:3); remembrance of Receiving the Torah on Mount Sinai (4:9–10); remembrance of the attack of the Amalekites (25:17–19); remembrance of the Golden Calf (9:7); remembrance of Miriam (24:9); and finally, remembrance of the Shabbat (Ex. 20:8).

These are but six specific biblical commandments that make constant demands upon us for reflection. But they do not exhaust the full significance of memory as the key link to our relationship with God. We are a religion rooted in history. Our identity stems from the stories of the patriarchs and matriarchs. Our commitment comes from the covenant agreed to by our ancestors. Our beliefs are shaped by truths transmitted through many generations.

It is no accident that when God chose to identify Himself in the first of the Ten Commandments, He did not do so by way of His role as Creator of the heavens and the earth. Instead He declared, "I am the Lord your God who took you out of the land of Egypt, the house of bondage" (Ex. 20:2; Deut. 5:6). As Rabbi Yehuda Halevi beautifully puts it, our God is a God of history – and only by way of our reverence for the past can we come to properly recognize Him.

This appreciation of history goes far beyond what the philosopher Santayana meant by his famous aphorism that "those who do not learn from history are condemned to repeat it." History is not intended merely to prevent us from continuing to make mistakes. It is to grant life meaning and purpose. It is to permit us to personally grow by standing on the shoulders of previous giants. It is to allow us to hear the messages of sanctity from the past that can transform us in the present.

And it is this almost obsessive relationship with the past that allowed for Judaism's second revolutionary idea about man's relationship to time: the idea that history is responsible for the concept of destiny. History that has meaning implies more than a haphazard series of happenings. History perceived as governed by God must be guided by a divine sense of order. Even as the major mitzva of Passover, the festival that introduced the Jews to the Creator as a God who continues to be involved in the story of mankind, is known as the Seder, so too there is *seder*, order, to the most important events of history.

In short, history viewed through a spiritual lens brings us a vision of destiny – the eventual fulfillment of a divine plan God has in store for His creations. With awareness in the present of the significance of both past and future, we remarkably find ourselves able to live at one and the same time in all three tenses. That is what allows us in some small measure to be similar to God whose four-letter name, the Tetra-grammaton, is a combination of the Hebrew for "was," "is," and "will be."

THE DUAL MESSAGE OF SHABBAT

"Remember the Shabbat day to keep it holy" (Ex. 20:8). The Shabbat commandment begins with a call to memory. It identifies its purpose as the desire to perpetuate the knowledge that "In six days the Lord made heaven and earth, the sea, and all that is in them, and rested on the seventh day; wherefore the Lord blessed the Shabbat day, and hallowed it" (Ex. 20:11). On every seventh day, we are prohibited from creating so that we may confirm the identity of the true Creator. On Shabbat we are to rest, just as God rested on the seventh day. Imitating Him is our weekly acknowledgment of His role in bringing the world into being. The Shabbat is a perfect illustration of how a law rooted in history is meant to bring about sanctity. We need to remember the past in order to live our lives with a true sense of the holy in the present.

But in a striking change from the Book of Exodus to the Book of Deuteronomy, we discover that there is a different biblical rationale given for the observance of the Shabbat as well. The Decalogue appears twice in the Torah. The first time records the words at the time they were given on Mount Sinai. The second time is when Moses repeats them in his parting speech to the nation. Biblical commentators discuss at great length how to reconcile the differences between these two versions, both of which seemingly claim to be a record of the words uttered by God as well as what was transcribed on the two Tablets. Their discussions are beyond the scope of this essay. Suffice it to point out that the Decalogue version in Deuteronomy differs from that in Exodus most markedly with regard to the fourth commandment, about Shabbat, and the reason given for Shabbat observance.

In Deuteronomy, the first word is no longer *zakhor*, remember; it is *shamor*, observe.[1] The rationale for keeping the Shabbat is no longer

---

1. In the Friday night service, this discrepancy is alluded to – and resolved – in the beautiful prayer of *Lekha Dodi,* composed by the great kabbalist Rabbi Shlomo Halevi Alkabetz, by way of the midrashic assertion that "observe" and "remember"

to serve as a reminder for God's having created the world in six days and having rested on the seventh; it is so that "You shall remember that you were a servant in the land of Egypt, and the Lord your God brought you out of there with a strong hand and an outstretched arm – therefore the Lord your God commanded you to keep the Shabbat day" (5:15).

It would seem on the surface that in spite of the different events, the Creation and the Exodus, alluded to in the separate occurrences of Shabbat in the versions of the Decalogue, there is one common denominator: The Shabbat speaks to the need for collective recollection about two major moments of the past. The emphasis is still history. The mitzva of Shabbat revolves solely around memory. But it becomes very apparent from Midrash, Mishna, and Talmud that Shabbat also has another totally different aspect. Shabbat is profoundly related not merely to what was but, perhaps even more significantly, to what will be. It carries within it the seed of a future Shabbat, foreshadowing a World to Come that will be defined by its spirituality and holiness. Shabbat is meant to be observed not just as history but also as destiny.

A midrash relates that at the time when God was giving the Torah to Israel, He said to them, "My children, if you accept the Torah and observe My mitzvot, I will give you for all eternity a thing most precious that I have in My possession." "And what," asked Israel, "is that precious thing that You will give us if we obey Your Torah?" God replied, "The World to Come." "Show us in this world an example of the World to Come," the Jews demanded. "The Shabbat is an example of the World to Come," was God's answer.[2]

The Mishna teaches, "Every day of the week the Levites sang a different song in the Temple.... What did they sing on the Shabbat? A Psalm, a song for the Shabbat day (Ps. 92:1) – a song *'le'atid lavo,'* 'for the Time to Come,' for the day that is all Shabbat rest in the eternal

---

were given "in one act of speech." Both words were recited at one and the same moment, an act impossible for humans but obviously presenting no difficulty for the Almighty. The purpose, as explained further in the Talmud, was to make the legal implications of both words inseparable. Whether this answer is sufficient to explain the far lengthier discrepancy between the two versions with regards to the reason given for Shabbat observance is a matter of serious conjecture.

2. Alphabet of R. Akiba, *Otzar Midrashim*, p. 407; see also p. 430.

life" (Mishna Tamid 7:4). The Talmud reiterates the same concept: The Shabbat, the rabbis assert, is one-sixtieth of the World to Come (Berakhot 57b).

In kabbalistic writings, much is made of this comparison. As the six-day workweek culminates in Shabbat, so too will the six millennia of human history prepare the world for a time of total spirituality and perfection corresponding to the day of completion of Creation. Rabbi Menaḥem Recanati, in his commentary on the Torah (Gen. 2:3), writes, "'And God blessed the seventh day'– The Holy One, blessed be He, blessed the World to Come that begins in the seventh millennium," that is to say, the Shabbat of Genesis alludes to the World to Come. In this he was anticipated by Nahmanides in his comment on the same verse, "The seventh day is an indication of the World to Come that is all Shabbat."

There is a wealth of rabbinic commentary that makes clear that the purpose of Shabbat is more than to serve as a reminder of God's role in the past. It is also a vision of the messianic future, a prelude to the ultimate divine plan for the universe. It has its roots not merely in memory but equally in anticipation; it is based on hope as much as on history. We might well ask where this insight finds expression in the Torah text itself. We have seen that the two sources that offer the rationale for Shabbat observance, the dual versions of the Decalogue, rely solely on events of the past and make no mention whatsoever of destiny. What is it that justifies our viewing Shabbat in eschatological terms as a vision for the future? I would like to offer a suggestion based on a profound idea propounded by Rabbi Yitzḥak ben Rabbi Yosef (Baal HaḤotem), known as the *Semak*, a major French commentator of the thirteenth century, in response to a difficulty presented by a famous talmudic passage.

We are taught that one of the first questions we will be asked when we face the heavenly court after our death is "*tzipita lishua*," "did you [during your lifetime] await salvation?" (Shabbat 31a) It seems we are expected to always optimistically await messianic Redemption. We must live our lives with ever-present hope or be held accountable at the time of our final judgment. The rabbis wonder, if this is such a serious obligation we are expected to fulfill, what is its Torah source? Where are we taught that our belief in God must be wedded to a belief in His role as eventual Redeemer? The *Semak* responds that it is implicit in the very first commandment:

> This is why everyone will be asked after death whether they believed in final Redemption. And where is this mitzva written? We may deduce that from this – the two ideas are interdependent. Just as we must believe that He took us out of Egypt, as it is written, "I am the Lord your God who took you out of the land of Egypt" [Ex. 20:2; Deut. 5:6], and this is a commandment, it also tells us that as I desire that you believe I was your Redeemer from Egypt, so too do I desire that you believe that I am the Lord your God and I am destined to gather you in and to finally redeem you. And so He will help us with His great mercy once again, even as it is written, "and [He] will return and gather you from all the nations where the Lord your God has scattered you." (Deut. 30:3)

The words "I am the Lord your God who took you out of the land of Egypt" are to be understood not simply as a statement of fact about the miracle God had just performed for the Jews whom He saved from the tyranny of Egypt. They are meant as the theological foundation of faith for all future generations. They are what must serve as the key to our relationship with God, rooted not only in gratitude for previous kindness but also in expectation of the fulfillment of divine promises yet to come.

The first commandment, with its reference to the Exodus, speaks *about* the past but also *to* the future. It contains the dual message of history and destiny. With this in mind, we may see in a new light the two different rationales given for Shabbat observance in the variant versions of the Decalogue. The text in the Book of Exodus, basing Shabbat on the act of Creation in which God rested on the seventh day, begins with the word *zakhor*, remember. It is clearly oriented to the past. Its purpose is memory. However, the rationale offered in the Book of Deuteronomy is to codify, on a weekly basis, the deeper meaning of the event recorded in the first commandment. Shabbat is linked to redemption.

That may well be why the Shabbat commandment in Deuteronomy begins with the word *shamor*, generally translated "observe." But in the Book of Genesis we find the word to have a special connotation that resonates with the interpretation the *Semak* offered to explain the first commandment. When the brothers of Joseph despise him for his dreams of rulership, the Torah cryptically tells us, "*ve'aviv shamar et hadavar,*" "and his father kept the saying in mind" (37:11). In his comment on this verse, Rashi tells us that the word *shamar* implies "*haya mamtin umtzapeh matai yavo,*" "he waited and anxiously hoped for the time when this would become fulfilled."

Shamor is connected to the future. The Shabbat commandment in Deuteronomy begins with this word. It emphasizes recognition of God as Redeemer. The two versions of the Decalogue now can be seen as the two sides of the coin representing our relationship to time. The *zakhor* of Exodus is the Shabbat of the past and of history. The *shamor* of Deuteronomy is the vision of the Shabbat of final messianic Redemption and of destiny.

THE THREE *AMIDA* PRAYERS OF SHABBAT

This duality helps us to understand a unique feature about the central prayer of Shabbat. We know that the *Amida*, the prayer in which we stand and speak directly to God, is condensed from its normal nineteen blessings on weekdays to seven on Shabbat as well as on holidays. The first and last sections, each consisting of three blessings devoted respectively to praise and thanksgiving, remain unchanged on Shabbat from their daily recitation. The middle weekday section, however, which is devoted to specific requests, is eliminated; on Shabbat and festivals we feel spiritually fulfilled, unburdened by the need to ask for anything else. Instead of *bakashot*, requests, we substitute one blessing, called *Kedushat HaYom*, identifying the sanctity of the day.

On every day of Yom Tov, the middle section of the *Amida* is the same for Maariv, Shaḥarit, and Minḥa – evening, morning, and afternoon. There is no reason for the words to change. Their purpose is merely to clarify the special nature of the day's holiness. Just as the reason for its sanctity remains constant, so too do the words of the blessing used to identify it. But strangely enough, that is not true for the prayers of Shabbat. The middle section intended to define the day is totally different on Friday night, Shabbat morning, and Shabbat afternoon. Although the blessing's conclusion in all cases is identical, "Blessed are You O Lord who sanctifies the Shabbat," the text leading up to the final phrase highlights a separate idea for each of the three services.

The Friday night prayer begins the *Kedushat HaYom* section with the proclamation that "You [Lord] sanctified the seventh day for Your name's sake as the culmination of the Creation of heaven and earth; of all days You blessed it, of all seasons You sanctified it." That is followed by the three verses from the Book of Genesis (2:1–3) that conclude the biblical account of Creation, beginning with "Then the heavens and the earth were completed, and all their array. With the seventh day, God completed the work He had done." The Creation theme is then expanded upon, leading to the concluding blessing of the Lord for the sanctification of the Shabbat.

On Shabbat morning, in contrast, Creation is no longer the prominent theme; what is stressed is Sinai. "Moses rejoiced at the gift of his portion when You called him faithful servant. A crown of glory You placed on his head when he stood before You on Mount Sinai. He brought down in his hands two Tablets of stone on which was engraved the observance of the Shabbat." This opening is also followed by a biblical quote. It is, however, not from Genesis. It speaks in legal rather than in descriptive language, beginning, "The children of Israel must keep the Shabbat, observing the Shabbat in every generation as an everlasting covenant" (Ex. 31:16). The blessing continues by emphasizing the unique role of the Jews in contrast to the other nations who did not receive the Law as a heritage. It does fleetingly add *"zekher lemaase bereshit,"* a reminder of Creation, but clearly it is the theme of the giving of the Law that is meant to be the main priority.

Shabbat Minḥa, the afternoon service, remarkably ignores both Creation and Sinai. The middle section of the *Amida* has no quote from the Torah to biblically validate its theme. It simply states, "You are One and Your name is One." It is a phrase that clearly echoes the verse from the prophet Zechariah with which we conclude every service: "And the Lord will be King over all the world, on that day the Lord will be One and His name will be One" (14:9). The descriptive section of the day's sanctity has moved from past to future. The first two services of Shabbat recall history; the concluding prayer asks us to focus on our destiny.

In his legal code, Rabbi Yaakov ben Asher, the noted halakhic commentator of the thirteenth and fourteenth centuries known as the *Tur*, takes careful note of the difference between the middle sections of the Shabbat and Yom Tov prayers and explains it as follows:

> And the reason they [the rabbis] decreed three different texts for the Shabbat service, and on holidays they decreed only one [the same] is because these three [Shabbat] prayers were decreed to correspond to the three Shabbatot: "You sanctified" corresponds to the Shabbat of Creation as becomes clear from its content; "Moses rejoiced" corresponds to the Shabbat of the Giving of the Torah, which according to all opinions was given on the Shabbat; and "You are One" corresponds to the Shabbat of the World to Come."[3]

Here we have clear support for our thesis that Shabbat is thematically linked to both past and future. As outlined by the *Tur*, the first two prayers, Maariv and Shaḥarit, link us to the seminal moments of both universal and Jewish history: Creation and Sinai. The concluding prayer, Minḥa, directs us forward to the glorious era that awaits us, a time whose spiritual perfection we were permitted to gain a small "one-sixtieth" glimpse of by way of the Shabbat. Schematically, we might say that Friday night takes us to the very beginning of human history. Shabbat morning brings us a step further with the selection of the Jewish people accepting the covenant to serve as a "light to the nations." Finally, Shabbat afternoon reminds us that history has a goal that includes final Redemption and universal revelation.

THE THREE ERAS OF HISTORY

This tripartite theme of three Shabbatot brings to mind very clearly another famous talmudic passage: "We are taught: We learned from the house of Elijah: Six thousand years is the length of time of this earth. This is divided into two thousand years of chaos [confusion], two thousand years of Torah, and two thousand years of the days of the Messiah"

---

3. *Tur, Shulḥan Arukh, Oraḥ Ḥayyim* 292.

(Sanhedrin 97a; Avoda Zara 9a). The passage takes as its premise a remarkable concept alluded to in the Book of Psalms: "For one thousand years in Your eyes are but a day that has passed" (90:4). The six "days" of Creation prefigure six millennia. According to the Gaon of Vilna, "Each day of Creation alludes to a thousand years of our existence, and every little detail that occurred on these days will have its corresponding event happen at the proportionate time during its millennium."[4]

And just as the six days of Creation described in the Book of Genesis were followed by Shabbat, so too will the six thousand years of history bring to a close the world as we know it, to be followed by a time of total spirituality: "Six thousand years were decreed for the world to exist in accord with the number of days in the week [of Creation]; and the seventh day of Shabbat refers the seventh millennium in which there will be rest and cessation."[5] As Nahmanides puts it, "The seventh millennium will be the Shabbat of the 'World to Come,' wherein the righteous will be resurrected and rejoice."[6]

That is why the Talmud identifies the first two thousand years of history as the "era of chaos and confusion." They are the two thousand years before Abraham discovered God. As Rashi explains, "The 'two thousand years of chaos' ended when Abraham was fifty-two years old. Abraham was born in the Jewish year 1948.[7] When he was fifty-two years old, exactly two thousand years after the Jewish count from the beginning of mankind, he brought back all the souls that he had acquired [converted] in Ḥaran, as stated in Genesis 12:5."[8]

The second two-thousand-year period is identified as the "era of Torah." The Hebrew calendar from the years 2000 to 4000, corresponding to from 1760 BCE to 240 CE, was highlighted by the age of the patriarchs, the Exodus from Egypt, the Giving of the Torah, the entry of the Jewish people into the land of Israel, and the building of

4. *Sifra DeTzeniuta*, ch. 5.
5. Rashi to Avoda Zara 9a.
6. Nahmanides, *Shaar HaGemul*, ch. 58.
7. I leave it to the reader to decide whether there is any significance to the year of Abraham's birth on the Hebrew calendar and its similarity to the date on the secular calendar for the modern-day establishment of the State of Israel.
8. Rashi to Sanhedrin 97a.

the two Temples, as well as the redaction of the Oral Law. The final era, in which we presently find ourselves, is bounded by the years 4000 to 6000, 240 CE to 2240 CE. It has so far included what one may certainly view as the prophetically predicted "birth pangs of the Messiah" – the dispersal of Jews throughout the world, the trials as well as persecution of the long exile, the Holocaust, and finally the ingathering of the exiles to the land of Israel and signs of the beginning of the final Redemption.

Perhaps the three prayers of Shabbat, identified by the *Tur* as the Shabbat of Creation, the Shabbat of Sinai, and the Shabbat of the World to Come, are meant to correspond to the three eras of history preceding the seventh millennium. Shabbat begins in darkness. Its prayer, Maariv, reflects the first two thousand years of history, a world of chaos without the missionizing presence of the first monotheist, Abraham. Its only claim to spirituality is an affirmation of God as Creator of the universe. Its biblical reference is the opening verses of chapter 2 in the Book of Genesis.

Morning brings with it both the light of day and an introduction to the light of Torah, key to the second two thousand years of history. The prayer of Shaḥarit reminds us of Moses and the joy of the Receiving of the Torah. Its biblical reference recalls our obligation to observe laws of Shabbat throughout the generations and to reaffirm our commitment to divine law. It is the paradigm of the middle of the three ages of mankind.

As the day progresses, and Shabbat brings with it higher and higher levels of holiness, we find ourselves drawn closer to the goal of our existence, with the Minḥa prayer reflecting the third two thousand years of history. We dream the dream of universal recognition of God. We dare to hope that we are approaching the fulfillment of the Messianic Era's promise. "You are One and Your name is One." That is the key to the central prayer of Minḥa on Shabbat.

Indeed, the three Shabbat prayers are in accord with the talmudic principle that we are always to "ascend with regard to the holy" (Berakhot 28a). They move us from history to destiny. They remind us that we come ever nearer to the day when the Messiah will bring the entire world closer to the spiritual fervor and joy that we Jews have been blessed with by way of the Shabbat throughout the generations.

These are the very themes we are encouraged to ponder as we prepare ourselves to celebrate the holiday of Passover. The celebration of Passover does not begin on the fifteenth of Nisan. Unlike all the other festivals on the Jewish calendar, Passover is singled out by the special emphasis placed on the Shabbat that precedes the festival. Indeed, it has even been given its own name, *Shabbat HaGadol*, the great Shabbat. It is the Shabbat that serves as a fitting prelude to the Yom Tov that focuses on the merging of these very same three themes – past, present, and future. We recall the Exodus of the past; we relive it in the present, as the Haggada states, "each person must see himself as if he himself had come out of Egypt"; and we pour a cup for Elijah and await the Messianic Era.

How fitting then that on the Shabbat before commemorating our redemption from Egypt, we preface our holiday with special emphasis on the day whose essence on a weekly basis focuses on the very same themes that imbue Passover with its full meaning. Passover is history merging with destiny. Passover is past mingling with faith in messianic fulfillment in the future. And it is on this Shabbat that we read the words of the *haftara* that express this day's ultimate message: "Behold, I will send you Elijah the prophet before the coming of the great and awesome day of the Lord" (Mal. 3:24).

The Three Festivals and Jewish Universalism

Aprofound question has often been raised about the covenant between God and the Jewish people: After Sinai, what does Judaism believe is the nature of the relationship between God and the rest of the world, who rejected His law? Put most succinctly, does God still care about people who refused His commandments or have they forevermore forfeited their right to providential concern?

UNIVERSALISM VERSUS PARTICULARISM

There are two ways in which one might view all of history in the aftermath of the Jewish people's acceptance of Torah. The first is to assume that God, the Creator of the heavens and the earth, sought a people who believe in Him and follow His ways. All the nations of the world, according to the Midrash, were offered the Torah but they declined. They were not willing to live by its restrictions. They felt it too confining for their lifestyles and values. Only the Jews said, "We will do and we will listen" (Ex. 24:7). From that moment on, it was the Jews who became the beloved children of the Almighty. All others exist merely to be tolerated, or perhaps to serve God's grander scheme to simply bring benefits to His chosen people. In this view, non-Jews were written off forever from divine favor. The world only exists for the sake of

Torah; gentiles who do not accept Torah are merely vestigial remnants of ancient times, consigned to eternal divine rejection.

In sharp contrast to this particularistic view, it is possible to believe that even after the covenant at Sinai was sealed between God and the Jewish people, the Creator of the entire world did not renounce hope and confidence in the rest of mankind. Judaism may well have a universalistic vision. After all, it was Adam, progenitor of *all* human beings on earth, who was created in God's image. That makes all humanity one, at least in some measure, with the Almighty. It lends all people on earth divine dignity. It sets humans apart from the beasts that preceded them in the act of Creation. Human existence is imbued with a level of holiness. This spiritual link to the Creator suggests that sin is but a temporary aberration; the refusal of non-Jews long ago to accept a covenant with God represents a failing in the past that will at some point be rectified. All the descendents of Adam must someday agree to live their lives as God had intended. The goal of history must be for Jews to serve as a catalyst for the rest of the world, to ensure that what they grasped at Sinai eventually becomes acknowledged by all of God's children.

Which is the correct interpretation of Judaism and its attitude to those outside of the covenant? The words of Isaiah come immediately to mind. We are to be "a light to the nations" (49:6). Our historically early acceptance of Torah places upon us an obligation to share its beauty with those who were not ready for its truths when first offered to them. Why did God give the Torah in the desert of Sinai rather than in the Holy Land? Our sages explain that God wanted to demonstrate that the Torah does not belong to one nation alone or even to one country. A desert is halakhically designated "a place free for all, without owner, no man's land," or better put, "*makom hefker*," "every man's land." The Torah was not given in the land of Israel, for that would have meant it was to be uniquely the Jewish constitution. It was given in a space owned by mankind equally, for it was intended for all. Its purpose is to turn a world without law – which, by definition, is barren desert – into a blooming, fertile, and productive place for human existence.

Yitro, the name of Moses' father-in-law, is also the name of the biblical portion (Ex. 18–20) in which we read the account of the most important event in Jewish history, the Revelation of the Decalogue. Strange that Moses does not receive the honor of having a Torah portion named for him. Stranger still that the portion has as its title the name of someone who was not even born a Jew, but who only later in life abandoned his false idols and recognized monotheism. Why choose him? Because he is the greatest illustration of what the Torah is meant to accomplish – to transform idolaters into believers, pagans into worshipers of God.

When the Jewish people stood at the foot of Mount Sinai and were prepared to accept the Torah, God defined their mission by telling Moses to instruct the people the following: "Now therefore if you will listen unto My voice and keep My covenant, then you shall be My own treasure from among all peoples; for all the earth is Mine, and you shall be unto Me a kingdom of priests and a holy nation" (Ex. 19:5–6). The commentators are intrigued by the phrase *"mamlekhet kohanim,"* "a kingdom of priests." Surely the Jewish people will not all be priests. The twelve tribes were divided into priests, Levites, and Israelites; most Jews are simply Israelites. Why does God say that the Jewish people in its entirety will become a kingdom of priests? Rabbi Yehuda Halevi explains that even as the priests were to be the teachers and holy leaders for the rest of the Jewish people, so too, the Jews have to become the holy leaders for the rest of the world. That is the meaning of "You shall be My own treasure from among all peoples." Not to be selected "from among" so that all others be discarded. Rather to be the *kohanim* who will ensure that all others eventually follow, for *"all the earth* is Mine."

This universalistic concept is even used by one of the talmudic sages to explain why Jews throughout history have been exiled around the globe. In a daring suggestion, R. Eliezer offers the possible rationale that this seeming punishment may have a totally different purpose: "The Holy One, blessed be He, did not exile Israel among the nations save in order that proselytes might join them, for it is said, 'And I will sow her unto Me in the land' (Hos. 2:25). Surely a man sows a *se'ah* [biblical measure] in order to harvest many *kors*" (Pesaḥim 87b). Jews must spread the knowledge of one God. The existence of the Jews allows for an awareness of Torah in the greater world community.

THE THREE PILGRIMAGE FESTIVALS

In this light we may understand a deeper reason behind the sequence of the three pilgrimage festivals, Passover, Shavuot, and Sukkot. Three major moments are commemorated in these holidays. Passover, the time when the Jews left Egypt, is identified always as *"zeman ḥerutenu,"* "the time of our freedom." Shavuot, referred to as *"zeman Matan Toratenu,"* recalls "the time of the Giving of the Torah" fifty days later. The forty years of wandering through the desert, leading up to the entry into the land of Israel, is marked by Sukkot, *"zeman simḥatenu,"* "the time of our rejoicing."

These descriptives attached to the festivals all recall their historic component. Yet another aspect is also incorporated into every one of them. The historic events of our people coincide with specific seasons. And the agricultural phenomena of these seasons are crucial to the proper observance of the festivals, so much so that whenever we refer to these holidays, we allude to their links with nature as well.

Passover is also called *"Ḥag HaAviv,"* "the Festival of the Spring." So important is this connection that although Jews observe a lunar calendar, we are commanded to insert an extra month in the year if the sages determine that Passover, because the lunar calendar is shorter than the solar, would occur too early and thereby lose its required link with spring. The emphasis on the season in nature in addition to the historic basis for Passover is true for the other two festivals in the series as well. In the Bible, Shavuot is referred to as *"Ḥag HaBikkurim,"* "the Festival of the First Fruits." Farmers saw the first of the harvest ripen at this time of year. They would take their first fruits that bloomed and bring them to Jerusalem. Sukkot, the last in the series, must always occur in the fall so that its agricultural title applies: *"Ḥag HaAsif,"* "the Festival of the Harvest." Spring, first fruit, and harvest are not simply addenda to the historic moments that these holidays commemorate. By way of metaphor, they offer the most profound insight into the meaning of the historic moments they ask us to recall.

To what may Passover best be compared? God finds a people He feels worthy of deliverance. To them He will subsequently give the Torah. They would be bearers of His mission. After the long darkness of historic winter, God's people begin to "blossom." It is spring. God and Israel meet as lovers. The Song of Songs, the love song of Solomon, is read in many synagogues during Passover. But the relationship has not yet borne any fruit. Without Torah, one cannot speak of any real fulfillment. Spring is but the season of promise, projected in terms of budding and blossoming. It is Ḥag HaAviv. It remains for Shavuot, the time of the Giving of the Torah, to metaphorically coincide with Ḥag HaBikkurim. The messages of historic Revelation and of nature's sending forth its fruits are in fact identical. Just as the farmer longs for his fruit to come forth from the seed, so too did God gratefully recognize the spiritual birth of the Jewish people. The world bore its first fruit when the Jews said, "We will do and we will listen" (Ex. 24:7).

Yet that moment of revelation in nature is not the final harvest. It is merely synonymous with the "Festival of *First* Fruits." The agricultural comparison assumes powerful meaning when we note the word used by God to describe His people. At the Burning Bush, God informs Moses that he would one day warn Pharaoh about the plague of the firstborn. The reason for this tenth plague was given: "And you shall say unto Pharaoh, 'Thus says the Lord: My son, My firstborn, is Israel, and I have said unto you, let My son go that he may serve Me. And you have refused to let him go. Behold I will slay your son, your firstborn'" (Ex. 4:22–23).

The firstborn of Egypt were slain, measure for measure, because Pharaoh had harmed God's firstborn, "*beni vekhori Yisrael*," "My son, My firstborn, is Israel." In what sense is Israel the firstborn of God? The commentator Ibn Ezra explains, "They were the first of My children to serve Me." Even as the uniqueness of the Jewish people is expressed in these words, God makes clear that He has many children. He is Father to everyone on earth. What makes Israel special is not that we are His "only" child, but rather that we are His first, the first to acknowledge Him. We are, as it were, the first fruits of the Almighty. How appropriate that the time when the first nation to submit to God as Master and accept His will as law appeared on the scene of world history is the time when nature offers up its annual message of fulfillment by way of *bikkurim*.

But first fruits are not the final harvest. Shavuot cannot be the end of the cycle of festivals. How could God, who created the entire world, be content if only a small portion of humanity is dedicated to Him? History must bring about recognition on the part of all; from first fruits we must eventually proceed to an ingathering of all the crops in the fields, a complete harvest. If Passover commemorates the Exodus and Shavuot the Revelation, then Sukkot speaks of the time that has not yet come to pass, the End of Days that the prophets spoke of with the certainty of their eventual arrival. Sukkot, agriculturally the time of the final harvest, affirms that history too will emulate the workings of nature. The "first fruits" of the covenant at Sinai will eventually be followed by a time of universal acceptance of God, a time for rejoicing in the fullest sense of the word, a *zeman simḥatenu* for all of mankind.

Sukkot is the holiday of universalism par excellence. On this holiday we are commanded in the Torah to offer seventy sacrifices – sacrifices on behalf of all of the nations of the world. The waving of the four plant species are to be directed to the four corners of the earth. We are to leave the confines of our homes that separate us from others and sit in booths under the heavens that look down upon all of God's children. And it is precisely on this holiday that the prophet Zechariah tells us, in the text that has become designated as the *haftara* reading for the first day of Sukkot, that "It shall come to pass that everyone that is left of all the nations that came against Jerusalem shall go up from year to year to worship the King, the Lord of hosts, and *to keep the Feast of Tabernacles*" (14:16). Sukkot will eventually be observed by the whole world because this is the holiday meant to fulfill the joy of the final harvest for God – a joy long delayed and overdue from the Shavuot moment when only the Jewish "first fruits" appeared on the scene at Sinai.

THE UNIVERSALISTIC VISION OF THE *SHEMA*

So important is this idea that according to Rashi, the prime commentator on the Torah, it finds expression in the verse we are commanded to recite twice daily to verbally summarize our commitment to God and our faith. The six words of the *Shema* have been translated in many ways. On the simplest level, "Hear, O Israel, the Lord is our God, the Lord is One" affirms no more than a belief in monotheism. But Rashi (Deut. 6:4) sees much more in this statement:

> The Lord is our God, the Lord is One – the Lord who at present is our God and not the God of the nations, He is destined

to become the One God, as it says, "For then will I turn to the peoples a pure language, that they may all call upon the name of the Lord, to serve Him with one consent" (Zeph. 3:9), and it says, "On that day the Lord will be One and His name will be One." (Zech. 14:9)

The phrase that summarizes our faith, the Torah verse we are to teach our children as soon as they learn how to speak and that, if we have the opportunity to do so, we are to recite before we go to our deaths, does not simply express belief in God. More than it advocates monotheism, it asserts total conviction that at some future time all of mankind will share this knowledge and join us in acknowledging the Creator of the heavens and the earth.

And it is this interpretation of the *Shema* that seems to be the way the Talmud understands it as well. In the Musaf prayer for Rosh HaShana, the rabbis arranged a series of ten verses to confirm the concept of *Malkhuyot*, Kingship, God's role as King and Ruler. The first three verses come from the five books of Moses; the next three from the portion of the Torah known as *Ketuvim*, the Writings; and then three more from the Prophets, followed by a concluding verse once again from the Pentateuch. Each one of these verses is meant to connect, to clarify, and to amplify the meaning of the others. The last quote from the Prophets, and the one preceding the final verse from the Pentateuch, is "And the Lord will be King over all the world, on that day the Lord will be One and His name will be One" (Zech. 14:9). We then recite, "And as is also written in the Torah, "Hear, O Israel…the Lord is One."

Clearly, the line of the *Shema* is to be understood as a more succinct and shorter version of the verse from Zechariah. Both of them emphasize eschatology, the End of Days, and the universal acceptance of God. So crucial is this connection that many siddurim make note of the custom in numerous communities to follow the recitation of the last line of the *Aleinu*, taken from Zechariah, with the addition of the words "as is written in Your Torah, 'Hear, O Israel, the Lord is our God; the Lord is One.'"

No wonder then that the verse from Zechariah that clarifies the real meaning of the *Shema*, with its confident expression of the eventual fulfillment of the messianic dream, deserves the distinction of ending every one of our prayer services. And no wonder as well that it is the perfect choice for serving as *haftara* for the first day of the festival of Sukkot, the very holiday that eventually all the nations of the world will join us in celebrating. As we celebrate Passover and give thanks for our national beginnings and deliverance, we need to recognize that it is but the first step of the historic journey of mankind. We have already been blessed with the freedom of Passover and the moment of Revelation of Shavuot. What remains is for us to play a role in bringing about the glorious time of universal worship of God, symbolized by the message of Sukkot – the end and goal of the *Shalosh Regalim*.

The Three Festivals and the Three Kinds of Love

Passover is a holiday that does not stand alone on the Jewish calendar. It is part of a trilogy. Together with Shavuot and Sukkot, it comprises the group known as the *Shalosh Regalim* – three festivals that are linked into a thematic unit. The three historic holidays share a number with profound significance in Judaism.

We are all familiar with the penultimate prayer of the Haggada that alerts us to the connection between numbers and concepts. "Who knows one?" asks the text, and responds, "I know one: Our God is One, in heaven and on earth." The number two is identified with the two Tablets on which the Decalogue was given. The number three is a reminder of our patriarchs, Abraham, Isaac, and Jacob. The linkage is not meant to be gratuitous. It is the key to a profound insight of our sages: *Numbers resonate with hidden meanings – they are often meant to serve as codes for profound concepts.*

"Three times in the year all your males shall appear before the Lord God" (Ex. 23:17). This verse is the source for the proper observance of the pilgrimage festivals. Three times a year, Jews were commanded to make their way to the Temple in Jerusalem. Three – just like the number of patriarchs. On the simplest level, the link between the *Shalosh Regalim* and the *Avot*, fathers or ancestors, is obvious: The three festivals are meant to commit the Jews to the teachings of their three founding fathers.

But that alone is no more than a superficial understanding of the relationship between Passover, Shavuot, and Sukkot, and the patriarchs. To truly appreciate the intimate connection between them, we need first to analyze another grouping of three that finds a prominent place in the Torah and in Jewish tradition. Its source is the mitzva, recited twice daily as part of the *Shema*, that demands of us nothing less than the total love of God.

"LOVE GOD" – HOW?

"And you shall love the Lord your God" (Deut. 6:5). Biblical commentators long ago recognized the difficulty posed by this vaguely worded commandment. Love, after all, is an emotion. Judaism is primarily concerned with halakha, with deed, and with a way of life. How is love to be transformed into action? What will demonstrate the extent of our commitment? How do we prove our passionate devotion?

The Torah follows the commandment to love God with three phrases: "with all your heart, with all your soul, and with all your wealth." Here is a start to resolving our inquiry. But for clarity we need more than words. Ideally, we would be served best by illustrations. *And because the number of phrases meant to shed light on our responsibility is three, we have our first clue to the way we are meant to fulfill the mitzva of love of God.*

The three phrases – "with all your heart, with all your soul, and with all your wealth" – correspond to the three ways in which the patriarchs demonstrated their complete commitment to God. As the *Tur* brilliantly points out, *ve'ahavta* (spelled *vav, aleph, heh, beit, tav*), the Hebrew word for "and you shall love," is with but a slight rearrangement of its letters the same as *HaAvot* (*heh, aleph, beit, vav, tav*), the Hebrew word for "the ancestors." This is how the verse in the Torah commandment contains the solution to the problem of its vagueness. How shall we love God? Precisely because the mitzva is unclear, the Torah alludes to three paradigms – the lives of the three patriarchs – to define the ideal love relationship. It is to them that the three phrases apply, in their historic sequence. "With all your heart" was Abraham. "With all your soul" was Isaac. "With all your wealth" was Jacob.

THE LOVE OF ABRAHAM

The daily morning prayers offer a brief review of Jewish history. We begin with a selection from Nehemiah. The prophet quickly moves from the story of Creation to the founder of Judaism:

> You are the Lord alone. You created the heavens and the heavens of heavens and all their hosts, the earth and all that is upon it, the seas and everything that is in them. And You bring life to all and the hosts of the heavens bow to You. You are the Lord, God, who chose Abram and took him out of Ur Kasdim, and made his name Abraham. And You found his heart faithful before You. (9:6–7)

For this biblical summary of Abraham's greatness, one trait alone is singled out as the unique virtue that earned him the name change from Abram to Abraham, defining his mission as the father of many nations: "And You found his heart faithful [*ne'eman*] before You." The heart is the source of faith. The Bible constantly relates the two. To have unswerving commitment is to have a *lev ne'eman,* a faithful heart.

Abraham was the one who grew up in the home of Terah, the idol maker. Abraham witnessed paganism firsthand. He fearlessly destroyed the idols of his father and traveled from place to place to bring personal witness to the reality of monotheism. To worship God and to love Him, it is obvious you must first believe in Him fully. It is not enough to suggest that there *may* be a God. Total commitment demands unwavering certainty. If you proclaim, "Hear, O Israel, the Lord is our God, the Lord is One," then you must be prepared to shatter the false gods of your surroundings and to renounce the idols of your contemporaries. True love begins with a love as powerful as the one shown by the first of the patriarchs, who was the living illustration of the commandment to love God "with all of your heart."

THE LOVE OF ISAAC

Some illustrations of the biblical story of the Binding of Isaac portray an old man carrying an infant in his arms, ready to sacrifice his son in unquestioning obedience to God's commandment. That image is not true. Our sages relate that Isaac was thirty-seven years old when the incident took place. The meaning of the story therefore revolves not merely about a test of Abraham's faith. Isaac was already a mature, thinking adult capable of choosing his own response. Isaac knew that he was being taken to serve as a personal sacrifice to God. When the Torah tells us, "and the two of them walked together" (Gen. 22:6, 8), the implication is that they walked as one, in mutual recognition of what would transpire, both equally prepared to fulfill the incomprehensible commandment.

True, the Torah introduces the story with the words: "And it came to pass after these things that God tested Abraham" (Gen. 22:1). Why call it "the test of Abraham" if Isaac was the one who knowingly and willingly would have to offer his own life? The answer is a profound and yet simple truth: Jewish thought teaches that it was a far greater test to force Abraham to kill than to ask Isaac to be killed. Isaac would die once. Abraham, had he been allowed to carry out the commandment, would have subsequently endured a lifetime of everlasting pain, for which death would have been a far preferable alternative.

Be that as it may, it was still Isaac who had to be prepared to die. He was ready to do so. Thus, in the biblical sequence illustrating the patriarchs' love of God, if Abraham was the one who showed us what it meant to believe with his entire heart, then Isaac demonstrated the next dimension of love. It is a love that ascended to the level of "with all your soul" – a readiness to offer his soul back to the One who gave it. From Isaac we learn the mitzva of martyrdom. And from Isaac we learn the great truth that if you believe in something fully, you must be prepared even to die for it.

When R. Akiva, one of the ten martyrs selected by Rome for public execution, knew that he faced his last moments on earth, he smiled while enduring most painful torture. In response to his students who asked him how he could possibly accept his affliction in such manner, he said, "I rejoice because all of my life I recited the words 'with all your soul' and could not be certain if ever the time came for me to demonstrate my willingness to fulfill them, that I would be able to do so. I thank God that I have found within myself the spiritual power to demonstrate my love for God with all my soul" (Berakhot 61b). R. Akiva managed to merge Abraham's faith, with all his heart, to Isaac's willingness to accept martyrdom, with all his soul.

THE LOVE OF JACOB

Believe in Him. Be prepared to die for Him. What else could there possibly be? It was Jacob who made a great discovery about the ideal way in which we are meant to serve God. It happened on Mount Moriah, the very spot on which the Temple would eventually be built. Jacob had just fled from his home in fear of his brother Esau. Going to sleep at the site that would many years later assume such significance as the place of ultimate sanctity, Jacob had a dream about which the Torah tells us, "And behold a ladder was set up on earth, and the top of it reached to heaven, and behold the angels of God ascending and descending on it" (Gen. 28:12).

What was the meaning of this heavenly message? Jewish commentators identify the symbolic content of the dream with the essential message of Judaism. Indeed, the *gematria* of *sulam*, ladder, 130, is identical to that of the word *Sinai,* the mountain on which God gave us the Torah. The ladder of Jacob's dream linking heaven and earth was meant to demonstrate that service of God does not call for the renunciation of all that is earthly; humanity's role is not to forsake this world but rather to sanctify it.

Christianity would teach that "my kingdom is not of this world." Those who seek to be holy would be counseled to cut themselves off from society, to enter a monastery, to renounce the pleasures of this world, and to prepare themselves only for the next. Love of money was viewed as the root of all evil and in the words of the Christian Bible, "It is easier for a camel to go through the eye of a needle than for a rich man to enter into the kingdom of God" (Matthew 19:24).

Not so in Jewish teaching. A man does not become a saint if he takes a vow of poverty. He becomes holy if he uses his wealth to enhance and sanctify the presence of God on earth. The angels of God ascend and descend the ladder – the very ladder that in Hebrew is numerically equivalent not only to the word *Sinai* but also, amazingly enough, to the word *mamon,* money – because what God asks of us is to find a way to bring about a mutually beneficial merger between heaven and earth, to infuse the profane with the sacred so that every part of Creation can bring greater glory to God.

Symbolically, Jacob's dream is about Sinai and the proper use of material blessings. The metaphor of the ladder is meant to illustrate the ideal of holiness representing harmony between heaven and earth. The Christian mortifies the flesh in order to rise above it. The Jew sanctifies the flesh in order to elevate it. The Christian condemns wealth and takes a vow of poverty. The Jew controls wealth and seeks to utilize it in a way that will make the world a better place by spreading the message of Sinai.

Immediately after Jacob dreams the dream, the Torah tells us, "And Jacob vowed a vow saying, if God will be with me…. Then of all that You shall give me I will surely give the tenth unto You" (Gen. 28:20–22). The concept of tithing comes from Jacob, the Jacob who just had the vision of the ladder. Why would he have spoken of something as mundane as money immediately after experiencing the most sacred vision of his life? *Because that very vision enabled him to comprehend that one can and one must serve God even "with all your wealth."*

Is it necessary for the Torah to command loving God with one's possessions after it has already told us we must be prepared to die for Him? Remarkably enough, the Talmud tells us there are those whose money is dearer to them even than their bodies (Sanhedrin 74a). It is not enough to be willing to die for a cause; harder still is the strength to continue to live for it by sacrificing one's wealth and possessions. The three "love commandments" take us back to our three patriarchs. They serve as paradigms, living illustrations from our past to serve as role models for our relationship with the Almighty.

THE THREE LOVES AS THREE FESTIVALS

Let us now turn back to the *Shalosh Regalim* and see how this set of three resonates with the "love commandments" of the three patriarchs. We will discover that the calendar is yet another way in which we are meant to reaffirm the commitments of the *Avot* as they exemplified the meaning of true love.

The Love of Passover – "With All Your Heart"

Passover was the first step in our relationship with God. Its purpose was to achieve belief: "When Israel saw the great hand the Lord raised against the Egyptians, the people feared the Lord; and *they believed in the Lord* and in His servant Moses" (Ex. 14:31). Passover is the key to the first commandment, focused on faith: "I am the Lord your God who took you out of the land of Egypt, the house of bondage" (Ex. 20:2; Deut. 5:6).

Why did God bring ten plagues upon the Egyptians before He took the Jews out of Egypt? Could He not have started with the most severe one first and do away with the need for the nine others? And why when Pharaoh was ready to comply and let the Jews go did God harden his heart? God needed every single one of those plagues in order to bring destruction upon the ten major idols of Egypt, just as Abraham shattered the false gods in the shop of his father, so that the Jews who left Egypt would know of a certainty that the Lord alone is God.

The message of Passover is *emuna*, complete and total faith, "with all your heart." Small wonder then that the Midrash tells us that when the three angels came to visit Abraham, he was observing the holiday of Passover, although it was many years before the event it commemorates even took place.

The Love of Shavuot – "With All Your Soul"

The acceptance of Torah at Sinai coupled belief to total commitment, even at the possible cost of one's life. The Jews stood *"under* the mountain" – God lifted the mountain over their heads and said if you obey the commandments, well and good, but if not I will drop the mountain upon you and you will not survive (Shabbat 88a). Commitment to the law had consequences. Some of God's commandments at Sinai were as incomprehensible to human understanding as the binding of Isaac on Mount Moriah. Indeed, there is a midrash that Mount Moriah itself was moved to the range of Sinai so that the story of the *Akeda* be inextricably linked with *Kabbalat HaTorah*.[1] Sinai and Shavuot, with their allusion to the need to emulate Isaac's willingness to offer his life for God, add the component of "with all your soul" as the second message of the pilgrimage festivals.

---

1. *Midrash Tehillim* (Buber), *mizmor* 68.

The Love of Sukkot – "With All Your Wealth"

Sukkot is the Festival of the Harvest. It is the time when Jews of old found themselves with the greatest wealth. Their granaries were full; they felt themselves rich beyond measure. And with wealth came all the dangers of excessive material blessing. In the Book of Deuteronomy, Moses warns the people, "But Jeshurun waxed fat and kicked" (32:15); unbounded riches often create great and unmanageable temptation. Wealth can lead us to greed just as much as it can bring us closer to God.

Sukkot is the time when we are commanded to leave our homes – the key symbol of our possessions – to live in a fragile hut. It is meant to remind us that no matter the amount of our wealth, we live under the rule of the One above in the heavens who is ultimately responsible for all of our blessings. The book from the Bible we read in many synagogues during Sukkot is Ecclesiastes – written by Solomon, the wisest and wealthiest of all men – who shares with us his conclusion that "that is the last word: all has been said. Have fear of God and keep His laws because this is right for every man. God will be Judge of every work, with every secret thing, good or evil" (12:13–14).

The Festival of the Harvest is the time for us to put our possessions into proper perspective. It is the moment when we need to define the correct relationship between our faith and our finances. It is the holiday on which we need to dream Jacob's dream of the ladder in order to create the bridge between our bountiful goods here on earth and our spiritual values from heaven.

No wonder, too, that the very first mention of Sukkot in the Torah is in connection with Jacob: "And Jacob journeyed to Sukkot and built himself a house and made booths for his cattle; therefore the name of the place is called Sukkot" (Gen. 33:17). How appropriate as well that the Torah reading for Sukkot begins with the words, "And tithe you shall surely tithe" (Deut. 14:22), the mitzva first practiced by Jacob in the aftermath of his dream of the ladder. This, after all, is the holiday dedicated to the proper fulfillment of the third and final "love commandment" – "and with all your wealth."

Three patriarchs, three ways in which we are bidden to express our love for God, and the *Shalosh Regalim,* the three pilgrimage festivals, all share in developing the identical theme of how to fulfill the mitzva of *ve'ahavta*. The patriarchs are the paradigms of history. The three phrases that follow the "love commandment" are the guidelines incorporated into our daily prayers. The *Shalosh Regalim* are the annual reminders brought to us by the calendar. And every year, when we complete the cycle and absorb its threefold message, we know that we have brought into our lives *zeman simḥatenu*, the time of our rejoicing.

The Final Redemption: Nisan or Tishrei?

> *At the End of Days, He will send our Messiah*
> *to redeem those who await His final salvation.*
> (*Yigdal* prayer)

We believe with certainty that Passover will someday be overshadowed by an even greater miracle of divine Redemption. The Exodus from Egypt was merely the first step in a long process of historic revelation destined to conclude with the ultimate goal of the Messianic Era. It is the twelfth of the famous list of the thirteen cardinal principles of our faith as enumerated by Maimonides. It is key to the optimism of our people. It is the reason why memory plays such a crucial role in our prayers, in our holidays, and in our observances. The miracles of the past are but a prelude to our future. Our history represents the greatest assurance of our destiny. God was always with us, is always with us, and will always be with us – that is the very source of His four-letter name comprised of a combination of the words for "was," "is," and "will be" in Hebrew. Passover was only the first step. It was *geula*, redemption – but not *Geula Shelema*, the final and complete Redemption promised by our prophets.

Someday the Messiah will come. Nations will no longer lift up swords against other nations nor will they learn the art of war anymore.

Peace and prosperity will cover the earth as the waters cover the seas and the knowledge of God's rulership over the entire world will be the spiritual heritage of all mankind. It is surely tempting to seek the date for this global transformation. If only we knew the time of the Messiah's arrival! But much as we have struggled to find clues to the time for the fulfillment of this fundamental belief of our faith, we have been told that this information remains part of the biblical category of "the secret things belong to the Lord our God" (Deut. 29:28).

More, the Talmud tells us it is sinful to attempt calculations predicting the End of Days:

> R. Shmuel bar Naḥmani said in the name of R. Yonatan: Blasted be the bones of those who calculate the end. For they would say, since the predetermined time has arrived, and yet he has not come, he will never come. But [even so], wait for him, as it is written, "Though he tarry, wait for him." (Sanhedrin 97b).

Human calculations may be mistaken. Deferred hope may lead to national despair. Better to remain with the certainty of faith that the Messiah *will* come than to permit the possibility of the desolation of hopelessness brought on by unfulfilled erroneous expectations. The history of failed messiahs, most powerfully illustrated by the tragic story of Shabbetai Tzvi, surely validate the talmudic prohibition against predicting an exact date for the Messiah's arrival.

In light of all this, it is certainly amazing to find a talmudic dispute centering around the date marking our final Redemption – true, not by year, but even more specifically by actual month:

> It has been taught: R. Eliezer says: In Tishrei the world was created; in Tishrei the patriarchs were born; in Tishrei the patriarchs died; on Passover Isaac was born; on Rosh HaShana Sarah, Rachel, and Hannah were visited [remembered on High to be blessed with having a child]; on Rosh HaShana [i.e., in the month of Tishrei but more specifically on the very first day] Joseph went forth from prison; on Rosh HaShana the bondage of our ancestors in Egypt ceased [six months before their actual deliverance]; in Nisan they were redeemed but in Tishrei they will be redeemed in the Time to Come.

R. Yehoshua says: In Nisan the world was created; in Nisan the patriarchs were born; in Nisan the patriarchs died; on Passover Isaac was born; on Rosh HaShana Sarah, Rachel, and Hannah were visited; on Rosh HaShana Joseph went forth from prison; on Rosh HaShana the bondage of our ancestors ceased in Egypt; in Nisan they were redeemed and in Nisan they will be redeemed in the Time to Come. (Rosh HaShana 10b–11a)

The dispute between these two rabbinic giants revolves around both past and future. It is concerned with the exact time in terms of months for the events of greatest historic importance. The Creation of the world, the birth of the patriarchs (with the exception of Isaac whose birth on Passover is indisputable), and the date for final Redemption share the focus of their differing opinions. And we cannot help but wonder what motivates these scholars to choose either Tishrei or Nisan? Why does each one of them believe that the month they favor is more propitious to have been chosen by God as worthy for these major moments? And, perhaps most striking of all, why ignore the injunction against "reckoning the end" by delving into something as specific as the actual month of final Redemption? The answer is implicit in something that Jewish tradition maintains is a central feature of specific times of the year. Months have their own special meaning. Seasons bring with them specific messages.

Passover is in the spring. Although Jews biblically follow a lunar calendar, it is adjusted with a leap month seven out of nineteen years, precisely in order to ensure that Passover always remain "Ḥag HaAviv," "the Festival of the Spring." Spring is a time of love. Passover is the love story between God and the Jewish people, the story of the Song of Songs, the biblical book of the canon other than the five books of Moses selected for communal reading on this holiday. The Midrash makes clear that God redeemed us in Nisan solely as an act of love. He redeemed us although we did not deserve it. He took us out of the land of Egypt even though we were still far from perfect. Passover was an unearned and unmerited redemption. And that is why it happened in Nisan, the month set aside for God's attribute of total loving-kindness and grace.

There is another month, though, in which we are meant to deepen an awareness of God's judgment and justice. It is the month of Tishrei in which God calls us to reflect upon the scales on which our sins are weighed against our merits. Tishrei is the month of Rosh HaShana and Yom Kippur. Tishrei reminds us that we dare not rely on God's love alone without also acknowledging personal responsibility. God's kindness dare not be taken for granted; God's compassion may not be used as exemption from our own obligations. Where Nisan emphasizes love, Tishrei speaks of law. Where Nisan offers grace, Tishrei demands compliance. Where Nisan emphasizes *rahamim*, mercy, Tishrei stresses *din*, judgment. These are nothing other than the two aspects of divinity stressed by the two different names of God: Hashem and *Elokim*. It is the two rabbis, R. Eliezer and R. Yehoshua, who dispute the relative importance and relevance of these two months for the Jewish people – as well as for the world.

There is a remarkable synergy between the names of these two rabbis and the ideals that they espouse in this controversy. Names have profound meaning. In the words of the Bible, "As his name is, so is he" (I Sam. 25:25). Both rabbis have a Hebrew word for God in their name. The first two letters of the name Eliezer are the short form of the name *Elokim*, God in His attribute of strict justice. The name Yehoshua begins with the first two letters of the four-letter name of God, which represents divine mercy. R. Eliezer is spokesman for the month of Tishrei, the month of Rosh HaShana and Yom Kippur, the month of divine judgment. R. Yehoshua is more attuned to the month of Nisan, the month of Passover, the month in which God chooses to defer the demands of justice to the greater blessings rooted in overriding love.

There are two ways in which the Hebrew language expresses help and deliverance. The verse "And God delivered [*vayosha*] on that day Israel from the hands of Egypt" (Ex. 14:30) reflects on the meaning of the word *yeshua*. When Moses feared what would happen to the Jewish people as the Egyptian army approached, with no seeming possibility for escape, the Lord reassured him. Moses then told his people, "Do not fear; stand firm and see the deliverance [*yeshuat*] of the Lord that He will do for you today" (v. 13). "The Lord will fight for you and you shall remain silent" (v. 14).

The word *yeshua* implies total reliance upon God. It asks nothing of man. It is divine help without human assistance. And it is what R. Yehoshua believed represents the most fundamental description of our relationship with the Almighty. Small wonder that R. Yehoshua felt it necessary to claim that the world was created in Nisan. The world could only come into existence on a foundation of love and the world can only survive as recipient of divine grace, even if unearned. The patriarchs had to be born in Nisan to emphasize that truth. The first redemption, the compassionate deliverance from Egypt commemorated by Passover, had to take place in Nisan. In Nisan we were redeemed in the past and it is in Nisan that we will be redeemed in the future as well. Redemption will come independent of our worthiness. Redemption will be mandated by God's love even if not validated by the strict standards of God's law.

R. Eliezer, the man whose very name emphasized God's identity as strict judge and ruler, could not abide a theology rooted in the message of Nisan. True, at the very outset of our history as a people, we may not have been wise enough to be worthy. We may not yet have sufficiently absorbed God's teachings to *earn* redemption, so the Almighty was willing for a time to ignore our deficiencies. He chose, in our early youth, to overlook our failings and to redeem us in Nisan – solely out of love – in the expectation that with the passage of time we would mature sufficiently so that we might finally earn by our own actions what had previously been granted to us as gift.

The redemption of Passover, R. Eliezer admits, came in Nisan but surely the final messianic Redemption – like the Creation of the world as well as the birth of the majority of our patriarchs – will be a Tishrei experience. In the spirit of Rosh HaShana and Yom Kippur, our deeds will be carefully weighed to decide if we be found worthy. The world itself was created on that premise in Tishrei so that we forever know it is we who must join with God in order to ensure its survival.

R. Eliezer saw God as partner to our own efforts. Remarkably, that is presaged in the second part of His name. The word e*zer* means help – but it is the kind of request for assistance that assumes personal effort as well. The first time we meet the word in the Torah is when God informs us that He will create an *ezer kenegdo* for Adam, "a helpmate opposite him" (Gen. 2:18). Adam was not meant to face the challenges of the world alone. God granted him support. But help is no excuse for personal abdication of responsibility. Eve was not meant to replace Adam but rather to assist him. So too with regard to God, the Psalm of

David calls out, "Hear, O Lord, and be gracious to me; O Lord, *be my helper* (Ps. 30:11). We ask God to be our helper, not our sole support. We ask for God's love, but only as reward for our commitment to live up to our obligations to the very best of our abilities.

Tishrei and Nisan are the metaphors used by the talmudic rabbis who differ about our roles in the drama of the major historic events of our history. And if we might have failed to grasp what these sages really had in mind in their dispute, there is another passage in the Talmud that clarifies beyond doubt the ultimate meaning of their controversy:

> Rav said: All the predestined dates [for redemption] have passed, and the matter [now] depends only on repentance and good deeds. But Shmuel maintained: It is sufficient for a mourner to keep his [period of] mourning. [Israel's sufferings in the exile in themselves sufficiently warrant their redemption, regardless of repentance.] This [very same] matter is disputed by *Tanna'im*: R. Eliezer said: If Israel repent, they will be redeemed; if not, they will not be redeemed. R. Yehoshua said to him: If they do not repent, will they not be redeemed! [Of course they will, even if they do not deserve to be redeemed.] [R. Eliezer responded:] But the Holy One, blessed be He, will set up a king over them, whose decrees shall be as cruel as Haman's, whereby Israel shall engage in repentance, and He will thus bring them back to the right path [so that repentance will in fact be the reason for their final redemption]. (Sanhedrin 97b)

The argument between R. Eliezer and R. Yehoshua for choosing either Tishrei or Nisan was apparently but another way of couching their views about the role of repentance as a requirement for redemption. R. Yehoshua saw messianic fulfillment as a sequel to Passover. The undeserved love shown in the biblical story will similarly be sufficient to bring about the glorious End of Days. Nisan will once again be the key to the final chapter of our history. R. Eliezer however believed that our destiny demands our full commitment and cooperation. We have not struggled so long throughout our long exile without the hope that we will have earned our final redemption. The End of Days will be a divine response to our collective repentance on Tishrei.

Indeed, we cannot know the year of the Messiah's coming. However, to decide on the month is to make us aware of the extent of our responsibility. The dispute between the two rabbis deserves a final answer. Who is right? Which view has achieved the approbation of the sages? Remarkably, Maimonides in his major work of Jewish law, the *Mishneh Torah*, clearly chose to side with R. Eliezer:

> All the prophets commanded [the people] to repent. Israel will only be redeemed through *teshuva*. The Torah has already promised that, ultimately, Israel will repent towards the end of her exile and, immediately, she will be redeemed as the verse states, "There shall come a time when [you will experience] all these things.... And you will return to the Lord, your God.... The Lord, your God will bring back your [captivity]." (Deut. 30:1–3)[1]

For those of us who believe that the modern-day return of the Jewish people to the land of Israel – as well as the reestablishment of the Jewish homeland after almost two millennia of exile – carries the seeds of final Redemption, there is one last insight into the dispute between the two rabbis that still bears consideration.

Until now we have understood the view of R. Yehoshua as linked specifically to the month of Nisan. What is somewhat strange in the text in Tractate Rosh HaShana further explaining his source for the belief that all of the patriarchs were born in Nisan is the following: "R. Yehoshua said: From where do we know that the patriarchs were born in Nisan? Because it says: 'And it came to pass in the four hundred and eightieth year after the children of Israel departed the land of Egypt, in the fourth year in the month of Ziv' (I Kings 6:1) – that is, the month in which the brilliant ones [*zivtanei*] of the world were born" (Rosh HaShana 11a).

Rashi immediately addresses the problem. The month of Ziv is not another name for Nisan. It is in fact Iyar, the month following. How can R. Yehoshua prove a point for Nisan from a text that really

---

1. *Laws of Repentance* 7:5.

does not refer to it? A suggested answer is that Nisan speaks also of the season, the spring equinox of three months to which Iyar is central. The time of love that is linked to Passover and the Song of Songs includes Iyar and that, too, is what R. Yehoshua had in mind with his emphasis on Nisan.

Perhaps, then, contemporary Jewish history validates the view of R. Yehoshua. *Yom HaAtzma'ut*, Israeli Independence Day, is observed on the fifth day of Iyar. *Yom Yerushalayim*, Jerusalem Day, is on the twenty-eighth of that same month. Both are still in the period of love, the time – just as Passover – which demonstrates that even when we are not yet deserving of redemption by our deeds, the Almighty may grant us undeserved gifts before our complete repentance. Yet Maimonides decided that R. Eliezer was right.

Perhaps here is another example of the classic formula with regard to a dispute between two rabbinic giants that "*ellu va'ellu divrei Elokim ḥayim*," "these and those are both the words of the living God" (Eiruvin 13b). Both rabbis were right. How can that be? How can opposing views be correct?

Redemption, in the words of our prophets, has two moments. There is *atḥalta degeula*, the first stage of redemption, and there is *Geula Shelema*, the complete and final Redemption. R. Yehoshua and R. Eliezer made no distinction between them. They assumed the same date for both of them. God, however, chose to begin the process of redemption in the season of Nisan, in the month of Iyar, even before the Jewish people were truly worthy of *Yom HaAtzma'ut* and *Yom Yerushalayim*. These were momentous illustrations of God's compassion, of God's kindness, and of God's love for His children in spite of their imperfections. Yet, as Maimonides points out, complete redemption requires complete repentance. God wants us to earn the Messiah's coming. The firm conviction that the Messiah will come is a belief not only in God's grace but in our own potential for greatness. The Messiah will come because we will deserve his arrival. The certainty of Jewish repentance is the corollary to our faith in the Messiah.

Let us thank God for the fulfillment of the Nisan/Iyar stage of redemption in our own lifetimes. And let us hopefully help to hasten the day of the Tishrei completion when our *teshuva* serves to usher in the *Geula Shelema*.

Good Riddance:
The Burning of the Bread

There is a fairly new tradition in New York for the transition from one year to the next. It is called Good Riddance Day. It takes place in Times Square and, although it has no religious basis and does not occur on Passover, it resonates with a ritual that has great meaning for us as Jews in preparation for the holiday commemorating our redemption from slavery. Tim Tompkins, head of the Times Square Alliance, explained Good Riddance Day this way: "It's a great idea for all of those who treasure an opportunity to physically destroy reminders of negative events of the past year and to symbolically move forward to better days ahead." And sure enough, New Yorkers turn out in droves in midtown Manhattan just before New Year's Day with their own individual and highly unique ways of commemorating a day dedicated to removing the trash from their lives and to expressing their contempt for the most harmful items of the past.

Some used the moment to burn the letters from unfaithful spouses. Others dumped photos of former lovers. There were the parents who shredded the year-old medical diagnosis of their son's kidney cancer that has now thankfully gone into total remission. Then there were those who brought documents they wanted to destroy, like medical bills, and objects they wanted to smash with a mallet, as a way to vengefully say good-bye to the troubles of the past year. What all of them shared was a cry of "good riddance" to those aspects of their lives they visibly wanted to discard, a commitment to keeping bad memories from interfering with the future.

And as a rabbi, I could not help thinking that something very much like this has been part of Jewish tradition for thousands of years. We Jews are doubly blessed when it comes to New Year celebrations. We observe one in the fall, on Rosh HaShana, commemorating the birth of mankind. We have another in the spring, when the calendar marks Nisan as the first month of the year because of its association with the Exodus from Egypt and the birth of the Jewish people. Passover is the holiday that commemorates this beginning – and it is preceded on the morning of the night of the Seder with a symbolic burning that resonates powerfully with the theme of New York's newly established Good Riddance Day.

Most people know that on Passover Jews are commanded to eat matzot. At least as important in Jewish law is its corollary: for all the days of the holiday Jews are forbidden not only to eat leavened bread but also to have the smallest crumb in their home or possession as well. Bread is something that needs to be totally renounced. Whatever is left over before Passover begins must be ceremoniously burned and verbally negated. "All leavened bread that is in my possession that I have seen or not seen," Jews must recite, "may it be nullified and rendered ownerless as the dust of the earth." What is this sudden aversion to bread all about? What does the food we normally consider the staff of life suddenly represent that is so reprehensible? Allow me to offer a possible interpretation.

Do you know the identity of the first people to discover how to make bread? Historians tell us sourdough is the oldest and most original form of leavened bread and *the oldest recorded use of sourdough is from the ancient Egyptian civilizations*! Archaeological evidence confirms that yeast – employed both as a leavening agent and for brewing ale – was initially used in Egypt. Food historians generally agree that the land of the Nile, biblically known for its enslavement of the Hebrews, must be credited with the remarkable technological achievement that was to play such a crucial role in the progress of civilization. Egypt's expertise brought the world a great gift of nourishment and sustenance. Yet its "scientific breakthrough" was not matched by moral progress. The inventors of bread remained barbaric masters of slaves. The very people who discovered the staff of life did not hesitate to serve as the agents of death for the Hebrew children they drowned in the Nile.

It was a profound lesson about the disconnect between science and ethics that mankind learned millennia ago – and not much has changed to this day. In our own times, Albert Einstein famously warned us that "it has become appallingly obvious that our technology has exceeded our humanity." And he wisely cautioned us that "our entire much-praised technological progress and civilization generally could be compared to an axe in the hand of a pathological criminal." Martin Luther King put it beautifully when he said, "We have reached a time when we have advanced enough to have guided missiles, yet we still remain primitive enough to have misguided men." Technology has blessed us with smart phones but left us with stupid people in terms of ethical and honorable values.

It was left to the Jews to publicize by way of ritual this great dichotomy between mankind's achievements and its propensity to continue to embrace acts of evil. As the Hebrews were about to be freed from slavery, they were to symbolically rid themselves of Egypt's great technological innovation of bread to demonstrate that *scientific progress divorced from a moral code needs condemnation, rather than unqualified praise and acceptance.* Every year on the eve of Passover, Jews have a Good Riddance Day. The "villain" is not bread but what it came to represent to the Jews in ancient Egypt – a powerful symbol of intellectual progress by their oppressors, devoid of any humanitarian concern for those they oppressed. The pioneering Egyptians ate bread; their slaves, never granted the dignity of human beings created in the divine image, were forced to eat matzot, the bread of oppression. It is a message that bears repetition in the context of the pre-Passover ritual. It reminds us of the sin of technology without values, progress without prudence.

Jonathan Safer Foer, in an article on "How Not to Be Alone," makes this confession about technology:

> My daily use of technological communication has been shaping me into someone more likely to forget others. The more distracted we become, and the more emphasis we place on speed

at the expense of depth, the less likely and able we are to care. Everyone wants his parent's, or friend's, or partner's undivided attention – even if many of us, especially children, are getting used to far less.

Simone Weil writes, "Attention is the rarest and purest form of generosity." By this definition, our relationships to the world, to one another, and to ourselves are becoming increasingly miserly.

We need to burn bread, the *ḥametz* of our lives and symbol of technology devoid of morality in ancient Egypt. We need to remember, in a world of nuclear giants and ethical infants, that if we continue to develop our technology without concern for spiritual principles, our scientifically created servants may, God forbid, become our executioners.

The Seder and the First Commandment

What is the single most important idea of the Passover Seder? For me, it has always been captured best by the very word that gives it its name. The ritual of this night that commemorates the birth of the Jewish people on the eve of our Exodus from Egypt is called "Seder" because it summarizes our unique understanding of history and the role played by God in the course of human events. Let me explain.

The very first commandment of the ten given on Sinai links God's identity with the Passover story: "I am the Lord your God who took you out of the land of Egypt, the house of bondage" (Ex. 20:2; Deut. 5:6). It is, on the surface, a very strange way for the Almighty to define Himself. After all, it is the very first statement introducing us to the reality of an all-powerful being, of a deity worthy of being worshiped. Could God not have chosen something far more formidable to illustrate His greatness? Would it not mean much more to us if God's claim to our obedience were to have been expressed with the words "I am the Lord your God who created the heavens and the earth"? The fact that God liberated us from slavery was a wonderful achievement, but even human beings, like Abraham Lincoln, have been great emancipators. However, only God Himself can lay claim to the role of Creator.

It is a profound question that has intrigued countless Jewish commentators. In one of the most famous philosophic works of the medieval period, the *Kuzari*, Rabbi Yehuda Halevi puts this very difficulty into the mouth of the pagan king of the Khazars in the imagined dialogue between him and the Rabbi who was summoned to assist in his search for religious truth. Why would God, the king wonders, choose a relatively minor event to make His power known if He is in fact the Creator of the entire universe?

The answer is rooted in the reality that most people, in fact, are not atheists. It is hard to deny the existence of a higher divine power who brought this whole world into existence. Every part of the miraculous structure and design of our bodies, every glance at the heavens, and every glimpse of the wondrous workings of nature force us to agree with the psalmist that "the heavens declare the glory of God and the firmament shows His handiwork" (19:2). The true difficulty is not to convince people of the fallacy of atheism. Both intellectually and intuitively mankind knows there must be a God. The first commandment did not come to proclaim what was already self-evident. What is difficult to grasp, however, for the millions of people on this earth who feel estranged from God, is that *the Creator really cares about all those whom He created*. The heresy that needs most to be addressed is deism. Deism acknowledges that the brilliant design of the world forces us to accept a Designer, just as a watch must have had a watchmaker. But just as the watchmaker no longer has an ongoing relationship with the watch he brought into being, so too is God surely indifferent to the lives of the world's inhabitants or to its ultimate destiny.

To be a deist is to believe in God – but in a God who truly does not matter. A deist would hardly deign to pray, for after all no one is really listening. A deist would be hard put to follow any divine commandments since he is certain the commander is not concerned enough to take note of his compliance or disobedience. A deist could not possibly accept a concept like messianic Redemption at the End of Days since the Creator long ago lost interest in the meaningless meanderings of His creations.

The God whom we met at Sinai wanted above all to refute the heresy that denied not His existence but His ongoing concern. When He told us, "I am the Lord your God who took you out of the land of Egypt, the house of bondage" (Ex. 20:2; Deut. 5:6), He wanted to impress upon us the idea, as Rabbi Yehuda Halevi puts it, that He is *a God of history* who maintains a personal relationship with every one of us created in His image.

Note carefully, said the commentators, that in the Hebrew phrase for "I am the Lord your God," the word for "your" is grammatically in the singular. It is as if God is speaking directly to every one of us, promising an ongoing special relationship. And because God is a personal God who continues to care about us, about the fate of the Jewish people and the ultimate future of mankind, history becomes meaningful. It is orchestrated from Above. It has a preordained destiny.

The sages teach us that there are two possible ways to view the events that befall us. The first is the philosophy of "*leit din veleit dayan,*" "there is no justice and there is no judge." This statement is a heresy that adopts words like coincidence, chance, luck, or happenstance to explain the human story. It is a sacrilege whose sin goes to the very heart of our mutual love relationship with God, denying any link between the Creator and His creations.

In the biblical section known as the *Tokheḥa* – the concluding admonition of the Book of Leviticus with its threatened curses for future national disobedience – there is a recurring phrase to explain what will anger God most and be responsible for repeated affliction: "And if you will still not listen to Me but walk contrary unto Me" (26:27). The Hebrew for "walk contrary unto Me" is *vahalakhtem immi bekeri*. In a fascinating philological insight, Maimonides connects the Hebrew root of the word *keri* with that of the word *mikre,* chance or accident. The intent of the verse then gives expression to this very idea: If the Jewish people continue to attribute events that befall them to nothing more than pure chance, to *mikre,* instead of recognizing them all as a part of the divine master plan that guides human history, God will continue to afflict them until they "get it." The crime that God cannot countenance is the refusal to recognize His ongoing role in history – the very idea alluded to in the first commandment in the emphasis on God's role as the Redeemer of the Jews from the slavery of Egypt.

The antithesis of the heresy that "there is no justice and there is no judge" is that history has meaning and purpose. It is not haphazard. It has a plan. It follows a divinely ordained order, decreed by God who continues to be involved in every aspect of the story of mankind. And the word for "order" in Hebrew? Of course, it is *seder*! The Passover Seder is known by this name not so much because the meal follows a preordained order but because it is meant to affirm the major teaching about God that appears in the first of the Ten Commandments. Long after God created the world, He demonstrated His continuing love by intervening in history, punishing evildoers, and bringing freedom to those who suffered from the cruelty of their oppressors.

The Talmud teaches us that every blessing requires two elements: God's name and His kingship, as it is written: "*Kol berakha she'ein ba hazkarat Hashem eina berakha*," "any blessing that does not include in it a mention of God's name is not a [valid] blessing"; "*Kol berakha she'ein ba malkhut eina berakha*," "any blessing that does not include [a mention of God's] kingship is not a [valid] blessing" (Berakhot 12a). To speak of Him simply by way of His four-letter name "Hashem" without clarifying that He is also *Elokeinu Melekh HaOlam* – our God who *continues to rule over the world as a King*, involved, concerned, and personally connected – is to be blind to the true significance of our monotheistic faith and the meaning of "the God of Abraham, Isaac, and Jacob." It was on the first Passover that the Jews clearly witnessed God's intervention in human affairs. To celebrate Passover is to acknowledge the idea of *seder* – the concept of history that embraces God as the ultimate Director of events that proceed according to a divinely ordained order.

The Seder and the Calendar I: Passover and Tisha B'Av

J ewish tradition recognizes that God makes His voice heard in many different ways. One of them is by way of the connection between events and the calendar, the linkage between a particular date and a divine message associated with it on a recurring basis. The calendar makes clear that history is not haphazard. It expresses divine order. It indicates God's involvement in the affairs of mankind. It demonstrates the *seder* of heavenly curse or blessing. Two vivid examples stand out as prime illustrations. One speaks in the language of punishment and retribution, the other via the loving tone of reward and redemption. The first example is the tragic day of Tisha B'Av , the ninth of Av. The second example is the fifteenth of Nisan, the day commemorating our liberation from the slavery of Egypt, celebrated ever since as the festival of Passover.

The ninth day of the month of Av has for millennia been identified with the most terrible tragedies of Jewish history. It is almost beyond belief – and certainly far beyond statistical probability – that one and the same day could serve as the identical date for the greatest catastrophes to befall the Jewish people. On the ninth of Av, the First Temple was destroyed by the Babylonians. That alone would have been enough for it to become marked as a day of national fasting and mourning. But history reconfirmed the ninth of Av's tragic reality five centuries later.

When the Romans approached the Second Temple and put it to the torch, the Jews were shocked to realize that their Second Temple was destroyed *on exactly the same date as the first.*

A short time later, the Jews rebelled against Roman rule. They believed that their leader, Shimon bar Kokhba, would fulfill their messianic longings. But their hopes were cruelly dashed in 135 CE as the Jewish rebels were brutally butchered in the final battle, at Betar. The date of the massacre? Of course – the ninth of Av!

The First Crusade was declared by Pope Urban II on July 20, 1095 – and when Jews looked at their calendars they realized to their great consternation that the Hebrew date was the ninth of Av. Ten thousand Jews were brutally slain in its first month, and Jewish communities in France and the Rhineland were decimated; a grand total of 1.2 million Jews were killed by this crusade, which started on the ninth of Av. The Jews were expelled from England on July 25, 1290, the ninth of Av. Similarly, the Jews were expelled from France on July 21, 1306, the ninth of Av. In 1492, the Golden Age of Spain came to a close when Queen Isabella and her husband King Ferdinand ordered that the Jews be banished from the land "for the greater glory of the church and the Christian religion." The edict of expulsion was signed on March 31, 1492, and the Jews were given exactly four months to put their affairs in order and leave the country. The Hebrew date on which no Jews were allowed any longer to remain in the land where they had enjoyed welcome and prosperity for centuries? Oh, of course, you know it had to be – the ninth of Av.

More recently: Historians agree that World War II and the Holocaust were actually the long-drawn-out conclusion of World War I, which began in 1914. Barbara Tuchman wrote a book about that first great world war, which she called *The Guns of August.* Had a Jewish scholar written the book, perhaps it would have been entitled with a more specific date than just a month. Yes, amazingly enough, World War I also began, on the Hebrew calendar, on the ninth of Av, Tisha B'Av.

And still more: On August 2, 1941, on the ninth of Av, SS commander Heinrich Himmler received approval from the Nazi party for the "Final Solution." One year later, to the day, the plan was formally implemented, the plan for the genocidal elimination of the entire

Jewish people. On July 23, 1942, the ninth of Av in the year 5702, there began the mass deportation of all the Jews from the Warsaw ghetto, en route to the death camp of Treblinka. And yet still more: The Jewish community center in Buenos Aires was bombed, killing eighty-six and wounding three hundred others, on Monday, July 18, 1994. On the Jewish calendar, 9 Av 5754.

These cannot all be meaningless coincidences. Indeed, Jewish scholars long ago linked them to a biblical incident. Tisha B'Av has a Torah source. The tragedies of the ninth day of Av are all rooted in the same story responsible for the Jews being denied entrance to the Promised Land of Canaan on their journey from Egypt. The trip from Mount Sinai could have been a very short one. The wandering in the wilderness might have taken just weeks, instead of forty years, were it not for the Sin of the Spies – a sin that so greatly angered God that He decreed that entire generation needed to die out before the Jews could enter the Holy Land.

The Torah tells us the story. God had assured the people of the blessings of the land and of their ability, with divine assistance, to readily conquer it. But the people doubted God's word. They insisted on sending out spies to verify for themselves the truth of God's promise. Twelve spies, one for each tribe, scoured the land; ten returned with a fearful and negative report. When the Jewish people heard the pessimistic words, they wept. And God was profoundly angered by their lack of trust and faith. It was then that He decreed that this generation was unworthy of seeing the fulfillment of the promise that they doubted. They would need to spend forty more years in the desert until the last remnant of those people with insufficient faith passed away. The day of that sin, when the Jews wept for no reason, was the ninth day of Av. "You wept today for no reason," God declared. "Whenever there will be occasion in the future to weep, it will continue to be on this very day."

That edict was a powerful statement about the concept of calendrical linkage. God is not only the Creator of the universe. He continues to be involved with it. History is not a series of coincidences or inexplicable fate. And that truth is repeatedly demonstrated by the remarkable correspondence between specific dates and their significance for the Jewish people.

Tisha B'Av is rooted in tragedy. Its recurring message is the threat to Jewish survival. And yet, remarkably enough, there is within it a message of consolation and comfort. What is the name of the month whose ninth day has been so filled with misfortune? It is Av, the Hebrew word for father. No matter what happens, our Father is still in heaven and we are still His children. God knows what is happening. God cares. He will never forsake us. It is the message of the calendar and its seemingly impossible coincidences that at same time reassures us of God's presence in spite of all the calamities that befall us.

And that is how the tragedy associated with Tisha B'Av remarkably enough became linked with the joyous festival of Passover. Just as Tisha B'Av was destined for sorrow, Passover was set aside for salvation. And just as Tisha B'Av has its list of horrible events throughout history, the fifteenth of Nisan has its moments of divine intervention for blessing. The sorrows as well as the joys of the Jewish people share divine scrutiny and direction.

In the Haggada, towards the conclusion of the Seder, we read a beautiful poem by Yannai, one of the first and greatest of Jewish synagogue poets, who lived in the land of Israel at the end of the talmudic era. Its refrain is "*uvkhen vayehi baḥatzi halaila,*" "and so – it happened at midnight," midnight of the fifteenth of Nisan. Twelve events of the past are described:

- Abraham defeated the four Canaanite kings.
- God warned Abimelech, king of Gerar, that he would die unless he returned Sarah to Abraham.
- God appeared to Laban the night before his encounter with Jacob and warned him not to harm the third patriarch.
- Jacob struggled with the angel of Esau, a battle responsible for the blessing of the name change from Jacob to Israel.
- The tenth plague and death of the Egyptian firstborn.
- The defeat of the army of Sisera.
- The annihilation of the army of Sennacherib.
- The dream of Nebuchadnezzar in which he saw the collapse of his giant idol.

- The revelation to the prophet Daniel that Nebuchadnezzar's dream presaged the rise and fall of the four great empires of the world.
- The assassination of Belshazzar on the very night that he had desecrated the Temple vessels at a royal feast.
- The deliverance of Daniel from the lion's den.
- Haman's drafting of orders for the extermination of the Jews, which turned out to be the beginning of his downfall.

A thirteenth event is alluded to as well. It differs from the others because it has not yet occurred; it is not past, but future. It is the final Redemption.

It was on the fifteenth of Nisan that our ancestors in Egypt had the courage to take the blood of the lamb, the national god of Egypt, and smear it on their doorposts, the most public demonstration not only of their rejection of Egyptian idolatry but also of their faith in God. As reward, God proclaimed, "This is a night of anticipation for the Lord, to take them out of the land of Egypt; *this* night is the Lord's, guarding all the children of Israel *throughout their generations*" (Ex. 12:42). Because of the Jewish commitment to God on this night of the fifteenth of Nisan, this very date will be blessed with similar moments of joy and divine recompense in the future, culminating with messianic Redemption. It is the concept of calendrical linkage – but this time for a positive purpose.

The lack of faith of the Jews in the desert on the ninth day of Av a long time ago doomed it to perpetual mourning. The demonstration of faith by the Jews who observed the first Passover on the fifteenth of Nisan imbued that day with everlasting blessing. It is at the Seder that we open the door for Elijah, the prophet appointed to announce the Messiah's imminent arrival. It is at the Seder that we pour a cup of wine for Elijah to demonstrate how confident we are that we will surely be privileged to greet him. It is at the Seder, on the very same date of the fifteenth of Nisan when our ancestors were first redeemed, that we demonstrate our faith in a historic repetition of that moment.

It is at the Seder as well that we have a remarkable custom that seems very strange – a custom that links the two days we have seen were decreed to two such dissimilar and contrasting verdicts. On the very night we look forward to redemption, we have a tradition of eating a hard-boiled egg, which many commentators explain is meant to commemorate the meal of mourning immediately prior to beginning the fast of Tisha B'Av. What is the meaning of this seemingly bizarre connection?

It is the same truth that is expressed in yet another amazing way. Tradition teaches us that *the Messiah will be born on Tisha B'Av*. What can the two – the ninth of Av and the fifteenth of Nisan – possibly have in common? The answer is profound: From the tragedy of the one comes the redemption of the other. By rectifying the sin of the lack of faith responsible for the divine decree of Tisha B'Av, we will be worthy of the blessing of redemption. What both dates share is recognition of the *seder* of history. To grasp the recurring message of the calendar is to confirm God as the ultimate power behind human events – and to believe with certainty the fulfillment of our prophetically-promised destiny.

The Seder and the Calendar II: The A"T Ba"Sh Code

The English word "alphabet," according to *Merriam-Webster's Dictionary*, means "the letters used in writing a language arranged in their regular order." It is a perfect word because it contains within it reference to the first two letters of the Hebrew alphabet – *aleph* and *beit*. But Jewish tradition, especially in the writings of the mystic masters of Kabbala, makes note of a second Hebrew alphabet – an alphabet that follows precisely the reverse sequence of the one we are familiar with. Both alphabets are correct, but they each serve a different purpose – and with that as a starting point we can discover a remarkable code for another illustration of calendrical linkage. The reason for two alphabets stems from their two different sources. There is an alphabet "from below" and there is an alphabet "from above."

The alphabet of mankind, the one that captures our efforts of communication, works its way up. It starts with the letter that stands for the number "one" and proceeds upwards – from *aleph* to *tav*. We go from simple to more complex, from lower to higher. Not so for God. For God, there needs to be diminution in order to reduce His infinite wisdom into humanly comprehensible form. God's alphabet starts from *tav* and descends to *aleph*. Our alphabet, the one that goes in ascending order, is referred to as the *nigleh*, the revealed. It speaks in the language of human comprehension. The divine alphabet, that goes in descending order, is known as the alphabet of the *nistar,* the hidden and esoteric, which transcends our intellect.

If we were to create two columns for the Hebrew letters, one in ascending and the other in descending order, and then draw a line connecting each one of the letters – the English-language equivalent would be a line from A to Z, from B to Y, from C to X, and so forth – we would have the secret of the code of *A"T Ba"Sh.* It is a code that represents a perfect merger between the human and the divine, between earth and heaven. Let me give an illustration. The word for a divine commandment is *mitzva.* In Hebrew, the word *mitzva* is composed of four letters: *mem, tzadi, vav, heh.* The holy name of God, the Tetragrammaton, is also comprised of four letters. The last two are the same as the last two letters of the word *mitzva.* The first two letters of God's name in our alphabet are *yud* and *heh.* On the surface, they do not appear in the Hebrew word for commandment. Yet if we follow the code of *A"T Ba"Sh,* the "mate" of the *yud* is *mem* and the "mate" of *heh* is *tzadi.* That tells us a profound truth: every mitzva is a way in which we can get close to the essence of God – first in a mystical sense through the *nistar,* the hidden, and then through the *nigleh,* the revealed.

A"T Ba"Sh is, in short, a way of communicating on two levels. And with regard to Passover, it was Rabbi Yosef Karo, in his classic work the *Shulḥan Arukh,* the code of Jewish law, who formulated a remarkable idea of calendrical correspondence rooted in the sequence of days on which the holiday is observed. He noted that the days of Passover will always, in every year, have within them a reference to the observance of the other major holidays. The holiday whose major theme is *seder,* order, gives us a hint of the order of the festivals throughout the calendar year, based on the code of *A"T Ba"Sh.*

Whatever day of the week is *aleph,* the first day of Passover, will also be *tav,* the day on which Tisha B'Av will fall that year. If Passover starts on Sunday, then Tisha B'Av will also fall on Sunday.[1] Whatever

---

1. Another remarkable link between Passover and Tisha B'Av; for a fuller discussion of this idea, see the previous essay.

day of the week is *beit*, the second day of Passover will be *shin*, Shavuot, the festival of the Giving of the Torah (one day in Israel, two days in the Diaspora). Per our previous example, if Passover begins on Sunday and its second day is Monday, then Tisha B'Av that year falls on Sunday, and Shavuot on Monday.

Continuing the sequence, whatever is the third day of Passover in any given year, the *gimel*, in our example Tuesday, will be the *resh*, that is, Rosh HaShana. Whatever is the fourth day of Passover, in our example Wednesday, will be *kuf*, the day of *Keriat HaTorah*, more commonly referred to as Simḥat Torah. The fifth day, whose A"T Ba"Sh mate is *tzadi*, will always be matched by the *tzom* (fast) of Yom Kippur, per our example on Thursday. The sixth day, *vav*, partnered in the A"T Ba"Sh code with *peh*, will coincide with Purim, on Friday.

And that was it for the calendrical correspondence given to us by Rabbi Yosef Karo. Passover biblically is a seven-day holiday. Yet its basis as source for the dates of other major moments on the calendar was only able to offer the *Shulḥan Arukh* six illustrations. For centuries, we needed that to suffice even as we wondered why there was no link to an additional holiday corresponding to the concluding day of Passover.

By way of the letters used for the first six, we wished there would be a connection between the letter *zayin*, seven, and its A"T Ba"Sh mate, the letter *ayin*. And then miraculously, mid-twentieth century, it happened! The day the State of Israel was established in 1948, the fifth of Iyar, became a holiday. It is *Yom HaAtzma'ut*, Independence Day for the Jewish people. *Atzma'ut* in Hebrew begins with the letter *ayin*. *And it is a truth revealed by the calendar that in any and every year whatever is the seventh and concluding day of Passover, the* zayin, *is also the* ayin, *the day of the week on which we celebrate* Yom HaAtzma'ut.

The calendar continues to speak. True, it is not on the same level of *nigleh*, of revealed and open miracles as the ten plagues and the Splitting of the Sea, but it is with the divine speech of *nistar*, the seemingly hidden, with which God has enabled us to see the first step of final Redemption. The two alphabets have again merged in a magnificent message of God's *seder* for history.

The Seder of the Seder

The word *seder* means order – and yet the order of the Seder seems very strange. The ritual of Passover night is divided into three distinct parts. The first is comprised of all the readings from the Haggada until the section known as *Shulḥan Orekh*, Table Setting. At this point, we pause to eat our festive meal. Then we return to the text to conclude the readings and final portions of the holiday text. Simply put, it is recite, eat, and recite again.

Somehow that begs for an explanation. With regard to our morning prayers, Jewish law is quite clear. We must first take care of our spiritual obligations to God before we are permitted to satisfy our physical wants. We have to recite our prayers to completion before we are allowed to sit down for our morning meal.

Yet at the Seder, Jewish law seems unable to make up its mind about proper priorities. Yes, prayers to God and reciting and expounding the narrative of the Haggada do come first. We spend considerable time until we get to our food. But in what would appear to be "the middle of the book," we halt our "God-talk" to placate our hunger. We recline and leisurely eat until we are satiated, and then our slowly closing eyes are pulled back from their reverie to conclude the closing unit of the Haggada.

Is this simply a concession to human frailty, an acknowledgment that it would be too difficult to continue reading from a text without some sustenance? Is the placement of the meal in the middle no more meaningful than an intermission made necessary by a rabbinic recognition that people could not be expected to read and expound for so long a time without a break for nourishment? Or is there in fact some greater meaning, some profound order, to the *seder* of the Seder?

The answer becomes clear when we take note of the exact placement of the meal in context of the entire Haggada. Hallel is a magnificent selection from the Book of Psalms that is customarily recited on holidays. It consists of a number of chapters that together form a self-contained unit. When recited in the synagogue, Hallel begins with a blessing and closes with a blessing – a clear indication that it is meant to be uninterrupted, an organic whole with a clearly defined structure. How remarkable, then, that at the Seder we read but the first two chapters of Hallel, chapters 113 and 114 of the Book of Psalms, and then move on to the meal only to return to the concluding portion, chapters 115 through 118, after we have eaten our fill.

Our original question becomes even stronger. If we feel that it is only right, just as with our daily morning practice, to fulfill the spiritual obligation of praise to God before tending to our physical needs and we therefore recite the beginning of Hallel, why not at the very least finish it? Would it really be so hard to delay eating for just a little bit longer? And if indeed a complete Hallel is out of place because of its length, and the rabbis felt that the Seder participants were entitled at long last to start the meal, could they not have deferred the first two paragraphs to the location after the meal accorded to the major portion of the prayer?

Surely the exact place where we make the break in Hallel has a great deal of significance. And once we identify the thematic difference between the first two chapters of Hallel and the remainder, we will have the key to understanding the reason for the remarkable sequence we have identified as "recite-eat-recite."

The Seder consists of three main units because it is on Passover night that we as a people first came to accept and understand God. The English word "god" is a contraction of the word "good." It conveys only one aspect of God's being, His goodness. In Hebrew, the four-letter name of God, the Tetragrammaton, is a combination of three words that express the three categories of time. *Haya* means "was"; *hoveh* means "is"; *yihyeh* means "will be." These three words combined together are the most powerful way we refer to the Almighty. By using this name, we acknowledge God's presence for all time. God *was* in the past, the all-powerful Creator of the world who revealed Himself to our ancestors. He *is* in the present as the ongoing Source of all of our daily blessings. And He *will continue to be* in the future, fulfilling all the promises He made as part of our covenantal relationship.

To believe in a God who is limited to a presence that fails to encompass all three aspects of time is to make a mockery of His greatness. And so every year on the first night of Passover, we conduct a Seder divided into three acts:

- The first is devoted to explaining the role of God in the past.
- The second emphasizes His closeness to us in the present.
- The last stresses our firm belief that just as He redeemed us long ago from the slavery of Egypt, He will finally bring about the promised messianic Redemption in the future.

Look carefully at the prayers and the rituals before the meal and you will see that their intent is to elaborate God's role in the past. The response to the young children's four questions, the *Ma Nishtana,* about the meaning of this night, begins with the paragraph that recounts how "we were slaves to Pharaoh in Egypt, and the Lord our God brought us out of there with a strong hand and an outstretched arm." We go back to the time when our ancestors at first were idol worshippers and then how "the Omnipresent drew us close in His service." We talk about Laban, the wandering Aramean, and how we ended up in Egypt. We recite the ten plagues and, with *Dayeinu,* express our gratitude for all the things that God did for us, each one of which alone would have warranted gratitude. That, we then sum up, is why we have the Paschal lamb, the matza, and the bitter herbs.

And that is why we then recite only two chapters from the Book of Psalms, chapters 113 and 114, out of the larger prayer commonly recited as Hallel. These first two chapters share this emphasis on praise for *past* kindnesses. We who were once slaves to Pharaoh are now servants of the Lord (ch. 113). God intervened on our behalf with great miracles, with the Splitting of the Sea and the trembling of the mountains (ch. 114). We go no further at this point because we have not yet shifted our attention to the second major way in which we understand God's role in time as expressed by His very name: *hoveh*, He is.

An anonymous author put it very well when he said, "The past is history. The future is mystery. The here and now is a precious gift from God – and that's why we call it the present." We could not survive even for a moment without God's providential care. The most powerful way in which this is expressed is by way of our daily bread. Manna may no longer descend from heaven as it miraculously did for our ancestors in the desert, but we are spiritually sensitive enough to recognize that without the Almighty, we would not be blessed with the most basic requirements for our continued existence. To eat our food is to know God in the present. Fulfilling *Shulḥan Orekh,* the section of the Seder in which we partake of our meal, is to absorb in both a literal and metaphorical way the reality of God's nearness. He feeds us – so we know that He loves us.

The meal portion of the Seder is not an intermission. It is another moment of awareness, different and elevated. It moves us from the *haya* to the *hoveh.* It makes the concept of the God of the past developed in the first section much more meaningful, something that is relevant for us today. In this second section, the God of the present is personal. We sit at His table, and we know that just like a concerned parent, God nudges us, "Eat My child, eat."

We express all of this every time we recite the Grace after Meals. "Blessed are You, Lord [the One whose name includes a relationship with us in the present] our God, King of the Universe, who in His goodness feeds [present tense] the whole world, with grace, kindness, and compassion. He gives [present tense] food to all living things, for His kindness is forever…. He is God who feeds [present tense] and sustains [present tense] all, does good to all and prepares [present tense] food for all creatures He has created."

The Seder has brought us from the past to the present. But it is still not enough. The Seder still cannot be over. We need to move on to the final and most complete understanding of God's relationship with us. After the meal we at last turn to *Tzafun,* Hidden. It is characterized by the matza we set aside at the beginning of the meal to be "saved for later." It is not the matza of the past, but the matza of the future. It is not the matza of memory that recalls the Exodus from Egypt, but the matza of hope for an as yet unfulfilled redemption from the bitterness of the exile and the Diaspora. It is the matza that was wrapped up for the children in the firm belief that they will enjoy a long-awaited future of messianic joy. *Tzafun* serves as a bridge to the third part of the Seder, when we move from gratitude for what is to even greater anticipation of what will be.

It is the third part of the Seder that captures the real significance of the Passover festival. This is not meant to be a holiday designated primarily as a trip down memory lane, a nostalgic reminder of an ancient story that has no realistic relevance to us. The conclusion of the Seder comes to affirm that *what happened before will happen again.* The first *geula* was but a preview of coming attractions. There will assuredly be a *Geula Shelema*, a final and complete Redemption. And so we open the door for Elijah, the prophet Jewish tradition identifies as the one who comes to announce the arrival of the Messiah. Better yet, we ask our children to perform this task. After all, it is a ritual that relates to the future, and it is the young who will most benefit from its fulfillment.

We ask God to pour forth His wrath upon the nations who so viciously abused us. We recite those passages of Hallel rooted in our hopes for the future that we did not mention in the first section of the Seder, during which we concentrated on the past. We pray for the return to Jerusalem, not just the city but the *rebuilt* city, the city of King David's dreams and King Solomon's Temple. We close with *Nirtza,* Parting, in which we express the hope that soon and speedily God will redeem us "into Zion with great joy" and Passover will at last fulfill its full promise.

Recite, eat, and then recite again. The Seder captures the three tenses of God's name. It incorporates all of time. And that is what makes the Seder timeless.

The Seder of History I: Ḥad Gadya

There is a rule in Jewish law about any long blessing. In Hebrew it is expressed this way: "*Hakol holekh aḥar haḥitum*," "everything goes after the ending" (Berakhot 12a). It means that the sages, with the insight of great educators, always required that any blessing that contains more than one idea conclude with a succinct summary that captures the major intent of the entire passage. The ending is where you will find the punch line. It is the most crucial part of any prayer. This is true for a blessing and it is true for a book. The Haggada goes off in many different directions. It has stories and commentaries, laws and rituals. But when all is said and done, what is the main idea it wants to leave us with?

Final words are meant to linger with us, to leave us with the essence of everything that preceded. They represent the end of the journey. They are the destination to which we have been directing all of our efforts. "Everything goes after the ending."

So as we start our expedition of explanation of the Haggada, let us at the very outset have a look at our goal, the conclusion that its authors felt worthy of this position of prominence. The end of the Haggada should make for a better understanding of its major theme. We turn to the back of the book with great anticipation. But we cannot help being perplexed as we realize that the majesty of the retelling of the Exodus and the magnificence of the celebration that commemorates the birth of our people closes with a simple nursery rhyme about one little goat.

Had Gadya – "one little goat my father bought for two *zuzim*." What a peculiar tale. The little goat is devoured by a cat, which is bitten by a dog, which in turn is beaten by a stick, which is burnt by a fire, which is quenched by water, which is consumed by an ox, which is then put to death by a slaughterer who meets his own end at the hands of the Angel of Death, at which point the story finally and mercifully comes to a close. And as if we have not had enough of it, we go through the whole thing once more in the concluding paragraph: "Then came the Holy One and slew the Angel of Death, who slew the slaughterer who slew the ox who drank the water that put out the fire that burned the stick that hit the dog who bit the cat who ate the goat my father bought for two *zuzim,* one little goat, one little goat."

Surely the worst commentary I have ever seen that "explains" this remarkable ending to the Haggada is the one that claims that we close with a nonsensical nursery story "to maintain the interest of the children." At this point the children are long asleep. And nonsense has no place in a holy text, certainly not at the place where we are usually alerted to discover the most important meaning of a lengthy service.

To my mind, Had Gadya *deserves its prominence as bearer of the Seder's final message because it is a parable of the major idea the holiday of Passover seeks to teach our people.* God directs history. The course of human events is not meaningless. It follows divine direction. It has an ultimate and preordained destiny. In short, history has a *seder,* an order that will lead it to its prophetically predicted conclusion. And what is the *seder* of history? It is the closing story of Had Gadya that reveals it to us.

The father in the story is, of course, God. He is *Avinu she-bashamayim,* our Father in heaven. We, the Jewish people, are the little goat. The reason for this symbolism is fairly obvious. In the Book of Genesis, there is a story in which a goat plays a major role in gaining God's blessings for us. Isaac must decide to which one of his sons he will pass on the blessing given to him by his father, Abraham. It is the blessing that will determine who will carry the mantle of Abraham's monotheistic beliefs forward to the future. And Isaac was about to make the wrong choice. Isaac was fooled into believing that Esau was spiritually superior to Jacob. The Torah tells us that it was only because of Rebecca and her plan that the future of the Jewish people was secured and the blessing went to the righteous son, Jacob, later to become the father of the children of Israel.

Here is how the Torah describes it: "Rebecca spoke unto Jacob her son, saying…'Go out to the flock and fetch me from there two good kids of the goats and I will make them savory food for your father such as he loves and you shall bring it to your father that he may eat so that he may bless you before his death'" (Gen. 27:6–10). Two little goats. With them, Jacob was able to receive the blessing. (The question about the morality of this duping of Isaac, the father, is one that receives considerable attention from the rabbinic commentators and is beyond the scope of our present discussion.) Two little goats were needed to provide both the food requested by Isaac as well as the goat skins that Jacob used to cover his hands so that he might be mistaken for his hairy brother. It is this fairly obvious allusion to the biblical story describing how Jacob was able to receive the blessing that permits us to grasp the metaphor of the little goat as representative of the Jewish people. And that too is why we say Ḥad Gadya twice, for both of the goats in the story.

And what is the meaning of the two zuzim with which father acquired the little goat, the Jewish people? The key to this part is the use of the number "two" – something that the Haggada makes clear in the passage right before the recitation of Ḥad Gadya. "Who knows one?" we sang, and we immediately responded, "Our God is One, in heaven and on earth." "Who knows two?" was just as simple. "Two Tablets of the Covenant" – the Tablets that have inscribed upon them the Decalogue summarizing the concepts of all the biblical law. God "acquired" the Jewish people by giving us the Torah. The two Tablets are the covenant that binds us together forever. Ḥad Gadya, Ḥad Gadya – "one little goat, one little goat my father bought for two zuzim." So begins the story of our relationship, of our history, and of the path to our destiny.

Nations are often known by way of symbols. America's symbol is the eagle. The Soviet Union's was the bear. Empires of the past, too, had pictorial shorthands. And shorthands are used in Ḥad Gadya to convey the historic truth that great powers rise and fall with inexorable regularity. Empires, very much like human beings, have limits to their longevity. They come on the scene with seemingly relentless power, pre-vail over those who preceded them, only to fall victim to the very same cycle as they become weakened and are defeated by yet another nation waiting in the wings. The English historian Edward Gibbon published a famous six-volume series explaining the rise and fall of the Roman Empire. His insights have been applied by historians with equal relevance to almost all the major world powers. Rise and fall is the story of history.

It is the very story of *Had Gadya* as well. God took us to be His people, following which we became witness to the seemingly haphazard transfer of power from one empire to the next. Yet all the while God wants us to remember that these events are overseen by His guiding hands. They are *not* haphazard. They are part of a *seder*, an order decreed by the Author of history for His hidden reasons. History is *His*-story. And the story has a preordained conclusion.

We can hazard fairly good guesses at the empires hinted at by way of illustration in *Had Gadya*. The cat is Assyria. The dog is Babylonia. The stick is Persia. The fire is Greece. The water is Rome. The ox is Islam. The slaughterers are the Crusaders, misguided agents of Christianity.

Had Gadya is meant to be an overview of *all* of history. And that is why it adds prophecy to its description of past events and includes allusions to moments that have not yet occurred. Its message is meant to affirm that the end of the book of the story of mankind has already been decreed even though it has not yet transpired. The final chapter, the ultimate Redemption and messianic fulfillment, is guaranteed by the God who took us out of Egypt.

Geula Part I must be brought to completion by *Geula Shelema*. So the final paragraph reveals, prophetically phrased in past tense as if it already occurred, "Then came Holy One and slew the Angel of Death, who slew the slaughterer who slew the ox who drank the water that put out the fire that burned the stick that hit the dog who bit the cat who ate the goat my father bought for two *zuzim*."

Eventually, God will reveal Himself and replace all the powers that came before Him. The time will come when He will be crowned as the King of all kings. His rise is the only one that will not be followed by a fall. In the *seder* of historic cycles, the rulership of God is the sole heir to everlasting legitimacy. Every prayer service ends with this idea in the line that concludes the *Aleinu* prayer with the words of the prophet Zechariah that "in that day the Lord will be One and His name will be One" (14:9). Similarly, in allegorical form, it is the very same idea that brings the Haggada to a close – surely appropriate as the concluding message of the Seder.

But there is one thing that is extremely important to note. In this outline of the Seder of history, we should certainly ask, where are we at present? How far are we from the long-awaited conclusion of God's revelation to mankind presaged by the final paragraph of *Ḥad Gadya*? Unfortunately, we do not know when the Messiah will come. But the rabbis have prophetically left us one clue to alert us to his imminent arrival. It is recorded in the Midrash by way of a fascinating parable:

> A student once asked his rabbi, "We have been waiting so long for the Messiah to come, yet he still has not made his appearance. How will we, the Jewish people, know when he will at last reveal himself? What is the sign we can look for that will announce his imminent arrival?" The rabbi responded, "I will answer you by way of a story. A father and son journeyed together on a long trek through a desert. Their destination was a faraway city. Weary from the trip, the young boy pleaded with his father to give him some kind of sign so that he might know when they were close to the final destination. In response, the father told the boy, 'This will be a sure indication before you. Remember this sign. When you will see a cemetery, you will know that the city is near.' This parable," the rabbi continued to his student who had asked about a sign heralding the imminent arrival of the Messiah, "is the answer to your question. When you will see a cemetery, you will know that redemption is near. So too did God reveal to His children that in the aftermath of being beset by horrible tragedy, death, and destruction, the Almighty will have mercy and answer the prayers of the Jews, as it is written, 'And the Almighty will respond to you in the day of great hardship'" (Ps. 20:4).[1]

---

1. *Midrash Tehillim* (Buber), *mizmor 68*.

Messianic footsteps will become heard from a distance when we see a great cemetery. The midrash did not make clear how many people had to be buried in the cemetery to qualify for the horrific event necessary to evoke God's compassion, nor did it give any reason for this disturbing linkage. It simply made clear that the prelude to the final Redemption would be a Jewish graveyard unlike in magnitude any that came before it.

Surely we are the first generation in history to grasp the full meaning of this prophecy. The Holocaust exceeded the Jewish tragedies that preceded it, in scope and in number. When it came to a close in 1945, six million Jews had perished, victims of a genocidal plan that sought to destroy the entire Jewish people from the face of the earth. It was a cemetery beyond compare. And just three years later, in 1948, we witnessed the miraculous establishment of the State of Israel. The sign of mass destruction was soon followed by the first steps of final Redemption.

That is exactly the *seder*, the order of history, as recorded in *Ḥad Gadya*. The concluding paragraph is messianic. It speaks of the universal reign of God. Note carefully what precedes it. The paragraph before the last talks of the Angel of Death. It alludes to the cemetery of the story told by the father to his son when asked for a sign indicating that their longed-for destination was near. It is the cemetery the rabbi of the midrash advised his student would serve as the harbinger of redemption. It is the cemetery of the Holocaust of six million that finally stirred God to respond with the initial stage of salvation.

So where are we today in the outline of history set before us by *Ḥad Gadya*? I believe the answer is obvious. We are right between stanzas – between the penultimate and the concluding stanzas. We are a generation of survivors, the remnants of a people decimated by the Angel of Death. And we are also the blessed inheritors of a divine promise that – it is becoming clearer and clearer – we are on the cusp of soon seeing fulfilled.

True, we are not yet at the end of history described in the final paragraph of *Ḥad Gadya*. God has not yet revealed Himself fully. Israel is not yet the spiritual center of Jewish life, with the Third Temple rebuilt in the holy city of Jerusalem. But it is a start. It is a beginning that portends the complete fulfillment of all of our prayers.

The Seder of History II:
The Patriarchs

The Seder, as we have noted, is concerned with past, present, and future. It is not enough to recall that long ago God redeemed us from Egypt. Passover is meant to inspire us with the hope of a future redemption as well. And the Seder, with its emphasis on history following a pre-ordained divine order, has assured us for many centuries that in spite of our long exile, we would return to the land of Israel and reestablish it as our national and spiritual homeland.

Remarkably enough, at least part of this prediction has already come true. We have witnessed the rebirth of the State of Israel. Diaspora Jews in large numbers have come home, to the land biblically promised by God to the descendents of Abraham, Isaac, and Jacob. It is hard to see this as anything other than a miracle. It is nothing less than fulfillment of the words of our ancient prophets. It happened because it had to happen. Unlikely as it seemed ever to become a reality, the State of Israel came into being because it was God's divine plan. But if this was all predestined as part of a *seder*, an order, divinely decreed long ago, were we granted any hints about its imminent arrival? If this was our immutable destiny, did Jewish sources permit us an inkling of what to expect and how this would all come about?

To fully believe that history follows a *seder*, as the underlying theme of the Passover Seder emphasizes, it would be very helpful if we could point to some meaningful clues that demonstrate the truth of this remarkable concept. And fortunately, with a knowledge of traditional texts and commentaries, that is not really too difficult to do. Going back to Jewish sources of old, we can discover amazing hints about how the redemptive process would take place, predictions that we in our day have lived to see fulfilled.

The principle that is at the core of our major insight is the illuminating concept often referred to by Nahmanides, which he based on a passage in *Midrash Tanḥuma*: "*Maase avot siman levanim*," "Everything that occurred to our forefathers [Abraham, Isaac, and Jacob] is a sign of what will happen to their children" (*Lekh Lekha* 9). This means that prophecy is built into the biblical stories of our patriarchs. What at first glance seem to be merely passing incidents in their lives are actually precursors of comparable events that will be experienced by their descendents.

All of Jewish history has its seeds in the lives of the first three patriarchs. To read their biographies in the Torah is to be permitted a fascinating peek into a crystal ball highlighting future events. Hidden in the stories of the patriarchs that spanned but several hundred years in total are stenographic hints to the major moments that would play out over the thousands of years to follow.

What happened to Abraham serves as an outline for the first period of the history of our people. In the Torah we read how Abraham, driven by famine, goes down to Egypt. He and his wife Sarah fear Pharaoh, but God intervenes to save them from the harm the king intended. Not only were their lives spared but they leave laden with gifts and accompanied by some of the king's own people.

It is quite obvious for us to see the parallel of this story in the events that befell the Jewish people in the very beginning of their existence as a nation. What happened to our first ancestor was a preview of coming attractions for what occurred to his descendents during the first third of their history. Because of a severe famine, the children of Jacob found themselves forced to flee to Egypt for food. While at first given great respect, they suffered greatly there until God intervened to release them from bondage. Remarkably, just as what happened with Abraham, when they left they were also given gifts of gold, silver, and garments by the Egyptians, some of whom even joined them as converts. For Abraham, the story took place over a matter of days. For his descendents, the "replay" of his experience required 210 years. But in mini form, a major event in the life of Abraham found its sequel in the experiences of his descendents. What happened to the first forefather occurred once more, albeit in extended time, to the children of Israel.

The commentators find many comparable connections. Abraham lived 175 years. His life was a preview of a total of 880 years of Jewish history, from the very beginnings of the Jews as a nation with the families of the twelve sons of Jacob, through the years of wandering, and finally the conquest and settlement of the land of Canaan.

The life of Isaac corresponds to the period of national Jewish sovereignty. Isaac is unique among the three patriarchs in one all-important way. He is the only one never to have left the land of Israel, with the exception of a very short visit to the land of the Philistines. The events of his life, commentators point out, are linked to the stories that coincide with the First and Second Temples, a span of nine hundred years in all that marked Jewish residence in the land of Israel, with but a very brief interruption during the seventy-year Babylonian exile. And just as Isaac had twin sons, Jacob and Esau, who started life together but then split up to go their separate ways, so too the Jewish kingdom was originally united as brothers but then divided into two: the ten tribes of Israel, to the north, and the two that made up Judea, to the south. More, in the aftermath of this break, both Esau and the ten tribes became lost to Jewish history.

The year 70 CE marks the onset of an exile lasting almost two thousand years. It begins the story of the Jews in the Diaspora longing to return to the land from which they were forced to take flight. It is the era that was prefigured by Jacob, the third of the patriarchs, whose life was mainly defined by running and fleeing. Jacob's very name, based on the word *ekev*, heel, was perfectly suited for the man whose encounters with Esau and Laban forced him frequently to "take to heel" and choose flight over fight. Jacob is the perfect symbol of the Diaspora Jew, and his life story mirrored the tragic experiences that would be the fate of an exiled people. According to a famous kabbal-istic idea recorded in the Talmud, the world as we know it is meant to exist only until the year 6000 on the Hebrew calendar (Sanhedrin 97a). Today in the sixth millennium, the final era of human history, we must look to the life of the last of the patriarchs for the model of the events predestined for us.

The early years of Jacob surely prefigured the years of wander-ing and homelessness of the Jews until the mid-twentieth century. But it is profoundly significant that late in life, Jacob's story takes a dramatic turn. It is so important that it brings about a change of his very identity, as evinced by his gaining a new name. In the Torah a name defines us; a change of name implies a new person has made his appearance. The name "Jacob," from the Hebrew root for "heel," identifies him as the one who flees from confrontation and allows himself to be stepped upon by the heel of others. His new name, "Israel," meaning "the one who strove with God and with men," now defines him as a person will-ing to fight for survival.

The prophetic meaning of this story is clear. What happened to Jacob, the Diaspora Jew, is what would eventually be the destiny of his descendents. Just as Jacob became Israel, so too would this story be replayed thousands of years later for the Jewish people in exile. It is highly instructive to read the details of this life-changing event as it appears in the Book of Genesis. By analyzing the account carefully, we can note the amazing correspondence between the Jacob story of old and its contemporary parallel:

> And Jacob was left alone; and there wrestled a man with him until the breaking of the day. And when he [the man] saw that he prevailed not against him, he [the man] touched the hollow of his thigh; and the hollow of Jacob's thigh was strained, as he wrestled with him. And he [the man] said, "Let me go, for the day breaks." And he [Jacob] said, "I will not let you go, unless you bless me." And he said unto him, "What is your name?" And he said, "Jacob." And he said, "Your name shall be called no more Jacob, but Israel; for you have striven with God and with men, and have prevailed." (32:25–29)

For Jacob, the immediate prelude for his name change to "Israel" was an attack by an assailant. The Torah identifies the area of injury as the *yerekh Yaakov*, hollow of the thigh. The Midrash understands this as a euphemism. It was an attempt to prevent Jacob from procreating (see the expression, "*Vayehi kol nefesh yotze'ei yerekh Yaakov*," "And all the souls that came out of the loins of Jacob" [Ex. 1:5]). It was a blow meant to destroy Jacob's future. What it said by way of prophecy was that a time would come when an attempt would be made to obliterate Jacob's children, a genocidal plan that would call for the elimination of all of the offspring of Israel – a stark foreboding of the Holocaust. Shortly thereafter, the angel blesses Jacob by giving him the additional name of Israel. The physical blow is a prophetic reference to the Holocaust; the blessing that followed, a divine foretelling of the creation of the State of Israel.

The Talmud records the prayers of several sages who pleaded with God to send the Messiah but who added, "May I not live to see his coming" (Sanhedrin 98b). What prompted this strange request was their awareness, from numerous biblical sources, that immediately prior to the final Redemption there would be a period of unimaginable horror. The blow to the thigh before the blessing, the Holocaust before the establishment of the State of Israel – these were secrets of the *seder* of history understood by the rabbis. And much as they longed for the latter events, they wished they could be spared the former. This was what led the rabbi in the story we have previously noted, when responding to the student who asked for a sign indicating that the final Redemption is near, to recount the parable of the boy wandering with his father in the desert, desperately anxious to know when they would reach their destination, who was told "when you will see a cemetery, you will know that the city is near."

The Holocaust was the collective cemetery of six million. It ended in 1945. Three years later, the Jews assumed a new identity. No longer would they put their trust in others. If the world crushes the Jacob who chooses to be a *yoshev ohalim*, a peaceful dweller in the tents, who pursues only a life of study, then Jacob will become Israel, prepared to fight back against his attackers. And who gave Jacob this blessing? In the Torah story, it is the unnamed villain. It hardly makes sense, but the one who the sages mysteriously identify only as the "*saro shel Esav*," "the angelic representative of Esau," is the one who suddenly responded to his battered victim by blessing him with the new title "Israel." Nahmanides, perceiving the ultimate meaning of this story as prophecy, suggests that at some distant future the *saro shel Esav,* representing the united nations of the world, will take pity on the wounded Jacob and grant him the legitimacy of the name "Israel." So miraculously, in 1948, the United Nations did precisely that and the new State of Israel was born.

Five short sentences summarize the Torah's preview of the *seder* of the twentieth century. "And Jacob was left alone" perfectly describes the abandonment of the Jews by the entire world. The "Final Solution" was the avowed goal of the Nazi regime. Supposedly civilized countries responded by sealing shut their gates to immigration. The Jewish people were forsaken. Only after suffering the grievous "blow to the thigh" did they recognize, as did Jacob, that even those committed to peace must be willing to fight for survival.

Jacob fought and gained not only the respect but also the blessing of his enemy; that is how he became Israel. So too the Jews in the twentieth century transformed themselves from victims to victors. Holocaust survivors became Haganah fighters. More remarkable still, they achieved the stunning climax of the biblical story: The blessing of their new status of Israel was granted to them by the *saro shel Esav* – representatives of the very nations that had previously abetted the "Final Solution."

The *seder* of history has its roots in the story of the patriarchs.

The Seder of History III: The Jubilee Year

Passover is the holiday of freedom. The Jubilee year is its powerful legal sequel. The Torah commands that every fiftieth year all those who are enslaved shall be freed:

> And you shall number seven sabbaths of years unto you, seven times seven years; and the space of the seven sabbaths of years shall be unto you forty-nine years. Then shall you cause the trumpet of the Jubilee to sound on the tenth day of the seventh month, in the Day of Atonement shall you make the trumpet sound throughout all your land. And you shall hallow the fiftieth year, and proclaim liberty throughout all the land unto all the inhabitants thereof: It shall be a Jubilee unto you; and you shall return every man unto his possession, and you shall return every man unto his family. A Jubilee shall that fiftieth year be unto you: you shall not sow, neither reap that which grow of itself in it, nor gather the grapes in it of your vine undressed. For it is the Jubilee; it shall be holy unto you: you shall eat the increase thereof out of the field. In the year of this Jubilee you shall return every man unto his possession. (Lev. 25:8–13)

So revolutionary was this idea that the civic authorities who purchased the Liberty Bell, the iconic symbol of American independence, chose for inscription the words "Proclaim liberty throughout the land unto all the inhabitants thereof" as its central message. Slavery could not be permanent. Freedom is the right of every human being.

The very first law in the civil code of Judaism, presented in *Parashat Mishpatim,* imposes a limit on the length of time for a slave's confinement: "If you buy a Hebrew servant, six years he shall serve; and in the seventh he should go out free for nothing" (Ex. 21:2). Why does a law about slavery begin the lengthy list of legal prescriptions for leading a holy life? Nahmanides explains the reason behind the sequence of the laws recorded in the Torah following Revelation at Sinai: they follow the order of the Ten Commandments. In the first commandment, God identifies Himself as the One who took the Jews out of the land of Egypt, the house of bondage. So too, therefore, must we liberate our slaves after six years – a very significant step towards the ultimate goal of the elimination of slavery in entirety.

The Torah took one more crucial step in its approach to a condition clearly antithetical to divine morality. It completely changed the laws governing its practice. To speak of biblical acceptance of slavery without making clear how far Torah law removed it from the way it was practiced, even in the United States, until the mid-nineteenth century is to totally ignore the halakhic framework that circumscribed the relationship between slave and master. The Talmud makes clear that a Hebrew slave, unlike his counterpart in the world at large, has rights. If he is physically abused, he has to be set free. He cannot be compelled to do "meaningless work" (for example, to dig a hole and then fill it again) – work that has no purpose other than to prove his submission. In perhaps the most powerful illustration of the way in which halakha provides for the preservation of the slave's human dignity and concern for his welfare, the Talmud posits that if the master owns two pillows, he must share one with his slave; if the master owns only one, it must be given to the slave because the slave feels downtrodden enough and should not be made to suffer unduly for his condition of servitude. Indeed, the Talmud observes that "he who acquires a slave is as if he gains a master over him."

Biblical slavery should never be confused with its historic counterpart either in ancient Egypt or in America as depicted in *Uncle Tom's Cabin*. Yet even in its highly altered state, the Torah refuses to legitimatize it without limit. A week has a required time of rest every seventh day; so too every seventh year brings the legal period of servitude to an end. Having changed the very definition of slavery, though, and made its condition far less repugnant, the Torah is concerned with an unusual possibility. Perhaps the slave might come to be so habituated to his situation that he no longer desires freedom. What if a slave wants to stay with his master? What if a slave chooses security over selfhood, indenture over independence?

To this the Torah answers with a remarkable compromise. Free will allows people to make choices against their own best interest. The Torah opts for the ideal of freedom. It would prefer a six-year maximum for slavery. But for those incapable of handling freedom, God feels compassion and allows for an alternative: "But if the servant shall plainly say, I love my master, my wife, and my children; I will not go out free, his master shall bring him unto God [the court] and shall bring him to the door, unto the doorpost; and his master shall bore his ear through with an awl, and he shall serve him forever" (Ex. 21:5–6).

The rabbis of the Talmud explain the symbolic meaning of this seemingly incomprehensible ritual. What is the significance of piercing the ear of the slave who is entitled to freedom yet refuses to accept it? It is a biblical sign of disapproval for an action only reluctantly permitted.

The ear that heard the divine utterance, "for unto Me the children of Israel are servants" (Lev. 25:55), and yet preferred a human master, let that ear be bored. The ear that heard God proclaim on Mount Sinai, "I am the Lord your God who took you out of the land of Egypt, the house of bondage" (Ex. 20:2; Deut. 5:6) and voluntarily chooses slavery obviously has not heard God's will nor His message.

More, the piercing of the ear is to be performed on the doorpost. The link with the Passover story is stunningly obvious. The path to freedom required the Jews to slaughter a lamb, a god of Egypt, and smear its blood on the doorpost: "And the blood shall be to you for a sign upon the houses where you are, and when I see the blood, I will *pass over* you, and there shall be no plagues upon you to destroy you, when I smite the land of Egypt" (Ex. 12:13). Passover required an act of personal involvement in the process. We were to demonstrate our desire for freedom and our willingness to sacrifice for it at our doorsteps. The slave who chooses continued servitude has shown his rejection of this ideal of deliverance. He prefers to be confined rather than to leave. He rejects the open door of liberty. He is permitted his choice, but he must bear a mark on his flesh, on the ear that has not heard God's will, and to bear witness to his folly at the very site biblically designated in Egypt for achieving our freedom.

The biblical passage, as we have seen, concludes "and he shall serve him forever" (Ex. 21:6). But according to the Talmud, that is not meant to be taken literally. The law of the Jubilee year in the Book of Leviticus makes clear that even the period of voluntarily chosen slavery has its limit. The Torah will simply not permit anyone to forfeit freedom forever. In the fiftieth year, everyone is to be set free: "In the year of this Jubilee you shall return every man unto his possession" (Lev. 25:13).

And one other major law takes effect in the fiftieth year. The Torah was concerned with a problem that today is receiving ever greater attention. Wealth transmitted from one generation to the next can create societies of considerable economic inequality. The rich continue to get richer, and the poor have no way out of their poverty. Bad financial decisions of one generation are paid for by those that follow. The middle class is squeezed out of existence, and society is beset by extremes of unlimited affluence and irremediable poverty. The Torah found a way out of the tragic consequences of unrestricted capitalism. Every fifty years land is restored to its original owners. Every fifty years everyone would begin with a renewed opportunity to improve their financial condition. No one generation could destroy the prospects for success of the next. The Jubilee year returns Jews to their land, just as it grants everyone their freedom.

In the context of the biblical text discussing this law, there is one word that strikingly calls out for commentary. It is a word that in the Hebrew original is written defectively, that is, missing a letter. It is not a scribal error but rather an intentional "misspelling." Every Torah scroll must be written with this word clearly missing a letter. So much so that if the grammatically correct letter were inserted by the scribe writing this passage in the *sefer Torah*, it would then become invalid! Only the "incorrect" way of writing the word is correct! The word in question is *tashuvu*, which appears in the verse, "In the year of this Jubilee you shall return [*tashuvu*] every man unto his possession."

Tashuvu is almost certainly the most significant word in this verse, which describes the legal effect of the Jubilee year. It means "you shall return." In this year of the Jubilee, you shall return – every man to his possession. You shall return – everyone to his freedom. And this word (spelled *tav, shin, beit, vav*) is written lacking the letter *vav* after the second letter, *shin*. The intentional "error" has long intrigued biblical scholars. What message could possibly be hidden in this spelling?

The Zohar, the masterwork of Kabbala, Jewish mysticism, offers the key to an explanation. In Hebrew, letters are also numbers. The *gematria* of a word, its numerical equivalent by way of the value of its letters, has special meaning. When the Torah writes "you shall return" with a missing letter in Hebrew, it incorporates into the language of law the additional message of prophecy. That deeper message is addressed on a more profound level to the Jewish nation as a whole. The Torah knew that a time would come when the Jewish people, by virtue of exile, would find themselves enslaved to foreign masters – a slavery to which they would become so inured that they would sink to even accepting it voluntarily. The Torah wanted to reassure the Jewish people that there would be a collective "Jubilee year" for the nation as a whole, corresponding to the Jubilee year for every biblical slave. It will be a Jubilee year bringing with it return of our ancient homeland as well as the freedom of self-government. And although not understood for centuries, the Torah concealed the very date of this national Jubilee in the "misspelled" word.

Tashuvu is a word, but it is also a number that can be understood as a year. A year of profound significance in modern Jewish history, 5708; the year 1948 in the secular calendar. That was the year marking the birth of the modern-day State of Israel. That was the year when we returned to the land of our forefathers. *And that was the year alluded to by the biblical verse legislating freedom and the blessings of the Jubilee.* Today we can confirm the incredible insight of the Zohar. "You will return," the Hebrew word *tashuvu*, predicted national redemption in a year corresponding exactly to its numerical value.

More, it also lacked the letter *vav*, which stands for the number six. Perhaps, as a student of mine suggested, we may now understand it as prophesying our collective return to our national homeland but lacking an important "six" – the six million who perished in the Holocaust and who, for reasons known only to the One Above, did not merit to live to be a part the modern-day miracle. Or perhaps, as someone else proposed to me, it was a hidden suggestion that this would take place in the sixth millennium, the thousand-year period in which we presently find ourselves.

A remarkable mishna in *The Ethics of the Fathers*, quotes Ben Bag Bag, who taught, "Delve into it and delve into it for everything is within it" (5:21). Amazingly, we in our generation have become privileged to understand the profound significance of a biblical word as prophecy. We can only pray that as we have merited the Jubilee blessings of land and of freedom, we will live to see complete and final messianic Redemption.

The Seder and the
Secret of Sentences

The assertion that history follows a *seder* has yet another remarkable confirmation. It is probably the most powerful proof of all. The day that I first heard it changed my life. I was in Israel on a congregational tour when a friend shared with me some remarkable stories about a saintly scholar in the city of Safed. Those who knew him well were sure that he was one of those known in Jewish tradition as "the thirty-six righteous men" – those holy and pure people in whose merit the entire world is maintained.

I did not dare hope that I would have the opportunity to actually meet him, but fate and divine destiny somehow brought us together. The details of our meeting were so incredible that I have to believe God Himself brought it about. But what I learned after we spent memorable hours together has indelibly altered the way I now understand the Torah, Jewish history, and even life itself.

Why he took me into his confidence I still do not know. He is a man utterly immune to the enticements of fame and wealth. He shared with me a mystical secret on two conditions: that I not reveal it publicly until he informed me that the time is right, and that I never, ever, divulge his identity and disturb his lifelong pursuit of anonymity. For years, I kept the secret to myself. It allowed me to see things as no one else did. Yet I could not say a word because of my promise.

And then a few years ago he called me and told me simply, "Now is the time." I have no idea what had changed. Perhaps it was because the world is today more attuned to the mystical and more receptive to its profound teachings. Perhaps it is because people have already been introduced to the concept of biblical codes and will not be overly cynical about a somewhat comparable approach. Or perhaps it is simply because there is something this secret can teach us today that the world desperately needs for its enlightenment, for its inspiration, and for its very survival. Let me therefore share it with you precisely the way I heard it.

We had spoken of miracles. He told me that miraculous events did not end with biblical tales. They are ongoing, occurring throughout all of history, including in modern times. The creation of the State of Israel, for example, he said, happened as an expression of God's will exactly when it was predicted to occur in the Bible. "Predicted exactly when it was supposed to?" I asked. "I do not recall the promise of return to the land being identified with a specific year." He replied, "Then perhaps it is time for me to reveal to you the secret of sentences."

I had no idea what he meant. Sentences? What secret could he possibly be referring to? "Let me show you something," he told me. And then he confided in me an insight he had received from his teachers that literally left me gasping. "The year that the State of Israel was born was 1948 on the secular calendar. In our traditional way of counting, the date was the year 5708. Know that the verses in the five books of Moses, the Torah, correspond to the years of history. Every major event of all times will have some allusion to it, direct or indirect, in the verse that is linked to it by number. Do you know," he asked me, "what the 5,708th verse in the Bible is?" Of course I had no idea.

So he told me, and I subsequently verified it. "It is Deuteronomy 30:3: 'And the Lord your God will turn your captivity and have compassion upon you, and will return and gather you from all the peoples where the Lord your God has scattered you.'" It was amazing. And it seemed too good to be true. Perhaps it was just a remarkable coincidence, one of those quirks that are more entertaining than instructive. But it was certainly intriguing: The one verse that speaks of return to the land after centuries of exile is actually *the very same biblical sentence* whose number corresponds to the year in which this unlikely event occurred in modern times!

In fact, Maimonides in his classic halakhic work *Mishneh Torah*, references one sentence from the entire Torah to validate the importance of belief in the prophecy of messianic fulfillment at the End of Days – *and it is precisely this verse:*

> Anyone who does not believe in him [the Messiah] or does not await his coming denies not only the statements of the other prophets, but those of the Torah and Moses, our teacher. The Torah testified to his coming, as it is written: "And the Lord your God will turn your captivity and have compassion upon you, and will return and gather you from all the peoples where the Lord your God has scattered you."[1]

So I found the nerve to ask a follow-up question. "You mean," I hesitatingly inquired, "this is not simply an isolated instance? Is it a principle that relates equally to other major events? Could I, for example, find a comparable reference to the Holocaust just as well as we did for the time of national redemption?" He responded with a smile, "Why not try it yourself?" And so I counted the verses backwards, making note of the number as well as corresponding year. The previous chapter, Deuteronomy 29, is the one whose sentences correspond to the years of the Holocaust, from the mid-1930s to the end of World War II, in 5705 (1945).

With halting breath, I read the phrases that sprang out at me in the verses whose biblical placement was linked with the horrible years of genocide and the Germans' determination to implement what they called the "Final Solution." The words clearly spoke of that terrible time in history: "All the curses of the covenant…. The plagues of that land and the sickness with which the Lord has made it sick.… The whole land is brimstone and salt and a burning…. Like the overthrow of Sodom and Gomorrah.… Even all the nations shall say, why has the Lord done thus?" (Deut. 29:20–23). It was true! The sentences linked by number to the

---

1. *Laws of Kings* 11:1.

years of the Holocaust described – as if written at the very same time the events occurred – the horrors and afflictions of that unimaginable era.

But there was yet one more amazing revelation that appeared by way of this reading. The verse that corresponds to 5705/1945 stunned me with its powerful message. It is, of course, the sentence that serves as the Torah's final word on the Holocaust and its meaning. It is God's summary as well as His "explanation." And what do the words we are so anxious to hear have to tell us? Note carefully the text because I believe it represents the very best and most appropriate judgment that human beings can possibly offer as we consider the events of those days: "The secret things belong unto the Lord our God but the things that are revealed belong unto us and to our children forever, that we may do all the words of this law" (Deut. 29:28).

When all is said and done, God is wiser than we are. God understands more than we do. In the profound words of the eleventh-century sage, Baḥya ibn Pekuda, "If we could understand God, we would be God." At times, we may grasp some of His ways. As we probe for reasons and explanations, we can occasionally grab hold of some truths that illuminate God's compassionate guidance of our lives. In those moments, we are overwhelmed by His greatness.

And in those times of confusion when we cannot comprehend how God could possibly seem so immune to our suffering, we reassure ourselves that God's love for us is the constant that will never, ever change. The biblical epitaph to the Holocaust must be our response to the travails of everyday life: "The secret things belong to the Lord our God." There are some things we will never understand. But our faith must be stronger than our misfortunes. Our belief can survive questions that have only partial answers. What remains for us is acceptance of God's will, to carry out the words of His law. In them we will find purpose to our lives and meaning for our existence.

No one can ever explain the Holocaust. But historically, the Holocaust was followed by national redemption, by the return of our people to our ancient homeland – something that no historian considered possible and that those who considered us eternally cursed as "the wandering Jews" predicted would never ever happen. I believe Elie Wiesel, an eloquent spokesman for Holocaust survivors, put it best when he said of our times, "We are the most cursed of all generations and we are the most blessed of all generations. We are the generation of Job but we are also the generation of Jerusalem."

To realize that both the curse and the blessing were secretly recorded and predicted in the Torah by way of the correspondence of sentences is to recognize that history, the bad and the good, are part of a divinely told tale with a conclusion meant to bring about messianic fulfillment. And that is precisely the truth we proclaim as we choose the word *seder* to identify the chief ritual of Passover, the festival commemorating God's active role in history.

The Seder and Looking Backwards

The Torah, as the word of God, is filled with many levels of meaning. According to tradition, there are four main ways in which we are to study and understand its content. They are alluded to by way of acronym in the word *pardes*. *Pardes* means "garden," but its four Hebrew letters refer to the four approaches to text that collectively allow us to grasp the full meaning of Torah:

- *Peshat* – the "plain" (simple) or direct meaning;
- *Remez* – the "hints" or deep (allegoric: hidden or symbolic) meaning beyond just the literal sense;
- *Derash* – from *darash*, "inquire" (seek), the comparative meaning, as given through similar occurrences;
- *Sod* – the "secret" (mystery) or the mystical meaning, as given through inspiration or revelation.

The sequence of the approaches that are hinted at in the word *pardes* is significant. We are first and foremost obligated to study Torah texts by way of their literal meaning. "*Ein mikra yotze midei peshuta*," "a verse must be understood simply for what it says," in spite of any additional insights it may contain hidden within it. Indeed, one is not even permitted to enter the realm of *sod*, the kabbalistic secrets of Torah, until reaching the age of *bina*, wisdom and understanding, after having already mastered the previous three levels of interpretation.

Look carefully at the three letters that comprise the Hebrew word *seder* (*samekh, dalet, resh*) and you will note something remarkable: it contains three of the four letters of the word *pardes*, in reverse order, excluding only the one (*peh*) that alludes to *peshat* – the simple and literal meaning. If we think of *seder* as an acronym for the ways in which to review the Torah story of the Exodus from Egypt, we are told that Passover night is not a time to concentrate on the simple story of the events as they occurred, but to delve deeper, beyond the *peshat* – and the more one increases probing deeper, "the more admirable it is." At the Seder we are to transcend the literal. And more, we are not only permitted to enter the realm of *sod*, the mystical secrets of the events that gave birth to our people, but we are even encouraged to reverse the normal order and begin our study there. *Sod, derash, remez* – that is the order of the Seder.

The Seder asks us to view history from a backward perspective. It is an allusion to a famous story in the Book of Exodus in which Moses pleads with God to allow him to "see" the Almighty. "Show me, I pray You, Your glory" (33:18), Moses begs. The response seems incomprehensible on the surface: "You cannot see My face, for man cannot see Me and live.… Behold there is a place by Me, and you shall stand upon the rock, and it shall come to pass while My glory passes by, then I will put you in a cleft of the rock, and will cover you with My hand until I have passed by. And I will take away My hand and you will see My back, but My face shall not be seen" (vv. 20–23).

One of the thirteen fundamental principles of Judaism according to Maimonides is that God has no body. How is it then that Moses asked to "see" God, if the Almighty has no form and is invisible? And how could God possibly promise to fulfill Moses' request by allowing him a view of His back, a corporeal dimension that clearly has no relationship to His being?

The classical commentators explain that Moses asked not so much to see God as to understand Him. Not, as it were, "show me what You look like," but "allow me to perceive Your glory." As the Talmud puts it,

Moses pleaded for the answer to the most perplexing theological problem of all: let me understand why the righteous suffer and the wicked
prosper. I want to worship You and revere You but I have difficulty com-
prehending Your ways. It is Your *kavod* – Your glory – that I beseech
You to explain (Berakhot 7a).

In that context, we can grasp God's response: "You…cannot see
Me and live." During the abbreviated span of human lifetime, God's
management of the universe appears inexplicable. But there will come
a time when you will see My back and you will understand. Looking at
events from the perspective of hindsight they will make sense at last. In
retrospect everything will become clear. This is what Kierkegaard meant
when he said "the greatest tragedy of life is that it must be lived forward
and can only be understood backward."

The very name of Moses in Hebrew, *Moshe*, magnificently makes
the point. There were surely many moments when Moses might have
doubted his mission, when the difficulties he confronted could have
caused him to question God's justice. Yet Moses' name in Hebrew when
read backward is *Hashem*. At the end of his life, seeing everything in
retrospect, he could understand that everything he experienced was
divinely directed. The perspective that allows us to view life in retrospect is crucial for all of history.

The Torah tells us that when God finished creating the world, He
"saw every thing that He had made, and, behold, it was very good. And
there was evening and there was morning, the sixth day" (Gen. 1:31). To
our finite eyes the world seems to be filled with imperfections. Yet God
calls it "very good." What is the difference between our appraisals? God
is not limited by time. He has an overview of past, present, and future
merged into one. We witness history unfolding beginning with the
story of Adam, progenitor of all mankind. The letters of Adam's name
in Hebrew refer to the three key figures of history in the chronological
order of their appearance – beginning, middle, and end. The *aleph* is
Adam himself; the *dalet* is David; the *mem* is *Mashiaḥ*, Messiah. According to Kabbala, these three share the same soul, by way of *gilgul*, reincar-
nation. We humans are restricted to a sequential view of the stories that
play out on earth as we move from beginning to end. God, however, is
always aware of the final destination, the *mem* of *Mashiaḥ*, and the steps

necessary to reach that goal. With the vision of the end at the beginning, God can declare that the world is not only good but good to the *n*th degree The word *meod*, very, is an acronym for *Mashiah*, Adam, David.

The *sod*, the secret that enables us to cope with the tragedies of history and survive all of our exiles, is the conviction that someday in the future we too will be able to look back at everything that happened and recognize that in retrospect the world and the story of the Jewish people are part of a divine plan that is "very good." And the word *seder* asks us to begin this way of analyzing our history, from back to front, with the *mem* of *Mashiah* at the forefront of our consciousness.

The Seder and Its Fifteen Parts

Numbers have meaning. At the very end of the Seder, we sing a song that alerts us to the idea that every number has special significance. *"Eḥad Mi Yode'a,"* "Who Knows One?" teaches us the linkage between the first 13 numbers and their respective profound biblical implications. Once we understand the concept, it behooves us to apply it beyond the illustrations of that hymn, which stops at 13.

The secret of number 15 is one that is fairly obvious. The very way in which it is written in the Hebrew alphabet makes clear its cardinal meaning. Normally, the short way to transcribe a number between 10 and 20 is to write *yud*, corresponding to 10, followed by the Hebrew letter for 1 through 9 that would add up to the desired total. The number 11, for example, would be written as *yud* followed by *aleph* (10+1); 12 as *yud, beit* (10+2); and so on. Not so, however, when it comes to writing the number 15. We would expect *yud* followed by *heh* (10+5), but that is not what is done. Instead we write it as *tet, vav* (9+6). Why? Because the word that is formed by *yud* followed by *heh* spells one of the names of God – and that is something that we do not allow for secular usage, to merely indicate a specific number.

No surprise then that the holiday of Passover, on which the Jews as a nation became witnesses to the Almighty's existence and power, took place on the 15th of the month of Nisan, corresponding to His name. Not only the events that occurred on this day but the date itself proclaimed divine authorship. Nothing was coincidence. The story of the Exodus was the great hand of God revealed by the calendar as much as by its miracles.

The number 15 becomes a theme repeated numerous times, in the Seder as well as in subsequent Jewish history. The Seder itself, as we have noted, is divided into 15 parts. In the beautiful *Dayeinu* song, in which we enumerate all the things God did for us, each one of which alone would have warranted our unbounded thanks, we make mention of precisely 15 aspects of our redemption. The Holy Temple in Jerusalem had exactly 15 steps leading up to it that the Levites would ascend while singing 15 different songs, taken from the Book of Psalms of David, known as the 15 Psalms of Ascent.

And yet even while the number 15 alludes to one of the names of God, a biblical story makes clear that this is not really the ideal way in which He wants to be known. It expresses the reality of God in a way that bespeaks a limitation – not a limitation, of course, in God Himself, but rather in the way in which He is recognized and acknowledged by mankind. The story appears in chapter 17 of the Book of Exodus, shortly after the miracle of the Splitting of the Sea and the deliverance of the Jews from the genocidal efforts of Pharaoh and the Egyptians:

> Then came Amalek, and fought with Israel in Rephidim. And Moses said unto Joshua, "Choose us out men, and go out, fight with Amalek; tomorrow I will stand on the top of the hill with the rod of God in my hand." So Joshua did as Moses had said to him, and fought with Amalek; and Moses, Aaron, and Hur went up to the top of the hill. And it came to pass, when Moses held up his hand, that Israel prevailed; and when he let down his hand, Amalek prevailed. But Moses' hands were heavy; and they took a stone, and put it under him, and he sat thereon; and Joshua discomfited Amalek and his people with the edge of the sword. And the Lord said unto Moses, "Write this for a memorial in the book, and rehearse it in the ears of Joshua: for I will utterly

blot out the remembrance of Amalek from under heaven." And
Moses built an altar, and called the name of it Adonai-nissi. And
he said, "The hand upon the throne of the Lord: the Lord will
have war with Amalek from generation to generation." (vv. 8–16)

In Jewish tradition, Amalek is not simply the name of a particular people who long ago attacked the Jews. It is a code word for anti-Semites
of every age, for those who have attempted to annihilate us throughout
all the generations.

That is why it is highly significant that verse 13 teaches that Joshua
"discomfited" Amalek. The Hebrew word really means "weakened" – they
were weakened, but not destroyed. They would still be around many
times in the future to cause us grief throughout our history. Amalek
represents the threat to our survival, be it under the guise of the Cru-
sades or of Nazi Germany, of Russian pogroms or of Arab jihadists. But
the story of our first encounter with Amalek closes with prophetic consolation. God promises by way of an oath that He Himself will join us
in this battle. He will be at our side to insure not only our survival but
our ultimate victory. And the reason? Because God has a personal and
vested interest in seeing to it that Amalek and all that he represents will
eventually be defeated.

As the enemy of the Jews, Amalek is also the enemy of God.
Amalek, the paradigm of the anti-Semite, represents those who stand
in the way of the world receiving the message of Torah from the Jewish people. That is why there is a remarkable linguistic "mistake" in two
of the words written in verse 16. This is the way Rashi, the preeminent
biblical commentator, puts it:

> Why is the Hebrew word for throne *kes* [*kuf, samekh, aleph*],
> rather than *kise* [*kuf, samekh, aleph*], and the name of God is
> similarly defective [*yud, heh*, lacking the additional two letters,
> *vav* and *heh*, that make up the more usual spelling of the Tetra-
> grammaton, Y-H-V-H]? To teach us that God's throne and God's
> name remain incomplete as long as Amalek maintains his power
> and influence.

God's rulership ideally ought to extend over the entire earth. But the truth is that there are still many who do not as yet acknowledge His kingship. It is the mission of the Jews to be, in the words of Isaiah, "a light to the nations" (49:6). Amalek is the reason why so many yet prefer to live in darkness. The time will come however, as the prophet Zechariah predicted, when "The Lord will be King over all the world, on that day the Lord will be One and His name will be One" (14:9). And as long as God's throne is incomplete, His full four-letter name, denoting complete dominion, is equally inappropriate. Until Amalek is destroyed, God maintains an allusion to His two-letter name *to remind us that we have not yet reached our final destination.*

The deliverance of Passover that took place on the 15th of the month, precious as it was, brought us only to a partial redemption. We were enabled to see God, yet what was revealed was only half of the ultimate promise. The miracle of the Exodus was far from messianic fulfillment. *Geula* Part I was but a first step that would historically be followed by many years of exile, of Diaspora existence, of travails, and of tests to our faith and our worthiness. So too the Passover Seder is linked to the number 15, corresponding to "the incomplete name of God," to emphasize that what we have achieved until now is but half the story. God is patiently waiting with us for the time when we will deserve the Passover sequel, the *Geula Shelema.*

When the Jews successfully crossed the sea and witnessed the drowning of the Egyptians, they burst out into song. The Torah tells us, "Then Moses and the children of Israel sang this song to the Lord" (Ex. 15:1). But strangely enough, the Hebrew text does not use the grammatical form for the past tense, "sang." Instead the phrasing ought really to be translated in the future tense, "will sing." The Talmud picks up on this and from here infers that the Torah is hinting to us that at some future date they *will sing* the song of gratitude for final fulfillment. Note carefully, though, that the song of the future will not be addressed to the half name of God, to the name that is incomplete, to God of the number 15 represented by the Passover story. Then the *shira*, song, will be dedicated rather to Y-H-V-H, the complete four-letter name of God, marking Him as the accepted Ruler of all of mankind.

The commentary of the *Tur* points out that in all of the Tanakh we can find nine texts that are designated as *shira*. Nine times in our past we were moved to sing songs of exultation and thanksgiving. Prophetically, the verse in Exodus recounting the first of these songs in the aftermath of the miracle of the Splitting of the Red Sea, alluding to a future time of jubilation, uses the word *yashir* – a word that can be divided into *yud*, the number 10, followed by *shir*, which also means also song. The hint is to a tenth and final song, not yet biblically recorded because it is part of our destiny rather than our history. In this light, the many allusions to 15 on Passover, including the very date of its occurrence in the month of miracles in Nisan, serve to remind us that on the first Passover, God revealed Himself – but only an "abridged" version of what He has in store for us at the End of Days.

The Four Cups I: The Expressions of Redemption

On Passover night we drink not one, but four cups of wine. The most famous reason given is taken from the Jerusalem Talmud. The four cups, we are told, correspond to "the four expressions [words] of redemption" used by God to Moses as He shared with him the prediction of future events before He sent him on his mission. Each one of the words is so important that it requires us to recall it by way of praise and of gratitude. The source of these four words is in the Book of Exodus:

> Wherefore say unto the children of Israel, I am the Lord, and I will bring you out [*vehotzeti*] from under the burdens of the Egyptians, and I will deliver [*vehitzalti*] you from their bondage, and I will redeem [*vegaalti*] you with an outstretched arm, and with great judgments. And I will take [*velakaḥti*] you to Me for a people, and I will be to you a God; and you shall know that I am the Lord your God, who brought you out from under the burdens of the Egyptians. And I will bring [*veheveti*] you in unto the land, concerning which I lifted up My hand to give it to Abraham, to Isaac, and to Jacob; and I will give it you for a heritage: I am the Lord. (6:6–8)

The source for the first cup of wine is the word *vehotzeti*; for the second, *vehitzalti*; for the third, *vegaalti*; and for the fourth, *velakahti*. That is what we are taught in the Jerusalem Talmud. But several questions immediately present themselves. Does this imply that the cups of wine we drink on Passover night simply correspond to words? And if so, why not a cup for every word in this prophetic section promising redemption – never mind how difficult this might be? Or, more logically, is the point that a cup is decreed for every phrase indicating a divine action – which then leads us to wonder why we totally ignore a fifth word, *veheveti*, introducing the beautiful promise expressed in verse 8 of God's leading us to the Promised Land?

More, why are these phrases, alluding to major aspects of the redemption from Egypt, spaced in such an unusual manner in the sentences? Verse 6 has three of them bunched together – "I will bring you out," "I will deliver you," and "I will redeem you" – while verse 7 only has one, "and I will take you," which is followed by phrases "and I will be to you" and "you shall know," which apparently are not significant enough to warrant an additional cup for each. There are clearly some important ideas concealed in the choice of the particular four words, of their spacing in the text, and of the omission of verse 8 entirely as source for an additional fifth cup of wine at the Seder.

The key to a correct understanding of the biblical passage as the basis for the halakha of the four cups is to be found in the beautiful commentary of the Seforno. What God was revealing to Moses was an all-important preview of the way in which the Exodus story would unfold. Deliverance would not be immediate; divine wisdom chose to bring it about in stages. Liberation from Egypt was to be not a single event but a process. The Jewish people needed time to acclimate themselves to freedom. Momentous changes are too difficult to grasp if they come too suddenly; neither are they sufficiently appreciated if there is no time to digest their import on a piecemeal basis.

The first thing God had to do was to allow slaves to regain their sense of selfhood. That is why the initial step was "I will bring you out *from under the burdens* of the Egyptians." As soon as the plagues started, the Egyptians no longer felt brazen enough to continue to persecute the Jews with heavy labor. True, they were not ready to free them. The plagues had not sufficiently frightened them. But the plagues had left their mark. The Jews were slaves who, for the first time, no longer had to groan from the whips of their masters urging them on to complete their hard work. And this was the first stage of redemption that halakha commemorates with the first cup of wine at the Seder.

"And I will deliver you from their bondage" was the second step in the redemptive process. The Jews could not be considered delivered from bondage until they were physically away from their masters. The first step had meant simply that the slave owners were temporarily afraid to afflict their slaves; now the Jews were "delivered" – they were no longer there, they were out of sight of their oppressors. The actual departure from Egypt is what warrants the second cup at the Seder.

Yet the Jews could not be considered redeemed until their masters were dead. The word *geula* could first be used after the Egyptians drowned in the sea. Then and only then, with the death of their former masters, could it be said that the Jews were no longer fleeing slaves. How very appropriate that the phrase, "I will redeem you," is followed by two expressions: "with an outstretched arm" and "with great judgments." This third link in the process, which refers to the events at the Red Sea, had two miraculous aspects: with an outstretched arm God enfolded His people and brought them to the safety of the other side of the sea; while at the same time with great judgments God brought about the punishment of the Egyptians by drowning – the very same way in which they had killed Jewish babies. This completes a trilogy of events – cessation of forced labor, leaving the land, and the death of their oppressors – that form one self-contained unit; hence, they all appear in one verse. The key words alluding to these three stages are the basis for the first three cups at the Seder.

But it is all important to remember that the point of the entire story of the Exodus was not simply to *get out* of Egypt but rather to *get to* Sinai. God first appeared to Moses in a burning bush. The Midrash points out that the bush was on the very spot that would serve as the site where God would later reveal Himself to the entire Jewish people as well. It was there that God would present the Jewish people with the two Tablets of the Law. The bush in Hebrew was called *sneh*, and the commentator Ibn Ezra points out that the name "Sinai" derives from *sneh*. The same place where God gave Moses his mission to redeem the Jews from Egypt was destined to serve as the location for the Giving of the Torah. God's message to the man He selected as leader of the Jewish people was not just to take them *from* Egypt but to bring them back *to* the very site where he received his commission.

Freedom without purpose is pointless. For the Jews to leave the servitude of Egypt only to become slaves to their own hedonistic passions and to live lives without meaning would render the Exodus worthless. It was the fourth step of the process of redemption that defined the purpose of the three that preceded it. That is why it deserved a verse all of its own: "And I will take you to Me for a people" – at the Giving of the Torah at Mount Sinai. Verse 7 predicts the fulfillment of the ultimate goal of the Exodus. It was at Sinai that the Jews would hear God proclaim, "I am the Lord your God who took you out of the land of Egypt, the house of bondage" (Ex. 20:2; Deut. 5:6). They would now replace mortal rulers with subservience to the King of kings and His laws. They would indeed be free, but free in a higher sense. Not free of any higher authority, but free by virtue of divine guidance to be themselves and to live up to their greatest potential by voluntarily accepting God's law. Verse 7 paraphrases the first of the Ten Commandments and its introductory word, "and I will take you," is the source for the Seder's fourth cup.

In light of this interpretation, we can readily understand an interesting halakha. Jewish law permits drinking wine between the first and second cups, and the second and third cups, but not between the third and fourth. There is to be no interruption between them. They must be directly linked with each other. Because of what the cups symbolize, the reason may well be this: Nothing is permitted to come between the preliminary steps of the actual Exodus and their purpose of Revelation. Just as Passover and Shavuot need to be connected by way of the counting of the Omer to make clear that the freedom of the first holiday acquired its significance by the commitment imposed by the second, so too the fourth cup commemorating our acceptance of Torah must be inextricably linked to what came before it.

Linking the four cups of wine to the four expressions of redemption incorporates yet another very powerful concept into the Passover story. It reminds us of a fact often forgotten. Passover was not a single event but rather a process. Those who lived through it required patience to wait for its complete unfolding. And that has very special relevance for us today.

We too await redemption, what we refer to as *Geula Shelema*. We long for the Messiah. We pray for the restoration of the Temple. We know that the modern-day State of Israel still lacks the spiritual fulfillment predicted by the prophets. And yet, in spite of its imperfections, we dare not negate its theological meaning simply because of its incompleteness.

Teaching us that the events of the Final Days would parallel the miracles of the Exodus, the prophet Micah predicts, "As in the days of your coming forth out of the land of Egypt will I show unto him marvelous things" (7:15). We do not know the exact correspondence planned by God between the past and the future, between the deliverance from our Egyptian oppressors and the end of our long exile in the Diaspora. But perhaps what the prophet intended was that just as God's first intervention on our behalf in history was played out as a process, so too will God's final intercession be defined not by a single event, but rather by a series of miracles culminating with the Messiah.

The creation of the State of Israel in 1948 was but a step. True, it was not accompanied by the government accepting Torah as its constitution. But neither did the moment correspond to "I will bring you out from under the burdens of Egypt"; that first step in the redemptive process marked only the end of physical servitude, a step that brought with it the spiritual blessings of Sinai. And still, as we see at the Seder, that first step warrants our blessing of gratitude and an uplifted cup. The year 1967 saw us regain the holy city of Jerusalem and the original site of the Temple. Again, that event represented an incomplete gift from God. The site is not the same as the reality of the Temple itself, with its holy items restored, its priests once again officiating, and the sacrificial service revived. May we rejoice for only partial salvation? The law of the Passover cups directs us to give a positive response. Every redemptive phrase fulfilled demands our thanksgiving. Every stage in the process calls for grateful acknowledgment. The three events commemorated by the first three cups all revolve around physical deliverance – our servitude ended, we were finally able to leave the land, and our enemies perished. These were all necessary; although in essence not spiritual, they paved the way for the moment of Revelation. To deny them their blessing is to be insensitive to God's role in history. Similarly, the contemporary events surrounding the birth of the State of Israel and its survival in the face of Arab hostility deserve equal recognition. To those who deny them any theological meaning simply because they have not yet been validated by the coming of the Messiah, we need to recall Micah's prophecy: the final Redemption will be just like the one out of Egypt – a process rather than an event, with redemptive stages that move from the physical to the spiritual.

And let us not forget the one question that remains to be answered. The Jerusalem Talmud bases the need for every one of the cups on a biblical phrase and comes up with a total of four. However, the verse beginning with the words, "And I will bring you," seems for some strange reason to be ignored. Why did the rabbis not decree the need for a fifth cup corresponding to the promise God made that He would bring us to "the land, concerning which I lifted up My hand to give it to Abraham, to Isaac, and to Jacob"?

The answer is obvious. That phrase has not yet been fulfilled in the way it was promised. God's oath implied not simply bringing them to the land, but turning it into the "eternal heritage" it was intended to be: the eternal spiritual homeland for the descendents of the patriarchs.

We do not drink a fifth cup at the Seder because the promise of the fifth word still remains for the future. And that may well be why we do pour a fifth cup that we do not drink, but rather reserve for Elijah. After all he is the one who will announce the Messiah's arrival. To indicate our firm belief that God's promise *will* be fulfilled, we prepare a cup for that moment – and when Elijah indeed comes it is *we,* not Elijah, who will finally drink all the required five cups out of gratitude for the fulfillment, at long last, of all five words of redemption.

The Four Cups II: The Miracles of Jewish History

One way to understand the four cups of wine at the Passover Seder, as we have seen from the commentary of the Jerusalem Talmud, is to view them as reminders of four different stages in the process of redemption from Egypt. A different approach may very well be inferred from a later passage in the Haggada recited shortly before we drink from the second cup. Tradition tells us that we are required to lift the cup when we say the words:

> Therefore it is our duty to thank, praise, laud, glorify, exalt, honor, bless, raise high, and acclaim the One who has performed all these miracles for our ancestors and for us; who has brought us out from slavery to freedom, from sorrow to joy, from grief to celebration; from darkness to great light and from enslavement to redemption; and so we shall sing a new song before Him. Halleluya!

On the surface, the intent of the text is simply to explain why we are obligated to offer praise on this night. We need to thank God, we explain, who performed for our ancestors and for us all these miracles – miracles that we then proceed to list by way of succinct summary: "You brought us out from slavery to freedom, from sorrow to joy, from grief to celebration; from darkness to great light and from enslavement to redemption." For all this we then conclude, "and so we shall sing a new song before Him. Halleluya!"

After looking carefully at the phrases chosen to reflect on past miracles, it becomes fairly evident that they refer not to one historic moment but rather to different times in our past when God made His presence known. The key words mentally jog us to recall four major events that are particularly noteworthy:

- The first of the four, "who has brought us out from slavery to freedom," is clearly a concise way to refer to the Passover story. The Haggada begins its recitation with the phrase, "We were slaves to Pharaoh in Egypt." It then goes on to tell the whole story of how this became the holiday known as *"zeman ḥerutenu,"* "the time of our freedom."

- The second phrase, "from sorrow to joy," takes us to the next stage in Jewish history. Our sins caused us to be exiled to Babylonia, "where we sat by its rivers and wept as we remembered Zion" (Ps: 137:1). But God took pity on us and brought us back to the Holy Land: "Then were our mouths filled with laughter, and our tongues with songs of joy.... The Lord did do great things for us and we rejoiced" (Ps. 126:2–3). It was a sequel to the Exodus story and surely worthy of commemoration.

- The third phrase, "from grief to celebration," brings us to the next time God intervened to save us from destruction. Now the Jews found themselves under the rule of Persia-Medea, confronted by the genocidal plans of Haman who wanted to kill "all the Jews, from young to old, infants and children, on one day" (Est. 3:13). The holiday of Purim commemorates the story of miraculous deliverance, a tale told in the Book of Esther. The celebration describes that the Jews went *"from grief to celebration,* to make these days of feasting and joy and the sending of portions every man to his neighbor and gifts to the poor" (9:22).

- The fourth phrase, "from darkness to great light," takes us to the events that we celebrate on the festival of Ḥanukka. It is the story of Jewish survival in the face of the Greco-Syrian attempt to assimilate us to their culture. The Maccabees fought brilliant victories, but the proof that ultimately it was divine intervention that prevailed was the miracle of the oil burning for far longer than physically possible. It was God who turned darkness into great light and assured the Jewish people that we could continue our prophetic mission to serve as "a light to the nations" (Is. 49:6).

On Passover night it is not sufficient to simply thank God for His role in the miracle of redemption from Egypt. One cup of wine would have sufficed for that. But we have come a long way since the Exodus. We have been privileged to witness more miracles. Three of them are so outstanding that we add an additional cup of wine for each one of them. On the night dedicated to gratitude, we declare that we need to thank God for *all the things He did for us and our ancestors.* And so, before we drink the second cup, we explain why on this night we do more than just the Kiddush, which commemorates the going out of Egypt, and list the additional miracles that warrant these avowals of our appreciation – redemption from Babylonia, from Persia-Medea in the Purim story, and from Greece on Ḥanukka, the festival of light.

But if you wonder, since there is a fifth phrase in the prayer, "from enslavement to redemption," why do we not drink a fifth cup at the Seder to correspond to this miracle? The answer is obvious. *Geula* in this context refers to the final Redemption. We cannot yet drink it because it still has not happened. Yet we believe with certainty that just as God fulfilled His promises four times in the past, so too He will surely keep His word with regard to His messianic promise. To indicate this we pour wine into a fifth cup, and although we do not drink from it yet, we call it the cup of Elijah. When the prophet will arrive proclaiming the imminent coming of the Messiah, as the prayer declares, "we shall sing a new song," a sequel to the song at the Red Sea – and celebrate the Seder by drinking five cups of wine in gratitude for the five major moments of godly intervention.

The Four Cups III:
The Names of God

The number "four" is a recurring theme throughout the entire Haggada. We are introduced to it in the requirement for the number of cups we drink at the Seder. It is the key to the number of questions our children ask about the way we observe the rituals of this night. We meet it again when we talk about the number of sons in the family. It is clear that there is a profound significance to the number four that links it to the major message of Passover. What is it that this number four represents?

In an important sense, it is a succinct numerical reference to one of the names of God. In the Torah, God is identified primarily by two different appellations. One is the four-letter name of God known as the Tetragrammaton, the name we are not permitted to pronounce as written because of its extreme holiness. It is the name we normally translate as "Lord." When we read it outside of the context of a prayer, we pronounce it *Adoshem*. The other name of God is *Elokim*, the name we render as "God."

The rabbinic commentators are in agreement about the reason for God having these two different names, as well as the difference of meaning between them. The name *Adoshem* is used to identify the Almighty in His merciful aspect. It connotes the Lord as He favors us with kindness and compassion even when we do not deserve it. It is identified as *middat harahamim. Reish, het, mem,* the root of the word *rahamim,* is also the root of the word *rehem,* womb. It brings to mind the kind of unconditional love a mother has for her child, a love that transcends worth and is granted simply on the basis of birth. The Lord loves us in the same way, with "motherly love," because in the most profound sense He is our Parent, our Creator, and in a remarkable way, suggested by the grammatical form of this name that concludes with a feminine ending, *kamatz, heh,* "He" is our Mother just as much as "He" is our Father in heaven.

But God relates to us in yet another way, an approach rooted in His "masculine" side rather than His "feminine" attribute. *Elokim,* translated as "God," represents the divine characteristic of judgment. With a grammatically masculine ending, it is God in His role as the Father, the One who makes demands and sets standards that dare not be compromised. Compassion is a wonderful trait, but when carried to an extreme it would lead to a lawless society, secure in gaining forgiveness whatever its sins. The Midrash puts it beautifully when it says, "He who is too kind to the wicked is cruel to the righteous." Just as parents need to find the correct balance between rigid discipline and unqualified devotion to their children, between strictness that creates necessary limits to their offspring's behavior and forgiveness for temporary lapses that deserve some leeway in recognition of human frailty, so too the God of law and the Lord of compassion combine to rule the world with the kind of love that is truly holy.

The verse that summarizes our acceptance of the kingship of God is "Hear, O Israel, the Lord is our God, the Lord is One" (Deut. 6:4). We begin this major declaration of belief by acknowledging both names of God, *Adoshem* and *Elokim* (in the verse, rendered *Elokeinu,* in the possessive). But then we conclude with the expression "the *Lord* is One." Our affirmation of the duality of God ends with the assertion that we understand that *both* divine characteristics, even the ones we might identify at first glance as overly harsh, are really also aspects of *Adoshem.* To comprehend the judgments of God correctly is to recognize that even when we think He is *Elokim,* His ultimate purpose is to grant us the love of *Adoshem.*

The parent who is strict with his child says, "Someday you will understand that I am only doing this because I love you." Hopefully, looking back, adults can come to see the wisdom of parental rules that so infuriated them when they were young. So too it is with God, who must necessarily at times treat us in ways we think are cruel but in retrospect are revealed to us as expressions of love. Both *Adoshem* and *Elokim* are in reality equally expressions of one and the same *Adoshem*. God in His infinite wisdom knows when to be strict and when to be merciful, when to judge us in accord with what we deserve and when to favor us with more than what is our due. His decision will determine whether He will deal with us in His role as stern God or as loving Lord.

The two divine attributes, of law and of love, are each identified by a numerical shorthand. The name that alludes to the "motherly" aspect of our Creator who loves us in spite of our failings is comprised of four letters. At the very end of the Haggada, we identify the significance of numbers "one" through "thirteen" in the song known as "*Eḥad Mi Yode'a*," "Who Knows One?" When we ask, "Who knows four?" our response is "I know four: four mothers." The number "four" corresponds to our matriarchs, Sarah, Rebecca, Rachel, and Leah. It alludes to those who epitomize motherly love. The four matriarchs and the four-letter name of God share the number that speaks the language of grace granted freely, without reference to whether or not it is earned.

Not so for the number "five." When we ask, "Who knows five?" our response is, "I know five: five books of the Torah." The number "five" represents the law. Five is the way God reveals Himself as *Elokim*. Five demands obedience. Five rewards those who deserve divine favor. And that is why there are four cups of wine used to commemorate the Passover experience of liberation from Egypt, and a fifth cup of wine set aside for Elijah, symbolic of the ultimate Redemption.

Biblical commentators all make clear that the Jews who were saved from Egyptian slavery did not really deserve the miracles performed for them. Were they to be judged on the scale of merit, they very well would have perished. But God saw their afflictions and knew that He could not remain silent. He had made a promise to Abraham, Isaac, and Jacob about their survival, and God realized that without His intervention at this moment in history there would no longer be a Jewish people.

The Exodus from Egypt and the entire story of Passover resulted from the divine characteristic of His four-letter name that willed the supremacy of love over law. The Lord, *Adoshem*, redeemed His people in the hope, as well as the expectation, that a time would come when they would eventually prove themselves *worthy* of divine miracles on their behalf. But on the Passover of old, even the Jews themselves recognized they did not deserve all the great things God did for them: "And Israel saw the great work that the *Lord* did upon the Egyptians, and the people feared the *Lord*; and they believed in the *Lord*, and in His servant Moses" (Ex. 14:31).

We drink four cups of wine at the Passover Seder because we acknowledge that when we were a young people, a nation of slaves not yet mature enough to earn divine favor, the Lord had faith in our potential for future growth and redeemed us by way of His four-letter name of love. But that redemption came with a demand for a commitment to the time to come. The Messianic Age is symbolized by a fifth cup, the cup for Elijah, because the redemption associated with Elijah's coming, unlike the redemption from Egypt, will need to be deserved.

The answer at the end of the Haggada to the question "Who knows five?" is "five books of the Torah." This is the response we are supposed to take to heart as we contemplate how we can hasten the day when we will drink a fifth cup of wine at the Seder. Elijah has a reserved place set aside for him with the cup whose number identifies the aspect of God that will permit him to make his appearance. When we were a youthful nation, the Lord was willing to bestow upon us an undeserved redemption; the Lord of the Tetragrammaton granted us miracles we did not merit. After all these years it is time for us to grow up as a people. God, the five-letter name, has a right to expect that we finally commit ourselves to the five books of Moses and earn the fifth cup.

Karpas-Yaḥatz: The Story Behind the Story

The mitzva on Passover night is to tell the story of the Exodus. It would seem logical, then, that immediately after the Kiddush we would go right into the *Maggid*, Telling. But we do not do that. Instead, we wash our hands for the *Karpas*, break the middle matza for the *Yaḥatz*, read the short paragraph welcoming the hungry and needy to join with us, and only then encourage the children to ask the four questions.

The Haggada by definition is *Maggid* – recounting the historic events associated with our deliverance. Why then is this mitzva delayed? Why do we not get right to it? What is it that makes the ritual of dipping the *Karpas* followed by the *Yaḥatz* indispensable introductions to the Passover narrative? The answer gets to the heart of a profound question we must ask ourselves as we celebrate and give thanks to God for bringing us forth from slavery to freedom. It is true that we have to be grateful to the Almighty for getting us out of Egypt. That certainly proved His love for us. But we surely have to wonder, if God really cared so much for the children of Israel, why did He permit the Egyptians to enslave us in the first place? Would it not have been far more appropriate, and a more powerful sign of divine love, if we never had to experience the horrors of bondage and oppression?

The question is not new. It was asked by none other than Moses himself. Our commentators see an allusion to it in the first stories recorded about the man who would become our national redeemer:

> And it came to pass in those days, when Moses was grown up, that he went out unto his brethren, and looked on their burdens; and he saw an Egyptian smiting a Hebrew, one of his brethren. And he looked this way and that way, and when he saw that there was no man, he smote the Egyptian, and hid him in the sand. (Ex. 2:11–12)

Prior to this incident, we had met Moses only as passive infant. We learned how divine providence saw to it that he survive Pharaoh's decree, but we knew nothing as yet about Moses the man. The very first story in the entire Torah that gives us some clue about Moses' character and personality is this incident. It stresses his sensitivity to the pain of others and his refusal to stand by as a witness to evil without intervening. "When he saw that there was no man" – Moses fulfilled what the talmudic sage Hillel centuries later would codify as a fundamental maxim of Judaism: "In a place where there are no men, strive to be a man" (Mishna Avot 2:5). Indeed, in all certainty this must have been the very trait that endeared him to God and made him worthy of being selected to lead the Jewish people. The fact that he cared so much proved he was the one best suited to become the nation's caretaker.

Remarkably, as well as providentially, the very next day provided a different encounter:

> And he went out the second day, and, behold, two men of the Hebrews were fighting together; and he [Moses] said to him that did the wrong, "Why do you smite your neighbor?" And he replied, "Who made you a man, a prince, and a judge over us? Do you plan to slay me, as you have slain the Egyptian?" And Moses feared, and said, "Surely the thing is known." (Ex. 2:13–14)

Rabbinic commentators are profoundly intrigued by this sequence of events. The first day introduces us to brutal Egyptian oppression. The second day shows us Hebrews fighting with each other. Worse still, in response to the attempt of Moses to break up the quarrel, there is an implied threat to inform against him to the authorities for his action of the previous day that obviously had not gone unnoticed. The theological link between the events of the two successive days is crucial. What happened on the second day allowed Moses to comprehend the tragedy of the first.

Why did God permit Jewish suffering? How could a God of justice countenance the injustice of Egyptian slavery? Rashi, the primary commentator on the Torah, asks what Moses meant when he said, "Surely the thing is known"? What was "*the* thing" to which he was referring? We assumed at first glance that Moses was concerned about his own safety and that "the thing" he was worried about referred to knowledge of the news that he had killed an Egyptian the previous day. A midrash reveals the rabbinic insight that Moses was not at all concerned about his own safety. Rather, Moses affirmed that "the thing" that had troubled him more than any other, why Israel out of all the seventy nations deserved their fate of servitude, finally became clear to him. He sadly concluded that Israel was being justly punished.

Deliverance could not come to the Jewish people until they atoned for the sin that was the true cause of their misfortune. The most important message we had to learn was the link between the horror of hatred of the Hebrews on day one, and the tragedy of hatred between Hebrews on day two. God allows the first, power given to our oppressors, only because of the second, our own failings in our relationships with one another. In a certain sense, the lesson of history may well be that *anti-Semitism is the divine response to internal Jewish divisiveness and needless hatred.* When we fail to come together as a people, it requires a common enemy to unite us.

That was the great discovery of Moses when he said, "Surely the thing is known." In retrospect, however, as we review the entire story of the Egypt experience, we can find an even greater confirmation of this concept. We miss the full meaning of the Egyptian exile if we do not go back to the very beginning of the story. Yes, we ended up as slaves in Egypt, but let us not forget how we got there. Our patriarchs began the story of our people in Canaan, the land of Israel. Our stay in the land of the Nile was an unfortunate interruption that required divine intervention to help us return to our homeland.

Our move to Egypt, the first of our exiles from the Holy Land, was precipitated by the sin of *sinat ḥinam*, needless hatred – the hatred of Joseph by his brothers. It is painful to remember that our ancestors could have been guilty of such a terrible crime. The cause, we are told in the Torah, was the jealousy engendered by Jacob's having given Joseph "a coat of many colors." This was the very coat the brothers dipped in animal blood, after they sold Joseph to a caravan that would bring him to Egypt, to prove to their father that his most beloved son was dead. In Hebrew that coat was called "*ketonet passim*" (Gen. 37:3). On that phrase, Rashi offers a remarkable explanation: "*Ketonet passim* is similar to *karpas*, a word mentioned in Esther 1:6." The coat of many colors is thus linked to the Aramaic word *karpas* – the very word used to describe the ritual performed at the Seder before we even begin the telling of the story of the Exodus!

And what do we do with the *karpas*? We dip it! Just as the brothers dipped the coat of many colors at the beginning of the story that led to our exile and slavery, so do we symbolically recall that crime at the very start of the Seder. Of course we dare not dip into blood – blood is forbidden to us. Instead, we use salt water, symbol of the tears that must be shed when we think of the consequences of family hatred and ill will between brothers. To start with *karpas* is to acknowledge our complicity in our exile. We do not complain about why a just God permitted our affliction because we recognize the part we ourselves played in bringing it about. *Sinat ḥinam* and anti-Semitism as cause and effect are as closely linked as the two stories of Moses.

Karpas is followed by *Yaḥatz*. What the brothers did with the coat of many colors caused the split symbolized by the splitting of the middle matza. The unity of the family was cast asunder, and the tragedy of Egypt followed. What must we learn then from this succinct summary of our first national tragedy? How can we insure that we don't again suffer a similar fate?

The answer is obviously to make certain we do not repeat the sin of the Joseph story. Rabbi Abraham Isaac Kook, the first Ashkenazic chief rabbi of British Mandatory Palestine, put it beautifully when he said that to atone for *sinat ḥinam* there is only one possible solution.

We must commit ourselves to *ahavat ḥinam* – to love of our people, no matter who they are, how much we may differ from them, or even how "undeserving" of our love they may appear to be.

And so there is still one more thing we do before we start the *Maggid* – the actual mitzva of the retelling of the biblical story. We recite *Ha Laḥma Anya*, a passage written in Aramaic rather than Hebrew. Obviously it was composed at a time when the Jews were no longer in Israel but in the exile of Babylonia. In a sense, they too found themselves once again back in Egypt. They were strangers in a foreign land. Yet they could celebrate the Festival of Freedom because they knew the secret – the secret of the cause of exile.

They took to heart the message of the *Karpas*. They prefaced their Seder with an open invitation to fellow Jews to come and join them. All who are hungry were welcomed to share their meal with them. All who are needy were asked to consider themselves members of the family and participate. They, the Jews of this renewed Diaspora, proclaimed their desire to atone for the particular sin that was biblically identified as the primary reason for Jewish exile.

The added paragraph is not only an invitation but also a declaration. Committing themselves to brotherly love, there is certainty that "Now we are here; next year in the land of Israel. Now – slaves; next year we shall be free." It is a passage equally relevant today as well. The Messiah has not yet come. The redemption from Egypt remains incomplete. Much as we rejoice in commemoration of the deliverance from the travails of Egypt, we recognize that we have not yet earned the fulfillment of God's final promise.

In all probability, the sin of the brothers of Joseph is still with us in some way – not because we are culpable for the crime of our ancestors, but because we continue to repeat it by way of our internal conflicts and failure to achieve Jewish unity. So before we start the Haggada, we dip the *karpas/ketonet passim*, we link it to the split that caused our exile, and we atone for that sin with the invitation that shows "we got the message." Having done all that, we can now proceed to the *Maggid* with the assurance that having learned from history we will not be condemned to repeat it.

Maggid: Why Does Jacob Become Israel?

It took a traumatic event in the life of Jacob to finally make him realize that a Jew dare not live by the code of "turn the other cheek." That moment became so central to his identity that it was responsible for a biblical change of name. The new name captured his mission and purpose; it redefined his character and personality. More, it became the way his descendents, the Jewish people, identify themselves to this day. We are the children of *Israel*. How Jacob became Israel is a story that not only is commemorated via an important Torah law but, as we will see, is also fascinatingly alluded to in the word that describes this key section of the Haggada, the *Maggid*.

Let us first remind ourselves why the name "Jacob" was initially such a fitting descriptive for him. Even before he was born, while still a fetus, he epitomized the root meaning of this name: *ekev*, heel. The Torah tells us, "And after that came forth his brother and his hand had hold on Esau's heel and his name was called Jacob" (Gen. 25:26). Holding onto the heel! Better put, being stepped upon.

The Midrash explains that Jacob actually had been conceived first. He should have been the one to leave the womb before his brother. Technically, he was the elder, with all the attendant privileges of primogeniture. However, his brother, Esau, pushed himself forward and forced himself over Jacob. What was Jacob to do? After all, even in the womb, it seems Jacob was guided by the philosophy that "nice boys do not fight."

He was content with simply being Jacob, trailing after his brother, being trampled upon because he assumed that a person with faith must live by the code that "God will take care of everything. He will right all wrongs. There is no need to fight if one believes in a righteous God who rules the universe." Jacob was the passive good guy who accepted the inequities of life as divinely decreed.

The twins, Jacob and Esau, grew up different as day from night. Jacob was righteous. Esau was a hunter, a man of the field who would not hesitate to kill – not just game, but even human beings who stood in his way. Yet, "Now Isaac loved Esau because he did eat of his venison" (Gen. 25:28). Esau was a hunter, to search for food, as well as to capture the heart of his father. He fooled him completely, as our sages point out, by posing questions of a religious nature as if he were concerned with correct halakhic procedure. And so he asked, "How shall I eat? How shall I bless?" Isaac was blind to the truth, even as his eyesight correspondingly failed him.

Nevertheless, the text tells us, "And Rebecca loved Jacob" (Gen. 25:28). Rebecca was not taken in by this sham. She knew the truth. Jacob studied constantly, and as the unassuming passive child, he was "a quiet man dwelling in tents" (v. 27).

The time came for Isaac to pass on the blessing he had received from his father, Abraham. To whom should he promise the destiny blessed by God? Isaac was about to make an error that would have had the gravest consequences for all of Jewish history. He wanted to bless Esau instead of Jacob. Once again, Jacob was prepared not to say a word. True to his nature, he would have allowed himself to be stepped upon because "nice boys do not fight back." "Somehow," he thought to himself, "God will help."

It was only thanks to Rebecca, his mother, who pushed him to act, that the tragedy of the blessing being given to the undeserving brother was averted. She insisted that Jacob disguise himself as Esau and bring the venison Isaac had requested. Jacob was afraid and tried to decline, preferring to do nothing and let events unfold on their own, without his involvement. But his mother insisted. Jacob went. That is why the blessing that sustains us to this day was uttered by Isaac to Jacob and not to Esau. But it is crucial to remember that Jacob, left to his own initiative, would have let the opportunity pass. But the story did not end there. Esau hated Jacob for what he had done. It became clear that he planned to wait a little while, until Isaac died, and then take his revenge, thinking, "Let the days of mourning for my father be at hand, then will I slay my brother Jacob" (Gen. 27:41).

Psychologists tell us there are basically two ways in which we can cope with the world. People are divided into two major types: those who favor fight and those who favor flight. Encountering any difficulty, one can either attempt to cope, grapple, and wrestle with an issue, and overcome it; or one can flee, giving up at the outset. Flight may even be rationalized as a correct religious response. Why take a chance, why get involved? Let me not do anything, and if God really desires a certain outcome, let Him handle it to His satisfaction.

What did Jacob, the man whose name is rooted in the word for "heel," do in the face of this threat? He "took to heel," he ran away, he fled so that there would be no encounter. That is how he came to the house of Laban, his uncle. And that is where he fell in love with Rachel, of whom the Torah says, "And Rachel was of beautiful form and fair to look upon" (Gen. 29:17). From the first moment Jacob saw her, he fell deeply in love. For seven years he was willing to work for the right to marry her, as Laban demanded. But Laban did not keep his word. He fooled Jacob into marrying Leah, not Rachel. And what did Jacob do when he discovered this horrible betrayal? What violence did he wreak? How much anger did he demonstrate? When Jacob questioned Laban's treachery, he was simply told, "It is not done so in our place to give the younger before the firstborn" (v. 26). That is the way we do things around here, no matter what I may have promised. If you really want Rachel, said Laban, "Then fulfill the week of this one and we will give you the other also for the service that you will serve with me yet another seven years" (v. 27).

Once again, Jacob acts as one might expect from his name. Fight is not an option. His approach remains consistent, to flee from confrontation and simply give in to evil. Jacob still has not changed from his time in the womb.

For the next twenty years, Jacob worked for his father-in-law. He made Laban a very wealthy man. In the process, Jacob also achieved a measure of security and riches for himself. It was then that he heard Laban's sons complaining, "Jacob has taken away all that was our father's, and of that which was our father's he has gotten all this wealth" (Gen. 31:1). Sensitive to this animosity and shocked that his brothers-in-law begrudged him even a small portion of the wealth for which he was responsible, Jacob decided there was only one solution. Faithful to his history of flight over fight, Jacob determined once again to run away. He would avoid confrontation, as it says, "So he fled with all that he had" (v. 21), until a moment came when even Jacob realized he could no longer live his life that way. Jacob finally changed – and that was when God changed his name.

Returning to Canaan, he heard the news that his brother Esau was coming towards him with four hundred men. Jacob had no clue whether the purpose of this meeting was revenge or reconciliation. He sent gifts ahead and he prayed. And then a remarkable thing happened. There was an enigmatic and almost incomprehensible encounter: "And Jacob was left alone and there wrestled a man with him until the breaking of the day" (Gen. 32:25).

Who was this mysterious assailant? What was this battle all about? Biblical commentators disagree. For Maimonides, it was but a dream. It was Jacob's fear about his imminent meeting with the brother who years before promised to slay him that was responsible for his nightmare. But Rashi and most other commentators accept it literally as an attack by the angelic representative of Esau. And this time the story had a totally unexpected ending.

The Jacob who until this moment had constantly fled from conflict, controversy, and confrontation finally recognized there comes a time when a man must choose fight over flight. This is the very first record of Jacob deciding to forsake a passive response and to wrestle with his opponent. They fought all that night. Who was the victor in this encounter? At first glance, it appears that Jacob was defeated: "And the hollow of Jacob's thigh was strained as he wrestled with him" (Gen. 32:26). Jacob was left limping. The injury was so significant that a biblical law was instituted to ensure that the Jewish people never forget it: "Therefore the children of Israel eat not the sinew of the thigh vein that is upon the hollow of the thigh, unto this day; because he touched the hollow of Jacob's thigh even in the sinew of the thigh vein" (v. 33).

But if Jacob lost the battle, how do we explain that he makes a demand upon his attacker? Jacob tells his opponent he will not release him until he gets a blessing from him. And, remarkably enough the attacker grants Jacob his wish: "Your name shall be called no more Jacob, but Israel; for you have striven with God and with men and have prevailed" (Gen. 32:29). Why does the angel now bless him? Why does he now call him "Israel"? *Because the name "Israel" refers to someone who has fought rather than fled, someone who has not simply allowed himself to be stepped on.*

That, indeed, was the whole point of the angelic encounter. God wanted Jacob to learn a different philosophy of life than the one he had espoused till that moment. Jacob may have suffered a blow. But he won the greater battle – the battle over his attraction to passivity, the battle over his previous unwillingness to ever engage in combat. *Jacob won the greatest victory of all: He finally managed to conquer his weakness of character and to stand up against evil.* And if he was left limping, what of it? That would simply mean *he would never again be able to run away* from anyone or any place, not even from himself. No longer would Jacob turn the other cheek. No longer would he refuse to face reality or to say, "If I believe in God, I will let Him do everything."

The name "Israel" defines someone who is willing to challenge iniquity and to wrestle the wicked in order to bring about a better world. When Jacob became Israel, he left a legacy for his descendents, the children *of Israel*, that in order to achieve a better world our role is to become partners with God in the struggle to perfect it.

It was a message the Torah considers so important that it was codified as a mitzva. We were forbidden to ever again eat of the *gid hanasheh*, the sinew of weakness. The law would force us to recall the incident when Jacob finally renounced self-demeaning passivity for active involvement. In that way, we would be inspired to make *Israel* and *his* approach to confrontation our role model.

Yet, what is exceedingly strange in the aftermath of this change of name is that in some later stories in the Torah we again find the third patriarch referred to as "Jacob"! The commentators wonder about this apparent reversion to lower status. What made Israel go back once again to being the meek, timid, and submissive Jacob personality we thought he finally outgrew in the encounter with the angelic representative of Esau?

The Zohar sees the answer clearly alluded to in the text: "And Jacob lived in the land of Egypt" (Gen. 47:28). In the Diaspora, the proud patriarch Israel is diminished. The reality of exile forcibly humbled him; and he – Israel – *lived as Jacob* in the land of Egypt. Only in the Holy Land, the Zohar concludes, was the more laudatory name of Israel appropriate.

That beautifully explains the strange usage of both names for the very same person in the opening verse of the Book of Exodus: "And these are the names of the *children of Israel* who came to Egypt *with Jacob*, each man and his household they came." His offspring are identified as the children of *Israel*. And then we are told they came to Egypt with *Jacob*? Israel and Jacob are one and the same person! Why would the Torah change the way it refers to our forefather in the very same verse?

This is the sentence that introduces us to the tragedy of our stay in Egypt, our first exile that brought us slavery as well as the threat of genocide. And so the text subtly teaches us how our stay in a foreign land altered our very personality. These are the names of the children of *Israel*. Born in the Holy Land, they shared the strength and the spirit of the man who wrestled with his opponents. But they came to Egypt "with *Jacob*" – brought back down to a weakened and passive mindset by the difficulties of the *galut*, exile.

The holiday of Passover marks this transition in reverse. It commemorates our move back from *galut* to *geula*. It is the story of *Jacob* once again becoming *Israel*. Freedom from slavery allows us to relive that momentous moment when we first renounced the role of victim and grasped the virtue of going to battle for survival. That was the story of the *gid hanasheh*. From it, all else follows.

And so the retelling of the Passover narrative from year to year, described in the Haggada as *Maggid*, may also be read "*megid*," "from the *gid*, sinew." Our history encompasses the *Jacob* as well as the *Israel* elements. The redemption from Egypt was meant to bring us back to the moment when we matured from the former to the latter. From there, from that incident, *megid*, we are on the night of Passover to perceive our mission and our destiny.

The Wicked Son

One of the famous four sons discussed at the Seder, the one who is wicked, is called *rasha*. From a Torah perspective, the use of this word places him in the category of those deserving of *malkut,* the biblical punishment of lashes, as it is written, "And it will be if the wicked one is deserving of being smitten…. He shall smite him with forty lashes" (Deut. 25:2–3). There are two things that are very striking about this punishment. The first is the precise number "forty" that has so many biblical parallels; the second, the fact that Jewish law insists although the Torah quite clearly states "forty," Jewish tradition by way of the Oral Law reduces it by one to thirty-nine.

What is the significance of the number "forty" that accounts for its prominence in the Torah? Clearly it has both meaning and message. Let us see if we can extrapolate its import from a closer analysis of the ways in which it played a role in biblical stories and laws. Here is a list of some of the most famous occurrences of the number "forty" with regard to events in the Torah:

- Rain fell for "forty days and forty nights" during the Flood.
- Spies explored the land of Israel for forty days.
- The children of Israel lived in the Sinai desert for forty years until a new generation arose.

- Moses' life was divided into three forty-year segments, separated by his fleeing from Egypt, and his return to lead his people out.
- Moses spent three consecutive periods of "forty days and forty nights" on Mount Sinai.
- Several Jewish leaders and kings are said to have ruled for "forty years," for example, Eli, Saul, David, and Solomon.
- Goliath challenged the Israelites twice a day for forty days before David defeated him.

In Jewish law we find a number of additional examples:

- A *mikve*, required for the immersion of converts to Judaism as well as for the purification of women after their period of menstrual impurity, consists of forty *se'ahs* (approximately two hundred gallons) of water.
- One of the prerequisites for a man to study Kabbala is that he be forty years old.
- There are forty days between the first day of Elul, when we begin to blow the shofar to prepare for Rosh HaShana, until Yom Kippur, the end of the annual *teshuva*, repentance, period.
- Forty days represent the time that an embryo takes to attain human form. An embryo does not have any status as a human being until forty days after conception.

Within the context of all of these illustrations we ought to have no difficulty understanding why the Torah prescribed precisely forty lashes for wicked sinners. *In every one of the instances cited above, the number "forty" clearly represents the idea of change and of transformation.*

The forty days of the Flood, the forty years of Jewish wandering in the desert, the forty days Moses spent on top of Mount Sinai, the forty years of reign by various leaders – all these permitted the required transformative changes to occur. The power of the *mikve* to transform a non-Jew into a full-fledged member of the Jewish people is predicated on the presence of its forty measures of water. The forty days from the first day of Elul through Yom Kippur allow us to become newly cleansed of our sins in the sight of God. Our very fundamental nature as human beings only comes about following the first forty days of conception. No wonder then that the number for lashes is forty, since their purpose is nothing other than to transform the sinner and make him change his ways.

But that leaves us with one major difficulty. We know that the Oral Law teaches that although the Torah says "forty," in this instance it really means thirty-nine. Ingeniously, the Talmud finds support for the oral tradition by virtue of the fact that the text does not read "forty in number" but rather "*in* the number forty" – that is, a number that is within forty rather than forty itself, that is, thirty-nine. Why then, we may well ask, did the Torah not state clearly, "thirty-nine," the actual number to be imposed by law, rather than to state "forty," which the Oral Law needed to amend? And further, if the purpose of lashes is to create change in the sinner, how would the number "thirty-nine" have any symbolic significance for this end? To answer these questions we will find it helpful to cite one other case from the halakhic tradition where we find both the numbers "forty" and "thirty-nine" playing a role.

In enumerating the categories of "*melakhot*," types of labor forbidden on Shabbat, the Talmud teaches us that there are "forty less one." As we know, these thirty-nine categories of forbidden labor parallel the types of activity that went into God's Creation of the world. Our own Shabbat rest parallels the Shabbat of Creation when God ceased His work and rested from any additional activity.

Our sages teach that the world was created through ten divine utterances. Mystically, each of these ten utterances manifests itself on four different levels – per the Tetragrammaton, the four-letter name of God – hence a total of forty. Here once again the number "forty" represents the profound change that describes the coming into existence of the universe. Yet on Shabbat, we refrain from but thirty-nine categories of forbidden labor. The Talmud refers to these thirty-nine as "forty minus one" because each one parallels one of the forty levels of Creation, *except for the highest level of Creation, the Creation of something from absolute nothingness, which has no parallel in our physical world.*

That is why the Talmud persists in referencing the forbidden types of labor as "forty less one" rather than simply saying "thirty-nine." It wants to emphasize that the source for these prohibitions is rooted within the theme to which only the number "forty" can give meaning. What we cannot do on the seventh day is to create, to change, to transform, all of which God ceased to do on the first Shabbat of history. But the first of the actions God performed, that of bringing about something from nothing, has no relevance whatsoever to human beings. There is no Shabbat labor that can possibly correspond to it. That is why the Talmud chooses to summarize what we need to know about what is not permitted to us as the "forty less one" forbidden labors.

When it came to the number of lashes to be imposed upon the wicked, the Torah also feels it necessary to use the number "forty" so that we conceptualize the punishment as a biblical effort to bring about the complete transformation of the sinner. Yet by having the Oral Law reduce the forty to thirty-nine, the Torah is teaching us an extremely profound idea about the extent to which a person, no matter how wicked, may be ensnared by evil. *No one can possibly become entirely depraved.* Within each one of us there is a spark of holiness that will always remain untouched by sin. Being created in God's image means that no matter how far we stray from the path of righteousness it is impossible for us to lose our seal of divinity. That is why even a *rasha* only requires thirty-nine lashes, not forty. And that is why even a *rasha*, in spite of his seemingly heretical question and his confrontational attitude, still sits at the Seder table – and is still viewed in our eyes with the potential for rehabilitation and return to the faith community that has its roots in the Passover story.

Pesaḥ-Matza-Maror: The Three Foundations of Faith

Rabban Gamliel would say: Anyone who does not say these three things on Pesaḥ has not fulfilled his obligation, and these are they: *Pesaḥ*, matza, and bitter herbs."

These words in the Haggada come directly from a mishna in Tractate Pesaḥim (116a–b). They add an unparalleled measure of importance to the text that follows. We are now told that everything in the Haggada that preceded may have been in vain, that all of our efforts until this point have as yet not fulfilled our obligation, unless and until we "say" these three things. Rabbinic commentators clarify: It does not simply mean "say" but rather comprehend. These three rituals have profound meaning. They represent the essence of the Seder and the ideas we hope to transmit to our children: *Pesaḥ*, the Passover sacrifice; matza; and *maror*, the bitter herbs – these embody the three keys to our faith. Let us see if we can understand why this is so.

THE THIRTEEN PRINCIPLES OF BELIEF

Judaism is primarily a religion of deed rather than creed. We are judged by our actions rather than our thoughts. Revelation at Sinai presented us with a lengthy list of commandments rather than a catechism of theological beliefs. The operative word of Judaism is "mitzva" – the act in accord with God's will is our mission and its fulfillment is what demonstrates our commitment.

And yet Judaism obviously requires a belief system as well. A mitzva, a commandment, only makes sense if there is a certainty in a commander. Deed without creed lacks a logical foundation. It is wrong, as some have suggested, that Jews do not require faith as long as they follow the law. The Talmud makes this clear in the opening mishna of the last chapter of Tractate Sanhedrin:

> All of Israel have a portion in the World to Come, for it is written, "Your people are all righteous; they shall inherit the land forever, the branch of My planting, the work of My hands, that I may be glorified" (Is. 60:21). But the following have no portion therein: he who maintains that resurrection is not a biblical doctrine, [he who maintains that] the Torah was not divinely revealed, and an *epikores*. (Sanhedrin 90a)

All of Israel have a share in the World to Come – but some of them do not? The mishna seems to contradict itself between its first sentence and the one that follows. If the mishna wanted us to acknowledge that there are exceptions to entry in the World to Come, should it not have simply stated that "all except the following three have a share in the World to Come"? The answer is obvious: the mishna wanted us to know that all of Israel start their lives with the gift of the promise of eternity. Everyone *does* have a portion in the World to Come – but it is theirs to lose. There are three who by virtue of their acquired heretical belief are no longer worthy.

Here is a remarkable passage that identifies belief as an indispensible requirement, so crucial to our identity as Jews that our afterlife depends upon it. Of course we must observe the mitzvot. But that still does not make us deserving of the rewards of Heaven. We also need faith. Faith in what are clearly considered the three theological cornerstones of Judaism.

The three are expressed as negations by those who lose their share in the World to Come. They refer to the heretic who denies the traditional belief in life after death; the heretic who denies the divine source of Torah and God's authorship; and finally the *epikores* – from the word that gave us Epicureanism, after the Greek philosopher Epicurus, whose philosophy of atomic materialism denied all belief in a God or a higher divine power – someone who rejects the existence of God.

Stated as positives, the three fundamentals of faith recorded in the mishna are resurrection, Revelation, and God. The mishna teaches us how one may lose a previously granted gift. Heretics begin gradually by attacking first what they consider nonessentials of faith. The journey to complete abandonment of God starts with an attack on a seemingly noncrucial issue. Belief in life after death, after all, is difficult to grasp intellectually. Surely it cannot be that important, says the heretic in his heart. From there the next step is to forsake the Torah. Without the context of eternity, eternal law as guarantor of eternal life no longer seems defensible. And with the passing of these two, resurrection and Revelation, the almost inevitable final heresy is *epikores,* rejection of God Himself.

It is on this mishna that Maimonides bases his famous thirteen principles of faith. They have become best known to us by way of their formulation in the famous *Yigdal* prayer, which made its way into the siddur:

1. Great is the living God and praised, He exists and His existence is beyond time.
2. He is One, and there is no unity like His. Unfathomable, His Oneness is infinite.
3. He has neither bodily form nor substance; His holiness is beyond compare.
4. He preceded all that was created. He was first; there was no beginning to His beginning.
5. Behold He is Master of the universe and every creature shows His greatness and majesty.
6. The rich flow of His prophecy He gave to His treasured people in whom He gloried.
7. Never in Israel has there risen another like Moses, a prophet who beheld God's image.

8. God gave His people a Torah of truth by the hand of His prophet, most faithful of His house.

9. God will not alter or change His law for any other, for eternity.

10. He sees and knows our secret thoughts; as soon as something is begun, He foresees its end.

11. He rewards people with loving-kindness according to their deeds; He punishes the wicked according to his wickedness.

12. At the End of Days, He will send our Messiah to redeem those who await His final salvation.

13. God will revive the dead in His great loving-kindness, blessed for evermore is His glorious name.

There is a remarkable difference, though, between the formulation as found in the mishna and that of Maimonides: The mishna lists only three foundations of faith, as opposed to the thirteen of Maimonides. How can we account for the larger number expounded by the great medieval sage? *It is because Maimonides, in a profound comprehension of the deeper meaning of the talmudic text, understood that every one of the three heresies singled out in the mishna required not one but several belief commitments to avoid sharing their contemptible and erroneous opinions.*

The *epikores* rejects God. We choose to affirm His existence. But it is not enough to simply say we believe in God. What *kind* of God do we believe in? Who is this God? What can we say about Him that makes Him uniquely the God of the Jewish people? Look carefully at the list of thirteen principles and you will note that the first five are all elaborations on the heresy of the *epikores* and his denial of God.

The first principle is simply that God exists. The second principle takes our belief an essential and necessary step further: The God we believe in is One and not the many of paganism, not the three of the Trinity, and not the two of Persian Zoroastrianism and dualism. More than one god profoundly diminishes each one of them. When there are two or more gods, none of them are supreme – and hence none of them are in truth what we mean by God. To really be God, God needs to be One.

The third principle teaches belief in God's incorporeality. A body by definition is a limitation. It is a limitation in space – if God is here, He is not everywhere; if God is contained within a fixed form, He cannot exist outside of it. A body is also subject to its physical frailty and weaknesses. To believe in God means to believe that "He has neither bodily form nor substance."

The fourth principle teaches that just as God cannot be limited in space if He is to be all-powerful, so too can He not be limited in time. "He preceded all that was created, He was first; there was no beginning to His beginning." His very name, the Tetragrammaton of four letters, is a combination of the Hebrew for the three tenses of being: was, is, and will be. The God in whom we believe always was, continues to be in an ongoing relationship with the world, and will never cease to be the eternal Ruler of the universe.

The fifth principle, perhaps not as clear as it should be in the *Yigdal* formulation, is best understood in the original. It is a warning against the worship of any intermediary to the Almighty, be it celestial or human, for fear that it will become an end in and of itself, just as the Golden Calf led the people away from the worship of God.

What Maimonides has done here is both striking and brilliant. Rather than counter the sin of the *epikores* with a simple declaration of belief in God, Maimonides has outlined five necessary additional components of that belief. Note also that Maimonides has reversed the sequence of the mishna for an obvious reason. The mishna spoke of those who *lose* their share in the World to Come because of their rejection of the fundamentals of faith. First they reject resurrection; from there they reject Revelation; and finally they reject God Himself. Conversely, the goal of Maimonides is to build the structure of faith by way of the sequence of its most logical development. His list is in the order of launching faith, rather than renouncing it. First, we need to establish firm belief in God. Only from there can we move forward to acceptance of Torah and of resurrection.

Principles six through nine are the four ideas Maimonides believes are essential to our understanding of Revelation and the divine source of Torah. The concept of prophecy, the sixth principle, is the first step. God can and did speak to mankind. More than that, as the seventh principle enunciates, Moses was unique among all the other prophets in the manner in which God communicated with him, "face to face." His was not a dreamlike vision but a veritable direct encounter. That is what lends such special significance to Torah as a Torah of truth, the eighth principle. Finally, the ninth principle teaches that Torah as the word of God is eternal, unchanging, and unalterable by any "new" or later testament. What the mishna described, in a negative format, as the belief that the Torah was not divinely revealed constitutes, in its positive format, four critical beliefs that correspond to our complete faith in divine Revelation at Sinai.

However, it is the last set of principles, the tenth through the thirteenth, that offers us an incredible way of understanding the mishna's emphasis on resurrection. Why, after all, is the belief in an afterlife so crucial to Jewish theology? Why is this one of only three ideas whose acceptance determines our final judgment? Maimonides guides us by placing it into the context of theodicy – the ultimate problem troubling mankind throughout all generations, the seemingly unanswerable difficulty that stands in the way of our acceptance of God and of Torah.

If God is good, why is the world so bad? If God is righteous, why do good people suffer and why do wicked people prosper? If Torah is true, why then are its followers not always blessed and why do those who disobey it so often flourish? It is the problem of Job – as it is the cause of our perplexed response throughout history to the apparent unfairness of life.

Belief in God and in Torah are powerfully appealing until they confront the ultimate religious question: How can an all-powerful God promise providential care and recompense when the world as we know it seems to operate in an unfair and indifferent manner, oblivious to reward for the righteous and punishment for the wicked? The only possible response is that our perspective is limited by our mortality, our judgment is made on the basis of the short biblical seventy years of our lives on earth, as opposed to the infinite duration of eternity.

Life is unfair. The lives lived here on earth, the lives measured solely by our experiences in this world, without consideration of what is yet to come. However, faith in God and faith in Torah require one more faith in order to make both of them sustainable and credible. We need to believe that *what happens in this world is not the end of the story*. Rewards not granted here are stored up for even more glorious delivery after our passing. Punishments not meted out to the wicked before our eyes are merely delayed for reasons known only to God.

The final four principles of faith listed by Maimonides conclude with resurrection – but they include God's knowledge of all of our actions here on earth (the tenth principle), reward and punishment for the righteous and the wicked (eleventh), the eventual fulfillment of the messianic process (twelfth), followed by the resurrection of the dead (thirteenth).

For Maimonides, the heresy of the one who denies resurrection was the denial of an afterlife and all that it means for our ability to respond to life's unfairness and injustices. The belief in the dual prophecies of the Messiah and *teḥiyat hametim,* resurrection, enable us to maintain our faith in the ultimate justice of God and of Torah – if not now, then in a preordained future.

THE REAL MEANING OF *AMEN*

Maimonides expanded the three ideas of the mishna into thirteen principles. We can, however, contract them as well into three simple words: God, Revelation, resurrection. There is yet another way we can summarize them: *El, Melekh, ne'eman.* Principles one through five would be *El,* God. Principles six through nine would be *Melekh,* King – as our Ruler who commanded us how to live our lives through Torah, He is also our King. Finally, principles ten through thirteen affirm that He is *ne'eman* – faithful to fulfill His promises, both to the righteous as well as to the wicked, in the Time to Come.

The word *amen* is our response to every blessing. Its letters form the root of the word *emuna,* faith or belief. The Talmud tells us that its three Hebrew letters, *aleph, mem,* and *nun,* are the first letters of precisely these three Hebrew words that summarize Jewish belief: *El Melekh ne'eman. Amen* therefore expresses not only the idea *that* we believe, but also hints at *what* we believe – the three fundamentals of faith that in their fuller form become Maimonides' list of thirteen.

THE THREE PASSOVER RITUALS

We began this discussion with the words of Rabban Gamliel. In order to fulfill our obligation on Passover night we must understand three mitzvot: *Pesaḥ*, matza, and *maror*. It is with these three mitzvot that we begin our historic narrative.

Pesaḥ was the Paschal lamb. It was the god of Egypt. The precondition for our deliverance was to slay the Egyptian god and to openly proclaim our rejection of this pagan idolatry by smearing its blood on our doorposts. Seeing this, God would pass over our homes, sparing us from the Angel of Death and designating us as worthy of becoming His people. This was our acceptance of *El*.

The matzot, spelled the same way in Hebrew as the word "mitzvot," were our introduction to Torah. Mitzvot, just like matzot, dare never be delayed in their observance lest they become "leavened." *Ḥametz*, representing a delay of time, is the enemy of matza as it is of every mitzva. Baking matza requires intense concentration and concern. Even a speck of *ḥametz* is prohibited. Matzot are the beginning of a "mitzvot relationship" with God – a relationship that will be fully consummated with the Revelation at Sinai. Matzot as mitzvot are the ritual symbol of God as *Melekh*.

The *maror,* bitter herbs, were the final faith lesson of Passover. Jews had to learn belief even in the presence of bitterness, faith even during the seeming triumph of injustice and unfairness. *Ne'eman* – God is faithful to carry out His promises even when they are long and delayed in coming. Bitter herbs are as much a part of life as the joyful events and blessings, which clearly come from God.

There is a beautiful story about the great sage the *Ḥafetz Ḥayim*, who once met one of his former students. The rabbi asked him how he was doing and he answered, "Oh, everything is so very terrible, everything is bad." The *Ḥafetz Ḥayim* vehemently shook his head and responded, "God forbid! Do not say that. Do not say it is bad. Say it is bitter." The student could not understand. Bad or bitter – what could possibly be the difference? Why was the rabbi so insistent on using one word rather than the other? "Rebbe, why is the word "bitter" more appropriate than bad?" he asked. To which the rabbi responded, "A medicine may be bitter – but it is never bad."

There are times when a righteous and loving God sends us bitter medicines, but the bitter has a purpose. That too is a crucial lesson we must absorb when we recall not only the Exodus from Egypt but the terrible times that preceded it as well. The key mitzvot of Passover are nothing less than a curriculum of *emuna*. Their three most important subjects are the ideas central to the thirteen principles of faith as outlined by Maimonides; the three prime heresies singled out as sufficient to deprive someone from attaining the eternal life in the World to Come; the three concepts the Talmud teaches us we ought to bear in mind every time we respond with the word *amen*.

Small wonder that *Pesaḥ*, matza, and *maror* deserve this overpowering emphasis at the Seder.

Redemption, Then and Now

MENORAH

REDEMPTION, THEN AND NOW

PESAḤ HAGGADA

WITH ESSAYS AND COMMENTARY
BY
RABBI BENJAMIN BLECH

Menorah Books

DEDICATION

There are very few individuals in one's life who have a formative and everlasting impact upon you; who change the way you look at the world around you; who affect your value system, your dreams, your aspirations. When I started learning Torah for the first time in my life, in the JSS (beginners) Division at Yeshiva University, Rabbi Benjamin Blech became one of those few inspirational figures, in my life, and the lives of many of my peers.

His *shiur* was only once a week, and for only one hour each time. It was called the Hashkafa Shiur. I've never heard of a shiur by that name, at any Torah institution, since. His insights, his proofs, his assertions, his untangling of complex ideas kept us fixated on every word he uttered, slowly. His personal stories of interactions with congregants, their questions, his answers, their dilemmas, his responses, their tragedies, his words of comfort and inspiration, put us on solid ground; his Torah armed us against the many assaults of the world around us upon our new convictions, commitments, and worldview.

Rabbi Blech empowered us to build our futures upon a divine gift from a very distant past. The words he spoke, we repeated to our children and we hear our children repeating them to theirs, and so the Torah is never forgotten. Thank you, Rabbi Blech, on behalf of your thousands of students, for giving us life.

Marc Belzberg
Jerusalem

Note to the Reader
For the accompanying essays on Pesaḥ turn to the other end of this volume.

Introduction

Seeing the Good in the Bad

The Talmud tells us that the structure of the Haggada is based on one major theme: "[When telling the story of the Exodus] begin with shame and end with praise" (Mishna Pesaḥim 10:4). We begin by recounting the bad, and then we conclude with the good. The sequence is meant to convey a fundamental truth of our faith. What appears at the outset to be a curse is in fact the key to a future blessing. We cannot judge whether something is truly good or bad until we have the ability to view it from the perspective of its final outcome.

The Talmud tells us that when Moses asked God, "Show me, I pray You, Your glory" (Ex. 33:18), he was really asking the ultimate question of theodicy: Why do bad things happen to good people? God's response was, "You will see My back, but My face shall not be seen" (v. 23). The commentators explain God's meaning: Events can never be understood as they occur, but only in retrospect, with the benefit of hindsight. Kierkegaard put it beautifully when he said, "The greatest tragedy of life is that it must be lived forwards and can only be understood backwards."

The Jewish people were first taught this truth through the story of Joseph. The tragedy of his sale by his brothers enables him to save his

family in the time of famine. At the end of the story, Joseph reassures his brothers that he will do them no harm: "And as for you, you meant evil against me, but God meant it for good, to bring to pass, as it is this day, to save many people alive" (Gen. 50:20).

The word "Haggada" in *gematria*, the numerical value of Hebrew letters, adds up to seventeen. That was the exact age of Joseph when he was sold into Egypt – the real beginning of the story of our Egyptian exile and ultimately of the Exodus commemorated by Passover. By numerical allusion, the Haggada reminds us of the terrible act that started it all. But there is yet another concept related to the *gematria* of seventeen; it is also the numerical value of the Hebrew word *tov*, good. We need to remember that the tragedy of Joseph's sale at the age of seventeen led to the miracle of our redemption and the Revelation at Sinai. No matter how black any event may appear at the time, the dark of night is always followed by the dawn. "And there was evening and there was morning" (Gen. 1) is the theme of our history – and the secret of the word "Haggada."

הגדה של פסח

THE PESAḤ HAGGADA

*The program for the evening is announced beforehand
in the following form:*

קדש / ורחץ / כרפס / יחץ

מגיד / רחצה / מוציא מצה

מרור / כורך / שלחן עורך

צפון / ברך / הלל / נרצה

KIDDUSH

WASHING

KARPAS

SPLITTING

TELLING

WASHING

MOTZI MATZA

BITTER HERBS

WRAPPING

TABLE SETTING

HIDDEN

BLESSING

PRAISING

PARTING

KADESH / KIDDUSH

The first cup of wine is poured. Lift the cup with the right hand and say the following:

On Shabbat add:

quietly: And it was evening, and it was morning –   *Gen. 1*

יוֹם הַשִּׁשִּׁי the sixth day.

Then the heavens and the earth were completed,   *Gen. 2*
and all their array.
With the seventh day, God completed the work He had done.
He ceased on the seventh day from all the work He had done.
God blessed the seventh day and declared it holy,
because on it
He ceased from all His work He had created to do.

---

piness, but it is up to us to add the work and the effort to make it happen. How appropriate to begin the story of our redemption from Egypt with a blessing over wine as a reminder that the ultimate Redemption will depend not only on God but on us as well.

The Symbolism of Wine

Wine has a special place in Jewish life and law. At happy occasions, we lift a cup of wine and toast each other with the word *lehayim*. Shabbatot and holidays begin with the Kiddush, verbal sanctification over a cup of wine. We follow King David's practice; to celebrate deliverance he declared, "I will lift up the cup of salvation and call on the name of the Lord" (Ps. 116:13).

What is wine's uniqueness? All things with which we are familiar become noticeably worse with age. Time is their enemy. Decay and deterioration are the natural result. But wine is different. It has the very special gift of improving with age. That is why it has such meaning for us symbolically. A blessing over wine is our way of expressing the hope that our lives will share this distinctive quality. As we get older may we, like fine wine, find ourselves always getting better and better. That is also why wine is such a perfect symbol for the festival of Passover, the story of our passage from our shameful beginnings as slaves in Egypt to deliverance and to the promise of ultimate messianic Redemption.

קדש

The first cup of wine is poured. Lift the cup with the right hand and say the following:

On שבת add:

quietly:

וַיְהִי־עֶרֶב וַיְהִי־בֹקֶר

בראשית א

יוֹם הַשִּׁשִּׁי:

בראשית ב

וַיְכֻלּוּ הַשָּׁמַיִם וְהָאָרֶץ וְכָל־צְבָאָם:
וַיְכַל אֱלֹהִים בַּיּוֹם הַשְּׁבִיעִי מְלַאכְתּוֹ אֲשֶׁר עָשָׂה
וַיִּשְׁבֹּת בַּיּוֹם הַשְּׁבִיעִי מִכָּל־מְלַאכְתּוֹ אֲשֶׁר עָשָׂה:
וַיְבָרֶךְ אֱלֹהִים אֶת־יוֹם הַשְּׁבִיעִי, וַיְקַדֵּשׁ אֹתוֹ
כִּי בוֹ שָׁבַת מִכָּל־מְלַאכְתּוֹ, אֲשֶׁר־בָּרָא אֱלֹהִים, לַעֲשׂוֹת:

KADESH / KIDDUSH

The Special Blessing for Wine

The blessing for wine is unusual. Wine comes from grapes, which grow on the vine. The blessing ought to be the same as the one for all other fruits, "…who creates the fruit of the trees." What accounts for this special blessing of *boreh peri hagefen*? The Talmud compares wine to one other food whose blessing is different than what we might expect. Bread comes from wheat. Its blessing should therefore be "…who creates the fruit of the ground." Instead, it has its own unique blessing: *hamotzi lehem min haaretz*.

What bread and wine have in common is the fact that God provides the raw ingredients, to be sure, but it is human initiative – the grinding of the wheat into flour and baking, the pressing of the grapes and storing in casks – that creates the matchless final product. When God and man partner to greatly enhance a natural object from its original state, that improved object is deserving of a blessing of a higher order. Bread and wine thereby become paradigms of a biblical ideal, described in the Jerusalem Talmud, that we are commanded to become "partners with God in the act of creation."

When we drink wine, we say, *lehayim*, to life. On a profound level, we are expressing the idea that the joy we find in the wine *we* created with God's ingredients is the secret of life itself. God gives us the wherewithal to find hap-

On other evenings Kiddush starts here:

When saying Kiddush for others, add:

Please pay attention, my masters.

Blessed are You, Lord our God, King of the Universe,
who creates the fruit of the vine.

On Shabbat, add the words in parentheses.

בָּרוּךְ Blessed are You,
Lord our God,
King of the Universe,
who has chosen us from among all peoples,
raised us above all tongues,
and made us holy
through His commandments.
You have given us,
Lord our God, in love
(Sabbaths for rest),
festivals for rejoicing,
holy days and seasons for joy,
(this Sabbath day and)
this day of the festival of Matzot,
the time of our freedom
(with love), a holy assembly in memory
of the Exodus from Egypt.
For You have chosen us
and sanctified us
above all peoples,
and given us as our heritage
(Your holy Sabbath in love and favor and)
Your holy festivals for joy and gladness.
Blessed are You, Lord,
who sanctifies (the Sabbath,) Israel and the festivals.

On other evenings קידוש *starts here:*

When saying קידוש *for others, add:*

סברי מרנן

בָּרוּךְ אַתָּה יהוה אֱלֹהֵינוּ מֶלֶךְ הָעוֹלָם, בּוֹרֵא פְּרִי הַגָּפֶן.

On שבת, *add the words in parentheses.*

בָּרוּךְ אַתָּה יהוה אֱלֹהֵינוּ מֶלֶךְ הָעוֹלָם,

אֲשֶׁר בָּחַר בָּנוּ מִכָּל עָם,

וְרוֹמְמָנוּ מִכָּל לָשׁוֹן, וְקִדְּשָׁנוּ בְּמִצְוֹתָיו

וַתִּתֶּן לָנוּ יהוה אֱלֹהֵינוּ בְּאַהֲבָה

(שַׁבָּתוֹת לִמְנוּחָה וּ)מוֹעֲדִים לְשִׂמְחָה,

חַגִּים וּזְמַנִּים לְשָׂשׂוֹן, אֶת

יוֹם (הַשַּׁבָּת הַזֶּה וְאֶת יוֹם) חַג הַמַּצּוֹת הַזֶּה

זְמַן חֵרוּתֵנוּ (בְּאַהֲבָה) מִקְרָא קֹדֶשׁ

זֵכֶר לִיצִיאַת מִצְרָיִם, כִּי בָנוּ

בָחַרְתָּ וְאוֹתָנוּ קִדַּשְׁתָּ

מִכָּל הָעַמִּים, (וְשַׁבָּת)

וּמוֹעֲדֵי קָדְשֶׁךָ

(בְּאַהֲבָה וּבְרָצוֹן)

בְּשִׂמְחָה וּבְשָׂשׂוֹן הִנְחַלְתָּנוּ.

בָּרוּךְ אַתָּה יהוה,

מְקַדֵּשׁ (הַשַּׁבָּת וְ)יִשְׂרָאֵל וְהַזְּמַנִּים.

On Motza'ei Shabbat, the following Havdala is added:

בָּרוּךְ Blessed are You, LORD our God,
King of the Universe,
who creates the lights of fire.

Blessed are You, LORD our God,
King of the Universe,
who distinguishes between sacred and secular,
between light and darkness,
between Israel and the nations,
between the seventh day and the six days of work.
You have made a distinction
between the holiness of the Sabbath
and the holiness of festivals,
and have sanctified
the seventh day above the six days of work.
You have distinguished and sanctified
Your people Israel with Your holiness.
Blessed are You, LORD,
who distinguishes between sacred and sacred.

בָּרוּךְ Blessed are You, LORD our God,
King of the Universe,
who has given us life, sustained us,
and brought us to this time.

Drink while reclining to the left.

URHATZ / WASHING

Water is brought to the leader.
The participants wash their hands but do not say a blessing.

On מוצאי שבת, *the following* הבדלה *is added:*

בָּרוּךְ אַתָּה יהוה אֱלֹהֵינוּ מֶלֶךְ הָעוֹלָם
בּוֹרֵא מְאוֹרֵי הָאֵשׁ.

בָּרוּךְ אַתָּה יהוה אֱלֹהֵינוּ מֶלֶךְ הָעוֹלָם
הַמַּבְדִּיל בֵּין קֹדֶשׁ לְחֹל
בֵּין אוֹר לְחֹשֶׁךְ
בֵּין יִשְׂרָאֵל לָעַמִּים
בֵּין יוֹם הַשְּׁבִיעִי לְשֵׁשֶׁת יְמֵי הַמַּעֲשֶׂה
בֵּין קְדֻשַּׁת שַׁבָּת לִקְדֻשַּׁת יוֹם טוֹב הִבְדַּלְתָּ
וְאֶת יוֹם הַשְּׁבִיעִי מִשֵּׁשֶׁת יְמֵי הַמַּעֲשֶׂה קִדַּשְׁתָּ
הִבְדַּלְתָּ וְקִדַּשְׁתָּ אֶת עַמְּךָ יִשְׂרָאֵל בִּקְדֻשָּׁתֶךָ.
בָּרוּךְ אַתָּה יהוה הַמַּבְדִּיל בֵּין קֹדֶשׁ לְקֹדֶשׁ.

בָּרוּךְ אַתָּה יהוה אֱלֹהֵינוּ מֶלֶךְ הָעוֹלָם
שֶׁהֶחֱיָנוּ וְקִיְּמָנוּ וְהִגִּיעָנוּ
לַזְּמַן הַזֶּה.

Drink while reclining to the left.

ורחץ
Water is brought to the leader.
The participants wash their hands but do not say a blessing.

KARPAS

A small quantity of radish, greens, or roots of parsley is dipped in salt water.
Say the following over the karpas,
with the intent to include the maror in the blessing:

בָּרוּךְ Blessed are You, LORD our God,
King of the Universe,
who creates the fruit of the ground.

Eat without reclining.

---

in the effort. The Jews, wanting to show their great loyalty to their host country, joined in enthusiastically. The next day, however, when the Jews arrived at the building sites, the Egyptians did not return. Shortly thereafter, the Jews found themselves surrounded by taskmasters who demanded that they perform the same amount of work that they had done of their own volition the day before. It was through soft and crafty words that Pharaoh lured the Jewish nation into slavery.

It was the desire of the children of Israel to demonstrate that they were "more Egyptian than the Egyptians" that brought about their first national tragedy. It is a trait that would manifest itself many times over by a people who found themselves a small group in a larger society, eager to prove that their religious difference did not preclude gratitude and allegiance to their host nation. In this spirit, Jews went overboard to show superpatriotism, just as in the era before the Holocaust many Jews delighted in demonstrating that they were "more German than the Germans." The end of each story all too often paralleled what happened in Egypt. Soft words resulted in rigorous labor and at times even brutal annihilation.

That is why the word *karpas*, which reminds us of this threat, assumes such a prominent place in the Seder. And that is why its meaning is hinted at by reading the word backwards – because this truth can never be understood at the time it occurs but only when viewed with the wisdom of hindsight, in retrospect. Looking backwards, we can understand how we were foolishly misled in Egypt as well as in all the other countries in which we assumed that greater patriotism guaranteed our survival.

There is a famous story about Henry Kissinger and Golda Meir. When the Israeli prime minister chided the American secretary of state to remember his Jewish origins, he replied, "Mrs. Meir, I am an *American* Jew – an American first." "Mr. Kissinger," Golda responded, "here we read backwards." And here too, with the *karpas*, we are reminded to read in the reverse direction as well.

כרפס

A small quantity of radish, greens, or roots of parsley is dipped in salt water.
Say the following over the karpas,
with the intent to include the maror in the blessing:

בָּרוּךְ אַתָּה יהוה אֱלֹהֵינוּ מֶלֶךְ הָעוֹלָם
בּוֹרֵא פְּרִי הָאֲדָמָה.

Eat without reclining.

KARPAS

Reading the Word Backwards

Karpas is an unusual word. Commentaries throughout the generations have offered a seemingly peculiar source as its meaning. It is related, they claim, to the verse in the Torah that describes the start of the enslavement of the Jews in Egypt: "And the Egyptians made the children of Israel labor with rigor" (Ex. 1:13). And what does the word *karpas* (spelled *kaf, resh, peh, samekh*) have to do with this? If we read the word backwards, the *samekh* could represent an abbreviation for the word *siman*, sign, with the remaining letters making the word *parekh*, rigor.

Two questions beg to be asked on this interpretation. First, why would the description of the way in which the Jews were enslaved, "with rigor," be given such prominence at the very beginning of the Seder? Second, why would the allusion to it be expressed in the manner of reverse order?

To answer the first question, we need to turn to a fascinating insight offered by the Talmud and elaborated on in the Midrash. In Sota 11b, R. Elazar explains that the Hebrew for "with rigor" is actually a combination of two Hebrew words *"peh rakh,"* "[with] smooth [or, soft] mouth." It was not by harsh decree that the Egyptians began their oppression. Their plan was far more ingenious. It was predicated on a soft approach, to seduce the children of Israel to become accomplices to their own enslavement. And tragically enough, the plan worked in Egypt just as it would subsequently play a significant role many times later in Jewish history.

Here is how the Midrash tells the story: When Pharaoh decided to enslave the Jews, he cunningly declared a national week of labor during which all good citizens of the realm were to come and help in the building of the great storage cities of Pithom and Raamses. This was to be a demonstration, he stressed, of willingness to assert national allegiance and citizenship. Pharaoh himself joined

YAḤATZ / SPLITTING

The middle matza is broken in two.

The bigger portion is then hidden away to serve as the afikoman with which the meal is later concluded.
The smaller portion is placed between the two whole matzot.

We break the matza into two parts to symbolize this concept. One part reminds us of Egypt, the other part of the Messiah. The first part we leave on the plate to be eaten in fulfillment of the mitzva of matza. The other part, the one demonstrating our faith in the divine assurance for a final Redemption, is wrapped up as the *afikomen,* to serve as *a gift for our children* – the future of our people. It will be eaten at the conclusion of the meal and identified in the fifteen sections of the Seder as *Tzafun,* hidden, the as yet unrevealed part of our history.

With this insight, we can readily understand the law meant to guide us to the proper fulfillment of the requirement of *Yaḥatz.* After breaking the matza into two, we will almost certainly have a division that leaves us with pieces of uneven sizes. We do not measure the break with a ruler; one part will surely be larger than the other. Which one shall we leave on the plate to be consumed for *Motzi Matza,* and which one is to be wrapped up as the *afikomen* for the children? The law is precise: The smaller one is to be designated as the matza commemorating the redemption from Egypt. The larger one is to be chosen as a symbol for the Redemption of the future. The reason? To emphasize the prediction of Jeremiah (16:14) that the time will come when we will no longer need to recall our deliverance from Egypt in light of the final and even more miraculous ultimate Redemption. What is in store for our future will be "bigger" than what happened to our ancestors.

יחץ

The middle מצה is broken in two.
The bigger portion is then hidden away to serve as the אפיקומן
with which the meal is later concluded.
The smaller portion is placed between the two whole מצות.

YAḤATZ / SPLITTING

Identifying the Bigger Part

We are required to break the middle matza into two. Symbolically, it is a profound statement. Matza reminds us of our dash to freedom when we fled from Egypt in haste and had no time to complete the baking of our bread. It is an everlasting sign of our miraculous deliverance. It is the quintessential mitzva of Passover. Yet central to its message – and that is why this idea is illustrated by way of the *middle* matza – is the recognition that the salvation we witnessed on that first Passover of history is only *part* of the story. True, we were redeemed from Egypt, but that moment did not mark the arrival of the Messiah. History still had millennia of exile and suffering in store for us. Passover was a *geula* but not a *Geula Shelema*.

One of the thirteen principles of our faith, as codified by Maimonides, is the belief in a final and total Redemption. On that day, as the prophet Zechariah predicted, "The Lord will be One and His name will be One" (14:9). The entire world will acknowledge the God who revealed Himself to the nation of Israel in the Passover story. Passover commemorates two redemptions, the one of history, as well as the one of destiny; the one that was, as well as the one that will be. The miracle of the past gains its greatest meaning by way of its promise for the future.

MAGGID / TELLING

During the recital of this paragraph
the seder plate is held up
and the middle matza is displayed to the company.

הָא לַחְמָא עַנְיָא

THIS

IS THE BREAD OF OPPRESSION

our fathers ate
in the land of Egypt.
Let all who are hungry
come in and eat;
let all who are in need
come and join us for the Pesaḥ.
Now we are here;
next year in the land of Israel.
Now – slaves;
next year we shall be free.

---

beginning the story of the twelve children of Israel and the creation of the Jewish people, we were given three paradigms of spiritual greatness, *each one of whom epitomized to perfection one of the traits singled out by the mishna.*

Abraham's greatness is manifested in his concern for others, his acts of lovingkindness. The very first thing we learn about him after he entered into his covenant with God by way of circumcision is that "he sat in the door of his tent in the heat of the day" (Gen. 18:1), waiting for an opportunity to host any strangers who might be passing by. His life teaches us the true meaning of *gemilut ḥasadim.* Isaac, who understood that his father was taking him to be sacrificed as an offering to God, willingly accepted his fate and was prepared to give up his life to fulfill a divine command, no matter how incomprehensible. He is the paradigm of *avoda.* Jacob "sat in the tents" (25:27), which the rabbis identified as the schools of Shem and Ever, studying the Torah traditions that

מַגִּיד

*During the recital of this paragraph
the* ‎קְעָרָה‎ (*seder plate*) *is held up
and the middle* ‎מצה‎ *is displayed to the company.*

הָא
לַחְמָא עַנְיָא
דִּי אֲכַלוּ אֲבָהָתָנָא בְּאַרְעָא דְמִצְרָיִם
כָּל דִּכְפִין יֵיתֵי וְיֵכָל, כָּל דִּצְרִיךְ יֵיתֵי וְיִפְסַח

הָשַׁתָּא הָכָא
לְשָׁנָה הַבָּאָה בְּאַרְעָא דְיִשְׂרָאֵל
הָשַׁתָּא עַבְדֵי
לְשָׁנָה הַבָּאָה בְּנֵי חוֹרִין.

THIS IS THE BREAD OF OPPRESSION

The Invitation to Guests

Before we begin with the recitation of the four questions, we preface the Seder
with an invitation to guests. We are taught in Ethics of the Fathers, "Shimon
the Righteous says that the world rests on three pillars: on Torah; on *avoda*,
sacrifice, worship; and on *gemilut ḥasadim*, acts of loving-kindness" (1:2). All
three are required for the world to deserve survival. The rabbis point out that
there is a striking correspondence between these three fundamental requirements and the number of patriarchs who served as founders of our faith. Before

rationale for the event of the first day became clear on the second. The condition of slavery was God's response to the sinful quarreling between Jew and Jew.

Matza is *laḥma anya*, the bread of oppression. Its name, connected to the Hebrew for strife and quarrel, captures the cause of our oppression throughout the ages. Jews fighting with one another is so grave a sin that God permits anti-Semites temporary victories in order to create Jewish unity in response to the possibility of communal annihilation. Matza is the annual reminder of a sin so egregious that we need a constant and annual reminder of its danger to our survival. And there is a simple antidote to its evil. Needless hatred, *sinat ḥinam*, the sin that caused our slavery in Egypt, must be countered with what Rav Abraham Isaac Kook famously called *ahavat ḥinam*, needless love, a boundless and inclusive love that overcomes all ill feelings.

There is a letter in Hebrew that conveys this idea of inclusiveness and togetherness. It is the letter *vav*, which means "and." It represents the idea of unity in its most powerful form. It is remarkable then that when the Hebrew word for matza, with its negative implication, has added to it this one letter, matza (spelled *mem, tzadi, heh*) becomes mitzva (*mem, tzadi, vav, heh*).

The Seder starts with an invitation. We demonstrate that we are no longer like those who fought with their brothers and brought about the punishment of slavery and exile. We treasure the idea of "and" – we know that the fundamental mitzva of our faith is to love each other, and so we invite guests to share the festive meal at our table in the hope that our unity will help bring about the final Redemption.

Our Mission in the Diaspora

The invitation to others is recited in Aramaic, not in Hebrew. This clearly marks the prayer as a product of the Diaspora, written after the expulsion of the Jews of the land of Israel in the aftermath of the destruction of the Second Temple, in 70 CE. Many theories have been advanced as to the reasons for our exile. On the simplest level, it was viewed as punishment for our transgressions. We were no longer in our homeland as a result of the sins we committed. But one opinion in the Talmud suggests something different and far more daring. In Pesaḥim 87b, we read, "The reason that the Jews were sent into exile was in order to increase the number of converts." It is to fulfill the vision of Isaiah that "it is too small a thing for you to be My servant to restore the tribes of Jacob and bring back those of Israel I have kept. I will also make you a light to the nations, so that My salvation may reach to the ends of the earth" (49:6). Exile allows us to be the bearers of the truths of Sinai to all the peoples of the world.

There is a remarkable hint in the Torah to this idea that predicts the time when the Jewish people will be cast out of Israel: "And cast them [*vayashlikhem*]

were transmitted even before the Revelation at Sinai. From the patriarchs, we were privileged to witness magnificent illustrations of the three ideals of the mishna.

The day when Abraham welcomed the three strangers – in reality angels, but perceived by him as passing Arab travelers – would many years later, by a remarkable "coincidence" of the calendar, become celebrated as Passover. Indeed, according to the Midrash, with divine intuition Abraham observed this holiday years before it was given to the Jewish people! In a sense, Passover is Abraham's holiday. Just as Abraham was deeply moved to intercede in order to prevent the pain and suffering of fellow human beings, God too intervened to redeem the Jews from the slavery in Egypt. The predominant characteristic of loving-kindness that marked our founding father was more than matched by the divine compassion demonstrated by our Father in heaven at the time of the Exodus. How fitting, therefore, that the Seder, at the very outset, takes note of this link by having us emulate Abraham's invitation to strangers.

Turning Matza into Mitzva

We know matza as an item of food central to the celebration of Passover. Yet strangely enough, the word has a totally different meaning in the later books of the Bible. In Isaiah we find it used as pejorative: "Behold for quarrel and strife [matza] you fast" (58:4). In Solomon's Book of Proverbs we find, "He who delights in transgression delights in quarrels [matza]" (17:19). The root meaning of matza seems to be identified with strife and quarrels. How could a word with such negative connotations come to play such a significant part at the Seder?

To answer, we need to remember the way in which Moses came to understand the Jewish suffering in Egypt. He was perplexed that God would allow the slavery of His people. In the first recorded incident of his life in the Torah, we read of how he went out to his brothers and witnessed their anguish. "He saw an Egyptian smiting a Hebrew, one of his brothers" (Ex. 2:11), and, unable to contain himself, he smote the Egyptian and buried him in the sand. But what troubled him more than anything else was how God could have allowed that to happen. Where was God's compassion, as He too was witness to this evil act? The Torah tells us that on the very next day Moses went out again, and this time he saw two Jews quarreling with each other. His attempt to intervene was rebuffed. Worse still, the fighting pair threatened to expose Moses for the events of the previous day. It was then that Moses uttered the fateful words, "Surely the thing is known" (v. 14). What was "the thing" that Moses now understood? Rashi tells us it was the very problem that had been troubling him so profoundly as he witnessed the seeming injustice all about him. What could the Jews have done to deserve such a terrible fate? Why did God permit them to suffer? The

The song *Eḥad Mi Yode'a*, Who Knows One, does not take us beyond the number 13, but rabbinic commentators long ago alerted us to the special meaning of other numbers. The number 28 in particular received singular attention because when viewed as written by the letters *kaf* for 20 and *ḥet* for 8, they make the word *koaḥ*, strength.

The very first verse in the Torah, "In the beginning God created the heavens and the earth" (Gen. 1:1), contains exactly 28 Hebrew letters. Creation of the heavens and earth clearly conveys to us the power of God. The verse that introduces the Revelation at Sinai and the Giving of the Ten Commandments is, "And God spoke all these words, saying" (Ex. 20:1). Once again, the sentence contains 28 letters, for this is the power of God as expressed by His code of law.

And what is the power of the Jewish people? It is the attribute we inherited from Abraham – the emphasis we place upon loving-kindness, compassion, and hospitality to strangers. No wonder then that this preface to the Seder, by which we invite others who are needy to participate with us, is comprised of exactly 28 words. This is our *koaḥ*. And perhaps this may account for the fact that the remarkable modern-day miracle of the reconquest of Jerusalem and its celebration as *Yom Yerushalayim* took place exactly on the 28th day of the month of Iyar. Jerusalem, as the spiritual center of Israel, is the power behind our national identity.

To Serve as God's Witnesses

The prayer that most succinctly summarizes our acceptance of God and His kingship is the *Shema*: "Hear, O Israel, the Lord is our God; the Lord is One" (Deut. 6:4). Every scribe is aware of the special law regarding the way in which two of the letters in this fundamental formulation of faith are to be written. The *ayin* of the first word *shema* and the *dalet* of the last word *eḥad* are enlarged. Our sages explain the reason. Together these raised letters, which spell *ed*, are to be viewed as one word which adds yet another significant dimension to our acceptance of God in our lives. It is not enough that we alone recognize the Almighty as Ruler of the universe. We have an obligation to the rest of mankind as well. The word *ed* means witness. Through the way we live our lives, we are to demonstrate the beauty of our faith and the splendor of following the path of a sanctified existence. We, who proclaim the truth of God, must also lovingly accept the mission of serving as witnesses of this reality to the world.

On a profound level, the rabbis see an allusion to deeper truths by taking note of the first letters of a sequence of words. The opening paragraph of the Seder is important enough to warrant this kind of analysis. We say, "*Ha laḥma anya di.*" The word *ha*, this, is followed by three words whose first letters make a word on its own: *le'ed* (spelled *lamed, ayin, dalet*), for witness. *This* – that is,

into another land as it is this day" (Deut. 29:27). But there is a strange feature
about one of these words in the verse. In every Sefer Torah, the letter *lamed*
in the word *vayashlikhem* is enlarged, in accordance with halakhic tradition.
Commentators have suggested a fascinating reason. *Lamed* is related to learning and teaching. Perhaps the verse is hinting at precisely the reason we have
suggested for exile. The Jewish people will be cast into another land for a positive reason, rather than as a punishment. It is as a people scattered among the
nations that Jews will have the opportunity to serve as teachers of the world,
living spokesmen for the moral codes given to them at Sinai. In this light, then,
the invitation, spoken in the language of our neighbors, may be meant to fulfill
our mission in the Diaspora – to allow others to witness the beauties of Jewish
life and observance.

Food for the Body, Food for the Soul

"All who are hungry" and "All who are in need" – What is the difference between
them? Are not the needy those who have no food, the very same ones already
described as the hungry? It appears the text is suggesting that there are two
different kinds of deprivation to which we need to be sensitive. The "hungry"
are those who lack physical nourishment. It is their stomachs that need to be
filled. Those "in need" are those who desperately require spiritual sustenance.
It is their souls that beg to be sustained so that their lives may have meaning.

There are two – and only two – blessings which have their source in the
Torah. The first is for food. When we complete a meal we are commanded,
"And you will eat, and you will be sated, and you shall bless the Lord your
God" (Deut. 8:10). The second is for the study of Torah: "For I will proclaim
the name of the Lord [the Torah], and you will ascribe greatness unto our God
[with a blessing]" (32:3). Why precisely these two? Because a human being is a
combination of body and soul, and both of these components require nourishment in order to survive. Food is what allows us to live; Torah is what gives us a
reason for living. Food sustains our bodies; Torah sustains our souls. Both are
essential. That is why both require a blessing.

And that is also why we invite two kinds of disadvantaged guests. The hungry are those who lack food. For them we provide physical nourishment. The
needy are those who seek meaning to their lives and who thirst for the peace
of mind that comes from faith and commitment to Torah. Let both be a part of
our Seder and become sated.

The Number 28 and the Power of the Jews

That numbers play an important role in Judaism is a concept we emphasize at the
very close of the Seder as we identify the significance of numbers 1 through 13.

The seder plate and the matzot are now covered and the second cup of wine is poured.
The youngest child asks the following questions:

מַה נִּשְׁתַּנָּה

WHAT MAKES
THIS NIGHT UNLIKE ALL OTHER NIGHTS,
so that every other night we eat either bread or matza,
> but tonight there is only matza?

And that every other night we eat many different greens,
> but tonight we will eat bitter herbs?

---

the key to our story of the trek from Egypt to Sinai, from Passover to Shavuot. Only with Torah did we become truly free.

That is why we need to add a second phrase after we plead for God to bring about a return to the land of Israel. Without a land guided by Torah, we would still be slaves – slaves to our passions, slaves to the idols of the marketplace, and slaves to the gods of contemporary fads and fashions. And that is why when we seek to comfort mourners for their personal tragedy and indicate that all of us share in their grief by way of our national tragedy of loss, we say to them, "May the Lord comfort you among the mourners of Zion and Jerusalem." What is the meaning of the double expression, "mourners of Zion and Jerusalem"? To mourn for Zion means to mourn for the land and to pray for the opportunity to physically return to its borders. To mourn for Jerusalem is to mourn for its sanctity and the Temple within it. We are grateful today that God has permitted our generation to achieve the first. We humbly recognize the challenge concerning the second.

WHAT MAKES THIS NIGHT UNLIKE ALL OTHER NIGHTS

The Dynamics of a Happy Family: Questions and Answers
One of the most famous lines in all of literature is Leo Tolstoy's opening sentence in Anna Karenina: "Happy families are all alike; every unhappy family is unhappy in its own way." But what is it that makes happy families happy? What is the common denominator of homes filled with joy and mutual love? In all certainty, homes are happy when their members share common values, when they treat each other with respect, and when they feel free to communicate openly without fear of being rebuffed or ridiculed. A happy home demonstrates the true meaning of family.

The קערה *and the* מצות *are now covered and the second cup of wine is poured.*
The youngest child asks the following questions:

מַה נִּשְׁתַּנָּה

הַלַּיְלָה הַזֶּה מִכָּל הַלֵּילוֹת

שֶׁבְּכָל הַלֵּילוֹת   אָנוּ אוֹכְלִין חָמֵץ וּמַצָּה
הַלַּיְלָה הַזֶּה   כֻּלּוֹ מַצָּה

שֶׁבְּכָל הַלֵּילוֹת   אָנוּ אוֹכְלִין שְׁאָר יְרָקוֹת
הַלַּיְלָה הַזֶּה   מָרוֹר

everything that we will be doing on this night – has a deeper purpose. It is to fulfill the mission of the *Shema*. It is meant not only for ourselves but for others as well, those whom we invite to the Seder and those who will hear of our retelling of the miracles God performed for us.

The Two Ultimate Redemptions

"Now we are here; next year in the land of Israel. Now – slaves; next year we shall be free." What is the difference between these two hopes? Is it not sufficient for us to pray for a return to the land of Israel, which by definition would make us free?

Obviously, our messianic hope consists of two parts. There are two stages we have always envisioned for our final Redemption. The first is physical, the second is spiritual. Return to the land is what we have been privileged to witness in our own lifetime. We now have the State of Israel. But that was never the ultimate dream. True freedom is connected to Sinai. We are told that when the Decalogue was given, it was "engraved on the Tablets" (Ex. 32:16). The mishna in Ethics of the Fathers, noting the correspondence of the word *ḥarut*, engraved, with *ḥerut*, freedom, tells us, "Said R. Yehoshua b. Levi: 'And the Tablets are the work of God, and the writing is God's writing, engraved on the Tablets'; read not *ḥarut* but *ḥerut*, for there is no free individual, except for he who occupies himself with the study of Torah" (6:2). Freedom without the constraints of law is not freedom; it is license, it is libertinism, it is anarchy. Freedom only becomes a goal to be treasured when it is constrained by the good and the right. Then it allows us to be free to be ourselves, to be true to our spiritual essence. That was

And that every other night we do not dip [our food] at all,
  but tonight we will dip it twice?
And that every other night some sit to eat and some recline,
  but tonight we are all reclining?

---

asking questions. In a happy family, parents encourage the give-and-take of discussion at a festive meal. That is why the Seder begins with the children asking their questions.

Four Questions and Four Sons

The children are the ones who ask questions – and soon we will learn that there are four different kinds of children. There is the wise son, the wicked son, the simple son, and the one who does not even know how to ask. Perhaps there is a profound connection between the number of questions and the number of children. And perhaps each one of the questions we find listed here is asked by a different kind of child, in the same order and sequence in which the Haggada later lists them.

The wise son asks about *ḥametz* and matza. The difference between them is miniscule. In fact they share the same ingredients. *Ḥametz* is matza just a little bit later. Even their Hebrew letters make this abundantly clear. *Ḥametz* (spelled *ḥet, mem, tzadi*) shares with the word matza (*mem, tzadi, heh*) two of its letters, the *mem* and the *tzadi*. The third letter of the former is *ḥet*, whereas that of the latter is *heh*, and that difference is no more than a little dot that marks the extension of the *heh* to a *ḥet*. On Passover we are extremely diligent to make certain that not even a small speck of *ḥametz* can be found in our homes. It is this extreme concern for every minor detail that distinguishes the wise son. His question marks him as someone who wants more than anything else to fulfill every mitzva punctiliously, without missing the slightest element necessary for its proper observance.

The wicked son asks the second question. Its emphasis is on the bitter herbs of the Seder. For him religious observance is nothing more than a burden. Rituals are unpleasant requirements he would as much prefer to avoid because he finds bitter foods distasteful. Why on this night, he wonders, must he yet again be forced to do something so unappealing?

The simple son is defined by inability to commit to or to focus on any one particular project. He moves quickly from one thing to another, without mastering any. He is an intellectual as well as an emotional "dipper," never fully partaking. For him the Passover Seder is a series of quick and disconnected moments,

שֶׁבְּכָל הַלֵּילוֹת   אֵין אָנוּ מַטְבִּילִין אֲפִלּוּ פַּעַם אֶחָת
הַלַּיְלָה הַזֶּה   שְׁתֵּי פְעָמִים

שֶׁבְּכָל הַלֵּילוֹת   אָנוּ אוֹכְלִין בֵּין יוֹשְׁבִין וּבֵין מְסֻבִּין
הַלַּיְלָה הַזֶּה   כֻּלָּנוּ מְסֻבִּין

And that was the way the Jews first came to Egypt. The opening verse of the Book of Exodus tells us, "And these are the names of the children of Israel who came to Egypt; with Jacob, each man and his household they came" (1:1). Note carefully the last phrase, "each man and his household." They came as family units. They understood they could survive as a people only on the foundation of strong family ties. The home was meant to be the source of their commitment to the ideals of the patriarchs. But in the six short sentences that follow, we learn the true prelude to the slavery that followed. The Jews became fruitful and multiplied, and increased greatly, and became ever stronger – and then there were sown the seeds of their future tragedy. Three Hebrew words say it all: "*Vatimaleh haaretz otam,*" "And the land was filled with them" (v. 7). The Midrash fills in the details. Whereas up to now their homes had been the focus of their lives, now the focus was the land – the land of Egypt and all of its tempting seductions; they filled the land, [that is] the theaters and the circuses. What happened outside of the home became far more important than what happened within it. And that is the biblical clue to the cause of what we are told in the sentence immediately following: "And a new king arose over Egypt who knew not Joseph" (v. 8), and who set in motion the enslavement of Jacob's descendents.

When the time for redemption finally came, God insisted that the Jews take "a lamb for every parental home and for every household" (Ex. 12:3). The first ceremonial ritual given to the Jewish people was to take place not in a communal gathering of the entire nation but rather within the confines of every individual home, within the borders of family units. The centrality of the home in Jewish life is what the Jews had lost; that was what was responsible for their downfall. That was the sin that needed to be rectified. Their homes had to be reestablished as the key to their covenant with God and to the values of their ancestors.

Passover as the festival which marks the birth of our people is the holiday devoted to family because the two are inseparable. On Passover we dedicate ourselves to strengthening family life as the foundation of national survival. Families thrive when they are nourished by free and open communication between all their members. In a happy family, children have no qualms about

The seder plate and the matzot are uncovered.

עֲבָדִים הָיִינוּ

WE WERE SLAVES
to Pharaoh in Egypt,
and the LORD our God brought us out of there
with a strong hand and an outstretched arm.
And if the Holy One, blessed be He,
had not brought our fathers out of Egypt –
then we, and our children, and the children of our children,
would still be enslaved to Pharaoh in Egypt.

The tragedy of the Jewish experience in Egypt was not only our slavery. It was that we too reflected this specific sin of their leader. In a world where speech lost its sanctity and was misused for vile ends, we also displayed some of the very same failing. We were not only slaves in Egypt but *slaves to Pharaoh*, imitating his ways as slaves are wont to do with their masters. How else could one describe the wickedness of the words thrust at Moses when he sought to intervene in the fight between two of his Hebrew brothers: "Who made you a man, a prince, and a judge over us? Do you plan to slay me as you have slain the Egyptian?" (Ex. 2:14) – with the implicit threat of informing on Moses to the authorities. Evil speech infected the Jews and threatened their spiritual status.

The story of the Exodus was meant not only to get the Jews out of Egypt but also to get Egypt out of the Jews. It was to turn mouths that had become accustomed to speaking evil into voices of kindness and prayer. It was no coincidence, the commentators tell us, that the name of the place the Jews camped before the destruction of the Egyptians at the Red Sea was *Pi HaḤirot* (Ex. 14:2), literally, the mouth of freedom – for it was there that mouths that had become enslaved to the mores of Egyptian culture became free of their subservience to Pharaoh's specific kind of evil.

And it is no coincidence as well that the night of Passover, commemorating this liberation of our speech to the pursuit of holiness, has as its major mitzva the reading of the Haggada – an almost uninterrupted use of our lips for good, to praise God, and to study Torah. "And the more one tells of the coming out of Egypt, the more admirable it is" – for this is the ideal way in which we continue to defeat Pharaoh and what he represented.

The קערה and the מצות are uncovered.

עֲבָדִים הָיִינוּ

לְפַרְעֹה בְּמִצְרָיִם

וַיּוֹצִיאֵנוּ יהוה אֱלֹהֵינוּ מִשָּׁם בְּיָד חֲזָקָה וּבִזְרוֹעַ נְטוּיָה.
וְאִלּוּ לֹא הוֹצִיא הַקָּדוֹשׁ בָּרוּךְ הוּא אֶת אֲבוֹתֵינוּ מִמִּצְרַיִם
הֲרֵי אָנוּ וּבָנֵינוּ וּבְנֵי בָנֵינוּ מְשֻׁעְבָּדִים הָיִינוּ לְפַרְעֹה בְּמִצְרָיִם.

without any unifying theme or meaning. He is intrigued by the dippings but fails to grasp the profound purpose of all the rest of the proceedings.

The child who does not even know how to ask wishes he could simply go to sleep. He witnesses the leaning going on all about him by the participants and assumes that everyone shares his fatigue and desire to bring the evening to a close.

But, of course, only the wise son has grasped that this is an evening filled with rituals of beauty and of purpose, of meaning and of message. Hopefully, what follows will inspire the other sons to a comparable level of insight and commitment.

WE WERE SLAVES

Defining the Passover Villain

The Haggada tells us we were slaves to Pharaoh in Egypt. Pharaoh is the key villain of Passover, and his Hebrew name adds a profound and deeper dimension to an understanding of the story. In Hebrew, Pharaoh's name is spelled *peh, resh, ayin, heh*. Central to this name are the two letters *resh* and *ayin*, which spell *ra*, evil. That is what defined his essence. Surrounding *ra* are two letters which when combined make the word *peh*, mouth. It was evil speech that most succinctly summarized the fatal failing of the Egyptian king. He pronounced genocidal edicts without the slightest compassion or conscience. When, as a result of the impact of the plagues, he made concessions to Moses, he had no compunction about failing to keep his word once he felt himself out of danger. His word could not be trusted; his speech was invariably marked by malevolence.

And even
were we all wise, all intelligent,
all aged and all knowledgeable in the Torah,
still the command would be upon us
to tell of the coming out of Egypt;
and the more one tells of the coming out of Egypt,
the more admirable it is.

AND THE MORE ONE TELLS

"Half to God, Half to You"

How should one best celebrate a holiday? Holidays are meant to be days of joy.
The mitzva is to be happy. In a famous talmudic passage, two rabbinic giants
argue about the way in which to ideally fulfill this requirement:

> R. Eliezer said: A man has nothing else [to do] on a festival except either
> to eat and drink or to sit and study. R. Yehoshua said: Divide it: [Devote]
> half of it to eating and drinking, and half of it to the Beit Midrash. Now
> R. Yoḥanan said with regard to this disagreement: Both deduce it from
> the same verse. One verse says, "a solemn assembly to the Lord your God"
> (Deut. 16:8), whereas another verse says, "There shall be a solemn assembly
> unto you" (Num. 29:35). R. Eliezer holds: [That means] either entirely to
> God or entirely to you; while R. Yehoshua holds, Divide it: [Devote] half to
> God and half to yourselves. (Pesaḥim 68b)

R. Eliezer believes that the road to happiness differs from person to person.
Some people find joy from spiritual fulfillment; others are more attracted to
physical delights and pleasures of the body. Holidays do not impose one kind
of enjoyment above the other. It is but the end result that is significant. We are
to choose either study, or food and drink; satisfying our souls, or our flesh,
whichever makes our holiday most enjoyable.

R. Yehoshua disagrees. Happiness by very definition is an amalgam of the
spiritual and the physical. Holidays demand *simḥa* – and *simḥa* is the product
of satisfying both aspects of our identity. On festivals we are commanded to eat
and to drink as well as to pray and to study: "Divide it: [Devote] half to God
and half to yourselves."

וַאֲפִלּוּ
כֻּלָּנוּ חֲכָמִים, כֻּלָּנוּ נְבוֹנִים, כֻּלָּנוּ זְקֵנִים
כֻּלָּנוּ יוֹדְעִים אֶת הַתּוֹרָה
מִצְוָה עָלֵינוּ לְסַפֵּר בִּיצִיאַת מִצְרָיִם
וְכָל הַמַּרְבֶּה לְסַפֵּר בִּיצִיאַת מִצְרָיִם
הֲרֵי זֶה מְשֻׁבָּח.

STILL THE COMMAND WOULD BE UPON US

Why Is the Command "Upon Us"?

A mitzva is a mitzva. All Jews are equally obligated. Everyone is required to recount the miracle of our Exodus from Egypt. Why then the phrase "*mitzva aleinu*," "still the command would be upon us"?

The answer is linked to a fascinating law connected to the cantor's repetition of the *Shemoneh Esreh*. It is customary for the cantor to recite aloud the entire *Shemoneh Esreh* after the congregants have prayed it silently. This institution was rabbinically initiated so that even those who were not learned enough to recite that important prayer themselves would have an opportunity to fulfill their obligation by responding "*amen*" to the cantor. This, based on the law that he who listens intently is as if he himself responded (Sukka 38b), makes it possible for the entire community to fulfill the mitzva of prayer. However, there is one blessing that the cantor does not recite aloud, and everyone in the congregation is required to personally say the words. It is the blessing of *Modim* – the one in which we give thanks to God for all the daily miracles of our lives.

Gratitude cannot be expressed by way of an agent. It is not enough to send someone in our stead to say thank you to someone to whom we are indebted. Appreciation is personal. On the night of Passover, the mitzva is to give thanks to God for our deliverance from Egypt. On this night, we not only recount but we relive. We are, each and every one of us, obligated to view ourselves as if we personally were redeemed. And that is why there is a mitzva "upon us" – no one else can say thank you for us.

pily reduce the amount of time we devote to the personal pleasures of food and drink in order to stress the spiritual joy of our intimate connection with God.

Praising God Too Much?

The theme of Passover night seems to be "the more, the better." The more we speak about the events, the greater the mitzva. The five rabbis stayed up all night, engrossed in their discussions, and would have continued were it not for their students informing them that it was time for the recitation of the morning *Shema*. Yet it would appear from the Talmud that excessive praise of God is not only unnecessary but indeed actually sinful: "Rabba bar bar Ḥanna said in the name of R. Yoḥanan: One who recounts the praises of the Holy One, blessed be He, to excess is uprooted from the world" (Megilla 18a). R. Elazar explained the rationale for this remarkable statement: "What is the meaning of the verse, 'Who can express the mighty acts of the Lord, or make all His praise to be heard?' (Ps. 106:2). For whom is it fitting to express the mighty acts of the Lord? For one who can make *all His praise* to be heard."

For a God of infinite power, words only serve to diminish Him. Praise is constricting. It puts into words only a limited amount of information. God is greater than the sum of what we may be able to say about Him. This, the commentators tell us, is what the Jewish people meant in the song they sang at the shore of the Red Sea after they witnessed the miracle of their deliverance and the death of their former oppressors: "Who is like You, O Lord, among the gods? Who is like You, glorious in holiness, fearful in praises, doing wonders?" (Ex. 15:11) God is too awesome for praise. It is fearful even to attempt it, as Rashi puts it, "lest they fall short – as it is written, 'to You silence is praise'" (Ps. 65:2).

How then did the Jews at the sea themselves sing their song unto God? And how then, in spite of the talmudic warning, do we laud unlimited words at the Seder? The answer lies in the profound difference between praise and gratitude. Praise has its limits when offered to the One whose greatness is so awe inspiring that it leaves us nothing less than speechless. Gratitude and its expression, however, have no boundaries. To say that we can never fully express what we owe to God and therefore prefer silence is to be guilty of the sin of ingratitude – a sin not merely to the Almighty but corruptive to our own selves and our moral sensitivity. It has famously been said that feeling gratitude and not expressing it is like wrapping a present and not giving it. At the Seder we are giving thanks to God – and that is an unlimited mitzva.

The final decision is rendered in accordance with the view of R. Yehoshua. It has a remarkable echo in the sacrifice offered in the Temple known as *shelamim*. Unlike the offering called *ola*, which was totally consumed on the Altar and meant solely for God, the *shelamim* was divided – half burnt on the Altar for God and the other half to be shared by the one who brought it together with his friends and family. It is this sacrifice of *shelamim* that the Talmud says was the unique religious contribution of the Jewish people to the world. Its name denotes wholeness and completeness. It teaches us to acknowledge both the physical and the spiritual in our service of God. That is why on Shabbat, the Kiddush over wine as well as the meals share the holiness of the day with the special reading from the Torah and the setting aside of time for study. And that is why at the Seder, our *simha* comes from the recitation of the Haggada as well as the *Shulḥan Orekh*, Table Setting – the words which lift our souls and the special foods which satisfy our bodies.

Yet there seems to be one problem with regard to our emphasis at the Seder. According to the view of R. Yehoshua, it seems that the division between spiritual and physical ought to be 50-50 – "divide it," were his words, "half to God and half to yourselves." But at the very outset the Haggada tells us, "And the more one tells of the coming out of Egypt, the more admirable it is." To increase means to go beyond half, implying that on Passover night there is a different equation. To stress the spiritual over the physical is commendable.

It is no coincidence that immediately after this statement, the Haggada tells us the story about the five rabbis who precisely followed this dictum. They stayed up all night discussing the miracle of the Exodus. Their meal surely took only a fraction of that time. The night was dedicated almost entirely to God. And in that story, the Haggada tells us that *one of those five rabbis was in fact R. Yehoshua* – the same rabbi famous for his teaching that the joy of a holiday is normally created by an equal emphasis on man and God, on food and faith.

If we may borrow the language of the Passover Seder, why then is this night different from any other holiday night? Why did even R. Yehoshua agree that his 50-50 division for the holiday was inapplicable to the ritual of this evening? There is a profound reason. On this night, we are to see ourselves as if we are actually reliving the experience. It is we who were saved from Egypt. It is we who were redeemed from slavery. It was we who were the beneficiaries of miracles.

And when we need to express gratitude for personal salvation, there is no limit to the thanks we owe our Redeemer. Whoever increases the praise he gives is himself more praiseworthy. We owe God our lives – and so we hap-

מַעֲשֶׂה

ONCE,

Rabbi Eliezer and Rabbi Yehoshua and Rabbi Elazar ben Azaria
and Rabbi Akiva and Rabbi Tarfon
reclined [for the seder] in Benei Brak.
And they told of the Exodus from Egypt all that night;
until their students came in and said,
"Teachers –
the time for saying the *Shema* of the morning has come."

Rabbi Elazar ben Azaria said: *Berakhot 12b*
I am almost seventy years old,
and never have I merited to find the command
to speak of the Exodus from Egypt at night –

---

siege observing the Seder in order to serve as inspiration for Jews in all times
never to give up hope for a better tomorrow – because that is as certain as the
fact that day follows night.

I AM ALMOST SEVENTY YEARS OLD

The Babylonian Exile
During the time of Roman persecution, the rabbis knew that generations before
their time, the First Temple had been destroyed by the Babylonians and Jews
had gone into exile. But they also remembered that just seventy years after
the destruction, God took pity upon the remnants of His people and brought
about their return to the Holy Land. The Jews of the First Exile might have been
tempted to believe they were forsaken by God. They could have renounced
the celebration of Passover as no longer relevant. But the God who redeemed
the Jews from Egypt continued His providential care of His people. The Jews
understood that Passover is an everlasting covenant whose message is relevant
even during those harsh times when we have difficulty understanding God's
seeming absence. R. Elazar ben Azaria was saying:

> Behold I am like one of the people of the seventy-year period of the First
> Exile. I too live in terrible times. But like them I will celebrate freedom even

מַעֲשֶׂה

בְּרַבִּי אֱלִיעֶזֶר וְרַבִּי יְהוֹשֻעַ וְרַבִּי אֶלְעָזָר בֶּן עֲזַרְיָה

וְרַבִּי עֲקִיבָא וְרַבִּי טַרְפוֹן

שֶׁהָיוּ מְסֻבִּין בִּבְנֵי בְרַק

וְהָיוּ מְסַפְּרִים בִּיצִיאַת מִצְרַיִם כָּל אוֹתוֹ הַלַּיְלָה

עַד שֶׁבָּאוּ תַלְמִידֵיהֶם וְאָמְרוּ לָהֶם

רַבּוֹתֵינוּ

הִגִּיעַ זְמַן קְרִיאַת שְׁמַע שֶׁל שַׁחֲרִית.

ברכות יב:

אָמַר רַבִּי אֶלְעָזָר בֶּן עֲזַרְיָה

הֲרֵי אֲנִי כְּבֶן שִׁבְעִים שָׁנָה

וְלֹא זָכִיתִי שֶׁתֵּאָמֵר יְצִיאַת מִצְרַיִם בַּלֵּילוֹת

───────────────────────

ONCE, RABBI ELIEZER

Night and Day

We know that these five rabbis lived in a period of terrible Roman persecution. They needed their students to tell them it was already day because they were in hiding. Yet they celebrated Passover. The reason is implicit in the two times set aside for the recitation of the *Shema*. We are commanded to fulfill the mitzva of acceptance of God not only when the sun shines but in the darkness of night as well. That is because we have a uniquely Jewish view of time and the definition of day. The secular world counts the day from midnight to midnight. Darkness on either side defines the meaning of life. Judaism has the day begin with the night before. "And there was evening and there was morning" (Gen. 1) is the refrain of the Creation story. And then, remarkably enough, even the night is called by the same word as the one for day: "And there was evening and there was morning, one day" (v. 5).

The darkness of night in retrospect becomes revealed as simply a prelude to the beauty of day. Faith allows those who suffer to believe in the certainty of better times in the future. The Haggada begins with a story of rabbis under

until Ben Zoma interpreted:
It is written,

"SO THAT YOU REMEMBER   *Deut. 16*
THE DAY OF YOUR EXODUS FROM EGYPT
ALL THE DAYS OF YOUR LIFE."

> "The days of your life" would mean in the days;
> "all the days of your life" includes the nights.

But the sages say,

> "The days of your life" would mean only in this world;
> "all the days of your life" brings in the time of the Messiah.

בָּרוּךְ הַמָּקוֹם

Blessed is the Omnipresent –
blessed is He.
Blessed is the One
who gave His people Israel, the Torah –
blessed is He.

---

very own lifetime. "All the days of *your* life" refers to us directly; even greater than our deliverance from Egypt are the miracles we experience in our own lifetime.

BLESSED IS THE OMNIPRESENT – BLESSED IS HE

The Four Blessings
Four times we recite the word *barukh*. Immediately after that we list four kinds of sons. The implication is clear. Our children may all be different, but every one of them remains a blessing. Even the wicked son is not to be despised; he is to be treasured as someone who has not yet chosen the right path. As the Lubavitcher Rebbe so beautifully put it, "There are only two kinds of Jews: religious Jews and not-yet-religious Jews."

עַד שֶׁדְּרָשָׁהּ בֶּן זוֹמָא

שֶׁנֶּאֱמַר

דברים טז

לְמַעַן תִּזְכֹּר אֶת־יוֹם צֵאתְךָ מֵאֶרֶץ מִצְרַיִם

כֹּל יְמֵי חַיֶּיךָ:

יְמֵי חַיֶּיךָ   הַיָּמִים

כֹּל יְמֵי חַיֶּיךָ   הַלֵּילוֹת.

וַחֲכָמִים אוֹמְרִים

יְמֵי חַיֶּיךָ   הָעוֹלָם הַזֶּה

כֹּל יְמֵי חַיֶּיךָ   לְהָבִיא לִימוֹת הַמָּשִׁיחַ.

בָּרוּךְ הַמָּקוֹם

בָּרוּךְ הוּא

בָּרוּךְ שֶׁנָּתַן תּוֹרָה לְעַמּוֹ יִשְׂרָאֵל

בָּרוּךְ הוּא

---

when I am not free because of my certainty in yet another redemption. Both in the days and in the nights, I will confidently recite the *Shema* because I believe in the eventual coming of the Messiah.

"All the Days of *Your* Life"

The story of the Exodus was filled with miracles. Our own lives replicate that story – but we all too often fail to take note of these wondrous events. We need to become attuned to the miraculous in the seemingly natural, the Divine in the daily stories of our life experiences. In the *Shemoneh Esreh* we verbalize that idea. We thank God "for Your miracles that are with us every day." The commandment to remember the miracles experienced by our ancestors includes those miracles even greater than our deliverance from Egypt, miracles we experience in our

כְּנֶגֶד אַרְבָּעָה בָנִים
The Torah relates
to four types of sons –
one who is wise,
one who is wicked,
one with a simple nature,
and one who does not know how to ask.

"I visited Vilna and saw a person who made a great effort to learn Torah all day. And I saw a person who spent all day thinking about how to make money. And I saw a person whose inclination raged within him every time he saw a woman in the street. And I saw a person who would always close his eyes so he would not stumble in seeing forbidden things. And I saw a person who always spoke gossip. And I saw someone who struggled to keep his mouth closed." They said to him, "What is so surprising – Vilna is a huge city with many Jews?" He said, "Yes, but what was remarkable is that it was only one person!"

The Haggada seems to speak of four different sons. Yet it keeps repeating the word *eḥad*, one. Perhaps the Haggada wants to emphasize the remarkable truth that these four different character types may in fact characterize one and the same person at different times. None of us are all wise or all wicked, all simple-natured or all insufficiently knowledgeable to ask the right questions. We are an amalgam of traits, a fascinating combination of types. By understanding the various selves of our being, we can find inner peace and tranquility.

The Wise and the Wicked
The word "wise" has to do with the intellect. The word "wicked" speaks of morality. How can they possibly be used as opposites? One could speak of the wise and the foolish, or of the righteous and the wicked. The wise and the wicked are not logical counterparts.

But perhaps they are, according to a remarkable talmudic insight. The rabbis ask, "What is the cause of sin?" The answer, based on an ingenious inference from the grammatical link between the Hebrew word for going astray with that for folly, is that "a person does not sin unless overtaken by a spirit of foolishness" (Sota 3a). Sin, more than a moral failing, is an act of stupidity. Its most powerful opponent is wisdom. The wise will choose not to be wicked. The Torah places its greatest hope for perfecting man's character in the study of its teachings. That is the best way in which a wicked person can be transformed into a wise person.

כְּנֶגֶד אַרְבָּעָה בָנִים דִּבְּרָה תוֹרָה
אֶחָד חָכָם
וְאֶחָד רָשָׁע
וְאֶחָד תָּם
וְאֶחָד שֶׁאֵינוֹ יוֹדֵעַ לִשְׁאֹל

FOUR TYPES OF SONS

The Sequence of the Four Sons

The list of the four sons seems not to follow a logical order. The two extremes, the wise and the wicked, ought to be at the ends with the other two in the center. What is the rationale for the sequence in which they are presented? Perhaps the reason is that we follow the simple rule of respecting age. The oldest is mentioned first, the youngest last. With that as our guide, the sequence makes perfect sense. The last, the youngest, is one who does not even know enough to ask. He is the child who is hardly old enough to speak. He is followed by the simple son, the one whose limited intelligence permits him to ask only, "What is this?" The one who is older still is the child of rebellious teenage years, going through a stage in which his striving for independence makes it difficult for him to accept parental values and guidance. It is one of the universal blessings that as children come to greater maturity, they find the wisdom to acknowledge that their parents are not as stupid as they believed them to be when the children were teenagers. In the profound words of Mark Twain, "When I was a boy of fourteen, my father was so ignorant I could hardly stand to have the old man around. But when I got to be twenty-one, I was astonished at how much the old man had learned in seven years." The four sons may in fact therefore not be speaking of four different children, but rather of four different stages in the life of every one of them – stages that take them from infancy through childishness, to rebelliousness and finally to true wisdom.

One Is Wise, One Is Wicked

The story is told of a Jew from the shtetl who for the first time went to visit a large city. He came back with an amazing story to share. He told his friends he could hardly believe what he saw there:

The
WISE SON
what does he say?
"What are the testimonies, the statutes and laws,   *Deut. 6*
that the LORD our God commanded you?"
> And you must tell him the laws of Pesaḥ:
> "After eating the Pesaḥ offering
> one does not eat anything more."

The
WICKED SON
what does he say?
"What is this service to you?"   *Ex. 12*
> "To you," he says, not to him.
> When he sets himself apart from the community,
> he denies the very core of our beliefs.
> And you must set his teeth on edge and tell him,
> "Because of this   *Ex. 13*
> the LORD acted for me when I came out of Egypt."
> "For *me*," and not for *him*;
had he been there he would not have been redeemed.

---

treasures life. The fool pursues sin and is soon snared by death. The wise son chooses life. That is why he wants to know all the details of Torah law which is "a tree of life unto all those who pursue it" (3:18). And whenever we make a toast with the word *leḥayim*, we are not only expressing a wish for life but also for wisdom.

THE WICKED SON – WHAT DOES HE SAY?

The Hypocrisy of the Wicked
A truly wicked person in Hebrew is called a *rasha*. The first and last letters of that word, *resh* and *ayin*, suffice to make the word *ra*, evil. The middle letter *shin* adds a powerful insight into the way in which the wicked are able to achieve

חָכָם

מַה הוּא אוֹמֵר

דברים ו

מָה הָעֵדֹת וְהַחֻקִּים וְהַמִּשְׁפָּטִים
אֲשֶׁר צִוָּה יהוה אֱלֹהֵינוּ אֶתְכֶם:
וְאַף אַתָּה אֱמָר לוֹ כְּהִלְכוֹת הַפֶּסַח
אֵין מַפְטִירִין אַחַר הַפֶּסַח אֲפִיקוֹמָן.

רָשָׁע

מַה הוּא אוֹמֵר

שמות יב

מָה הָעֲבֹדָה הַזֹּאת לָכֶם:
לָכֶם וְלֹא לוֹ
וּלְפִי שֶׁהוֹצִיא אֶת עַצְמוֹ מִן הַכְּלָל
כָּפַר בָּעִקָּר
וְאַף אַתָּה הַקְהֵה אֶת שִׁנָּיו, וֶאֱמָר לוֹ

שמות יג

בַּעֲבוּר זֶה עָשָׂה יהוה לִי בְּצֵאתִי מִמִּצְרָיִם:
לִי וְלֹא לוֹ
אִלּוּ הָיָה שָׁם, לֹא הָיָה נִגְאָל.

THE WISE SON – WHAT DOES HE SAY?

Wisdom and Life

The wisest of all men, King Solomon, teaches us in the Book of Proverbs, "The teaching of a wise man is the fountain of life" (13:14). The *gematria* of the word *ḥakham* is exactly the same as the *gematria* of the word *ḥayim*. The wise man

The
SIMPLE SON
what does he say?
"What is this?" *Ex. 13*
>   And you must tell him,
>   "With a strong hand the LORD *Ibid.*
>   brought us out of Egypt,
>   from the grip of slavery."

---

and destiny. The greatest sin of the wicked son is precisely his failure to understand this idea. He "sets himself apart from the community" and thereby denies this fundamental concept of Jewish unity.

THE SIMPLE SON – WHAT DOES HE SAY?

Why the Simple Son Is Simple
What is the simple son lacking that makes him simple? His name, *tam*, has two of the three letters that make the Hebrew word for truth, *emet* (spelled *aleph, mem, tav*). What he lacks is the first letter, *aleph*, signifying "one," which at the very end of the Seder we make clear is the number that represents God. Without God there can be no truth. Without God the two remaining letters in the word for truth connote "death." And without God the reverse of death is to be alive yet unaware of the true meaning of life – to be simple, to be merely a *tam*. It is the role of the simple son's parents to enlighten him about God and His role in history, that "with a strong hand the Lord brought us out of Egypt, from the grip of slavery" (Ex. 13:9). With the knowledge granted to him of the *Aleph* of the universe, the simple son will know the truth – and no longer be simple.

The Simple Son and Job
The simple son of the Haggada is most often viewed in negative terms, the child intellectually immature or perhaps – as we prefer to put it in contemporary terms – mentally challenged. Yet, remarkably enough, one of the most saintly and gifted heroes of the Bible is lauded with precisely this descriptive: "There was a man in the land of Uz, whose name was Job, and that man was *tam* and righteous, and one who feared God and turned away from evil" (Job 1:1).

תָּם

מַה הוּא אוֹמֵר

מַה־זֹּאת

וְאָמַרְתָּ אֵלָיו

בְּחֹזֶק יָד הוֹצִיאָנוּ יהוה מִמִּצְרַיִם

מִבֵּית עֲבָדִים:

שמות יג

שם

---

their ends. To make people believe in them and in order to gain acceptance, they make central to their very being the illusion that what they represent is the letter *shin*. That is the letter that stands for God. It appears on every mezuza as the shortened version for the name *Shaddai*. *Shin* represents the sacred and the holy. The greatest threat to society is the hypocritical rascal who claims that all his actions are in the service of "holy causes." It is evil that camouflages itself as saintly; it is the devil who masquerades as an angel. That is why the father is told to respond, "And you must set his teeth [*shinnav*] on edge" – remove from him the letter *shin* with which he hopes to deceive, the letter of piety that he uses to disguise his wickedness, so he will be unmasked by way of the only two letters that remain and all will know that he is simply *ra*.

"Because of *This*"

The father responds to the wicked son with a biblical verse: "Because of this the Lord acted for me when I came out of Egypt" (Ex. 13:8). What is the "this" to which the text alludes? In Hebrew the word "this" is *zeh*. Its deeper meaning is implicit in its *gematria*. Its two letters, *zayin* and *heh*, have the respective values of seven and five. Together the word is a reference to twelve. At the very end of the Seder we explain the deeper meaning of numbers: "Who knows twelve? I know twelve: twelve tribes [of Israel]." Twelve is the unity of our people. Twelve is the entire community. Twelve is a reference to our indivisible link rooted in family and common ancestry.

The sale of Joseph by his brothers, reducing the family to eleven sons, was ultimately the cause of our descent into Egypt and the disastrous slavery which followed. Passover, commemorating our redemption, was "because of *this*" – that we re-create the bonds of family and the recognition of our mutual history

And the
ONE WHO DOES NOT KNOW HOW TO ASK
you must open [the story] for him,
as it is said:

> "And you shall tell your child   *Ex. 13*
> on that day,
> 'Because of this the LORD acted for me
> when I came out of Egypt.'"

Neither theologians nor philosophers have ever been able to come up with a satisfactory answer. The Book of Job simply makes clear that God's ways are not our ways; that His wisdom transcends our understanding. The Torah tells us, "The secret things belong unto the Lord our God but the things that are revealed belong unto us and to our children forever that we may do all the words of this law" (Deut. 29:28). But there is one idea we need to emphasize when our faith is challenged by the incomprehensibility of life's seeming unfairness. *Bad things make us question God; good things force us to reaffirm His ongoing presence and involvement.*

In the aftermath of the death of a loved one, Jewish law demands that we recite the words uttered by Job in his similar circumstance: "The Lord has given and the Lord has taken, blessed be the name of the Lord" (Job 1:21). Precisely at the painful moment of loss, we need to acknowledge that it came about by the very same hands of the One initially responsible for the blessing previously given. Can we call death cruel when its cause emanates from the very same Source responsible for originally giving life to our loved one?

It is a truth poignantly illustrated in the aftermath of the tragic passing of the two sons of the second-century talmudic sage R. Meir. The scholar was giving a lecture at the synagogue one Shabbat afternoon. At the very same time, unbeknown to him, his two beloved sons suddenly died. The grief-stricken mother, Beruria, covered them with a sheet and waited until her husband came home after Shabbat. When R. Meir arrived and asked where his sons were, his wife begged her husband to first recite the Havdala service, marking the departure of Shabbat. Then, she said that she had a very important question to ask him.

וְשֶׁאֵינוֹ יוֹדֵעַ לִשְׁאֹל

אַתְּ פְּתַח לוֹ

שֶׁנֶּאֱמַר

שמות יג

וְהִגַּדְתָּ לְבִנְךָ

בַּיּוֹם הַהוּא לֵאמֹר

בַּעֲבוּר זֶה עָשָׂה יהוה לִי

בְּצֵאתִי מִמִּצְרָיִם:

Clearly, in this verse the word *tam* is meant to be complimentary. Following it we are told that Job was righteous, God-fearing, and someone who "turned away from evil."

Perhaps then, here too in the Haggada the descriptive is not to be taken in a derogatory fashion. This son is "simple" in the sense that, like Job, he is whole-hearted and unquestioning in his faith. He is totally committed and unswerving in his acceptance of God. But, also like Job, he is perturbed by the problem which has proven to be the most difficult test of our belief. Theodicy is the thorn in our attachment to our conviction that a just God rules the universe. Why do bad things happen to good people? Why do the righteous suffer, even as the wicked often prosper? Why does a God of love permit so much evil on earth? Indeed, there is a great similarity between the cry of Job and that of the "simple son." They are both saying, "What is this? How can this be happening? I do not understand."

The trauma of Job's personal calamities resonates with an earlier biblical national tragedy. Surely the collective body of the children of Israel must have had their faith equally challenged by the inequity of their enslavement, by the harshness of their mistreatment, and by the seeming silence of the Lord to whom they prayed since their ancestor Abraham's discovery of His existence. To teach our children on the night of Passover the story of the miracle of our redemption is to bring up to them as well the reality of our 210 years of slavery and subjugation. We must expect that at least one of them, a child of simple faith, will be moved to say, "How was this possible? What is this? I do not understand God's ways."

וְהִגַּדְתָּ לְבִנְךָ

"AND YOU SHALL TELL YOUR CHILD" –

One might have thought
this meant from the beginning of the month.
And so it says, "on that day."
Had it said only "on that day,"
one might have thought [the obligation] applied during the day.
And so it also says, "Because of this" –
"because of *this*" can only be said
when matza and bitter herbs are there before you.

---

us, we are not to curse the loss but rather to thank God for however much time
we were given to be blessed with His gifts.

"The Lord has given and the Lord has taken." The word used in the Hebrew
for "the Lord" is the specific name of God which represents His attribute of
goodness and mercy. The challenge for us is to acknowledge the Lord's goodness
not only when we consider what He gave us but even when we must cope with
the moments when by divine decree we face loss in our lives.

To the "simple" son who seeks solace and a measure of understanding for
the unfathomable, the father is told to teach that "with a strong hand the Lord
brought us out of Egypt, from the grip of slavery" (Ex. 13:9). True, we suffered.
Yet we prevailed. If God saw fit for a while to allow injustice to triumph, the end
of the story is by far the more important message. God intervened on behalf
of our downtrodden ancestors. God brought our slavery to an end. God took
us out of the house of bondage. The transitory success of evil is a challenge to
our faith – but the blessings of divine miracles and heavenly intervention are
sufficient responses to validate our continued trust in the Almighty.

וְהִגַּדְתָּ לְבִנְךָ

יָכוֹל מֵרֹאשׁ חֹדֶשׁ

תַּלְמוּד לוֹמַר: בַּיּוֹם הַהוּא.

אִי בַּיּוֹם הַהוּא יָכוֹל מִבְּעוֹד יוֹם

תַּלְמוּד לוֹמַר: בַּעֲבוּר זֶה.

בַּעֲבוּר זֶה לֹא אָמַרְתִּי

אֶלָּא בְּשָׁעָה שֶׁיֵּשׁ מַצָּה וּמָרוֹר מֻנָּחִים לְפָנֶיךָ.

Perplexed, but nonetheless acceding to his wife's wishes, R. Meir recited the prayer and then asked his wife to tell him her problem. She said, "Not long ago, some precious jewels were entrusted to my care. Now the owner of the jewels has come to reclaim them. Shall I return them to him?"

R. Meir was surprised by the simplicity of the question and his wife's need to ask him for guidance. "But of course," he said, "you yourself know the law very well. An object entrusted for a time must be given back when the owner demands it." Beruria then took her husband by the hand, led him to where the dead children lay, and drew back the sheet. R. Meir began to weep uncontrollably. "My sons! My sons!" he cried. Then Beruria tearfully reminded him of his own words, "Did you not say that we must restore to the Owner what He entrusted to our care? Our sons were the jewels that God allowed us to have for some years. Now their Master has taken back His own gifts to us. Let us, even at this tragic moment of loss, feel gratitude for the gift God gave us in all the time we were blessed to have these jewels, our precious children." So too we need always to remember that whatever we have is a gift from God. If it is taken from

מִתְּחִלָּה

IN THE BEGINNING,

our ancestors were idol worshippers.

BUT NOW

the Omnipresent has drawn us close in His service;
as it is said:
"Joshua said to all the people,   *Josh. 24*
'This is what the LORD God of Israel has said:
Beyond the river your ancestors always dwelled –
Terah the father of Abraham, the father of Nahor –
and they served other gods.

---

over story contains within it the dual themes of physical liberation and spiritual
fulfillment. God freed us from slavery and took us to Sinai. We needed the two
aspects of the Exodus to qualify it as the most significant turning point of our
history. Indeed, the Haggada does not choose the view of one to the exclusion
of the other. *It incorporates both opinions into the text.*

But the Haggada starts, as Shmuel has it, with a reference to our having been
slaves to Pharaoh in Egypt. Only after that does it tell the story from a spiritual
perspective, as Rav is anxious to emphasize. It may well be that the dispute
between Shmuel and Rav revolves precisely around sequence. Rav chooses to
be guided by the measure of ultimate importance. Clearly the goal of our redemption from Egypt was spiritual. It is not insignificant that Moses was given
the mission to take the Jews out of bondage at the *sneh*, the burning bush. Why,
asks Ibn Ezra, was Sinai called Sinai? It was named after the *sneh* – the burning
bush, located on the very same spot which would serve as the location for the
Giving of the Torah. The real meaning of the divine call to Moses was not simply
to take the Jews *out of Egypt*; it was *to bring the Jews to the place that would give
meaning to their redemption.* Physical freedom requires spiritual purpose in order
to imbue it with true value. That, according to Rav, mandates that our Seder start
with a review of our passage from paganism to divine service.

But Shmuel feels that a different order takes precedence. The story should
be told in historic sequence. The Jews were first freed from physical slavery.
Passover precedes Shavuot. After our bodies escaped from bondage, our souls
could fully connect with our Creator. The narrative of Jewish history decrees
that we come to God as a follow-up to our liberation.

מִתְּחִלָּה

עוֹבְדֵי עֲבוֹדָה זָרָה הָיוּ אֲבוֹתֵינוּ

וְעַכְשָׁו

יהושע כד

קֵרְבָנוּ הַמָּקוֹם לַעֲבוֹדָתוֹ, שֶׁנֶּאֱמַר
וַיֹּאמֶר יְהוֹשֻׁעַ אֶל־כָּל־הָעָם, כֹּה־אָמַר יהוה אֱלֹהֵי יִשְׂרָאֵל
בְּעֵבֶר הַנָּהָר יָשְׁבוּ אֲבוֹתֵיכֶם מֵעוֹלָם
תֶּרַח אֲבִי אַבְרָהָם וַאֲבִי נָחוֹר, וַיַּעַבְדוּ אֱלֹהִים אֲחֵרִים:

IN THE BEGINNING, OUR ANCESTORS WERE IDOL WORSHIPPERS

From Shame to Glory: The Proper Sequence

The Mishna teaches us that the sequence of the Seder is to be guided by the principle of "[When telling the story of the Exodus] begin with shame and end with praise" (Mishna Pesaḥim 10:4). We begin with the shameful part of our history and conclude with the glorious. It is only by remembering the unpleasant that we can fully appreciate the gift of a new beginning.

But what is the shameful part we are bidden to recall on Passover night? Two rabbis of great standing debate the matter immediately after the concept is stated in the Mishna (Pesaḥim 116a). Shmuel declares that our review of the story at the Seder should start with the fact that we were slaves to Pharaoh in Egypt. We were a physically subjugated people. What we lacked first and foremost was freedom. To be free is the prerequisite for being human. This is the story which needs to be stressed. His colleague, Rav, disagrees. For him the key to the Passover story lies elsewhere: "In the beginning, our ancestors were idol worshippers." Before Abraham, we were no better than the rest of mankind in our ignorance of the Almighty and in our understanding of His role as Creator and Ruler of the universe. Jewish history is primarily a narrative rooted in theology. On the night commemorating the beginning of our relationship with God as a nation, we need to tell the story as a journey from paganism to proud servants of God: "But now the Omnipresent has drawn us close in His service."

Perhaps, as a number of talmudic commentators point out, the dispute is not an either-or debate. Both Shmuel and Rav must have understood that the Pass-

But I took your father Abraham from beyond the river,
and I led him all the way across the land of Canaan,
and I multiplied his offspring and gave him Isaac.
And to Isaac I gave Jacob and Esau,
and I gave Esau Mount Seir as an inheritance,
WHILE JACOB AND HIS CHILDREN WENT DOWN TO EGYPT.'"

BLESSED IS THE ONE WHO HAS KEPT HIS PROMISE TO ISRAEL –

blessed is He.
For the Holy One calculated the end
and fulfilled what He had spoken
to our father Abraham
in the Covenant between the Pieces.

BLESSED IS THE ONE WHO HAS KEPT HIS PROMISE TO ISRAEL

Why Were We Not in Egypt for Four Hundred Years?

At the Covenant between the Pieces (Gen. 15:7–21), God revealed to Abraham the fate of his descendants in Egypt. The exile and slavery were foretold, together with the number of years they would be in effect. Four hundred years was the prediction – and yet the reality, thankfully, was only 210. We bless God for "hastening the end." "*Ḥishav et haketz*," "[For the Holy One] calculated the end" is the phrase that alludes to the difference between the numbers 400 and 210. We were spared 190 years of slavery and suffering – the exact *gematria* of the word *ketz*, whose first letter *kuf* is 100, and whose second letter *tzadi*, 90. But the question begs to be asked: In what merit did God shorten the time originally allotted?

Some suggest that the duration of bondage was reduced because Egyptian slavery was far more severe than that intended by God's decree, and the suffering experienced by the children of Israel during the 210 years equaled what should have been spaced out over 400 years. There is another possibility implicit in each of the letters of the word *ketz*. Our first patriarch wanted, more than anything else, to have a child in order to perpetuate his faith. Yet that was not to be for the

וָאֶקַּח אֶת־אֲבִיכֶם אֶת־אַבְרָהָם מֵעֵבֶר הַנָּהָר
וָאוֹלֵךְ אוֹתוֹ בְּכָל־אֶרֶץ כְּנָעַן
וָאַרְבֶּה אֶת־זַרְעוֹ, וָאֶתֶּן־לוֹ אֶת־יִצְחָק:
וָאֶתֵּן לְיִצְחָק אֶת־יַעֲקֹב וְאֶת־עֵשָׂו
וָאֶתֵּן לְעֵשָׂו אֶת־הַר שֵׂעִיר לָרֶשֶׁת אוֹתוֹ
וְיַעֲקֹב וּבָנָיו יָרְדוּ מִצְרָיִם:

בָּרוּךְ שׁוֹמֵר הַבְטָחָתוֹ לְיִשְׂרָאֵל
בָּרוּךְ הוּא
שֶׁהַקָּדוֹשׁ בָּרוּךְ הוּא חִשַּׁב אֶת הַקֵּץ
לַעֲשׂוֹת כְּמָה שֶׁאָמַר לְאַבְרָהָם אָבִינוּ בִּבְרִית בֵּין הַבְּתָרִים

What makes this so relevant to us today are the words of Micah, the prophet who told us that the End of Days would be "like the days I took you out of Egypt" (7:15). Micah did not clarify in which way the Messianic Age would parallel the Passover story. But perhaps his prophecy sheds light on the events of our generation. After almost two thousand years of exile, we have been witness to the miraculous return of our people to our ancient homeland and the reestablishment of the State of Israel. For those of us who see this as the first step of messianic fulfillment, we need to respond to those who claim that in light of its spiritual imperfections, the present-day State of Israel cannot possibly represent God's promise of the End of Days. The country is not as yet governed by the laws of Torah. Israel still lacks the promised Third Temple. Israel is still not a spiritual light to the nations. But perhaps modern-day Israel is, as Micah predicted, replicating the historic sequence of the Passover story. What we are achieving first is physical liberation. We are learning to live freely, in our own land, unfettered by the limitations to our independence imposed by life in exile in the Diaspora. Contemporary history, like the Haggada, follows the sequence of Shmuel. From slavery to freedom is but the first step. We fervently look forward to the next part of our journey – the spiritual fulfillment of Sinai which in the days of old followed the Exodus.

As it is said:

"He said to Abram,   Gen. 15

'Know that your descendants

will be strangers in a land not their own,

and they will be enslaved

and oppressed for four hundred years;

but know that I shall judge the nation that enslaves them,

AND THEN THEY WILL LEAVE
WITH GREAT WEALTH.'"

---

for preventing national suicide, and it proved to be the key to the miracle of our survival in Egypt.

The text tells us that Judah was sent *Goshna* (spelled *gimel, shin, nun, heh*), to Goshen (Gen. 46:28, 29). Those four letters many years later would serve to commemorate a similar miracle. The Ḥanukka story also constituted a threat to the spiritual survival of the Jewish people. The Maccabees fought a battle primarily against assimilation. Many Jews were tempted to embrace Greek culture with its emphasis on the holiness of beauty as opposed to the Jewish ideal of the beauty of holiness. They were known as the Hellenists and had their views prevailed, Judaism would have perished, God forbid. The miracle of the victory of the Maccabees is to this day recalled by way of oil in the Ḥanukka menora. Oil, the rabbis tell us, is the one liquid which refuses to lose its identity when mixed with others. When mingled with water, it stays separate and rises to the top. It is the paradigm of the message of the Maccabees – it will not assimilate.

Four Hebrew letters compose the acronym on the dreidel for this idea: *nun, gimel, heh, shin*. The first letters of each word in the phrase "*nes gadol haya sham*," "a great miracle happened there" are also the letters which constitute, in a different order, the word *Goshna*. The idea of old, that the children of Jacob maintain spiritual purity by refusing to intermingle with cultures antithetical to Jewish values, remains the key to the miracle of Jewish survival throughout the generations. "And this [idea] is what has stood by our ancestors and us." And perhaps it is the key as well to the fulfillment of our messianic hope – even as the word *Goshna* in *gematria* adds up to 358, the numerical equivalent of that of the word *Mashiaḥ*, Messiah.

שֶׁנֶּאֱמַר
וַיֹּאמֶר לְאַבְרָם
יָדֹעַ תֵּדַע כִּי־גֵר יִהְיֶה זַרְעֲךָ בְּאֶרֶץ לֹא לָהֶם
וַעֲבָדוּם וְעִנּוּ אֹתָם
אַרְבַּע מֵאוֹת שָׁנָה:
וְגַם אֶת־הַגּוֹי אֲשֶׁר יַעֲבֹדוּ דָּן אָנֹכִי
וְאַחֲרֵי־כֵן יֵצְאוּ בִּרְכֻשׁ גָּדוֹל:

longest time – until Abraham was 100 years old. His wife, Sarah, also shared the pain of childlessness for many years, until she was 90 and realistically despaired of ever fulfilling her dream.

Remarkably, it is at the Seder, surrounded by our own children, that we take note of the pain experienced by those not as fortunate and make reference to the idea that God Himself was profoundly aware of their agony. That is why He took it into account when He diminished the number of years originally scheduled for Egyptian slavery by the number of years each one of them had to wait until blessed by the birth of Isaac.

The Secret of Jewish Survival

God told Abraham, "Your descendants will be strangers in a land not their own" (Gen. 15:13). Not simply that they would be there, but that they would be strangers throughout their stay. They would remain separate, maintaining their own unique identity, beliefs, and values. In short, they would not assimilate.

The Torah tells us that Jacob sent Judah down to Egypt to make preparations for the family's stay: "And he sent Judah before him unto Joseph, to show the way before him unto Goshen" (Gen. 46:28). The intention was to create the first ghetto in history. It was not the much-later ghetto of Venice enforced by the church or the horrific ghetto of Warsaw of Holocaust Nazi infamy. Those were ghettos of hate instituted by Jewish enemies. Goshen was a self-chosen ghetto established by our ancestors to ensure continuity by way of proximity and preservation by means of communal reinforcement. It was a brilliant method

The matzot are covered and the wine cup is raised.

וְהִיא שֶׁעָמְדָה

AND THIS

[promise] is what has stood
by our ancestors and us;
for it was not only one man who rose up to destroy us:
in every single generation people rise up to destroy us –

BUT THE HOLY ONE BLESSED BE HE
SAVES US
FROM THEIR HANDS.

Saved *Through* Our Enemies

It is a recurring irony of history: We are saved not only *from* the evil intentions of our enemy but also *through* them; their own actions are the source of our salvation. God delivers us *miyadam*, by way of their hands. Pharaoh sought to drown every male Israelite. By the hand of Pharaoh's own daughter, Moses was plucked from the Nile and brought up in the very palace of the one who plotted to annihilate his people. Many years later, it was none other than Haman who gave the Persian King Ahasuerus the advice to get rid of the queen who refused his command, and replace her with someone more suitable – who turned out to be Esther, responsible for Haman's eventual downfall. The very gallows on which Haman was hung was the one Haman had prepared for his nemesis, Mordekhai.

In modern times, Nazi Germany sowed the seeds of its own defeat when it passed the laws which made into intellectual outcasts Jews in general and Albert Einstein as well as a coterie of scientific geniuses in particular. The discriminatory legislation prevented Germany from developing the nuclear expertise, which assured eventual victory of the Allied forces. Evil is responsible ultimately for its own demise.

The מצות are covered and the wine cup is raised.

וְהִיא

שֶׁעָמְדָה לַאֲבוֹתֵינוּ וְלָנוּ

שֶׁלֹּא אֶחָד בִּלְבָד עָמַד עָלֵינוּ לְכַלּוֹתֵנוּ
אֶלָּא שֶׁבְּכָל דּוֹר וָדוֹר עוֹמְדִים עָלֵינוּ לְכַלּוֹתֵנוּ
וְהַקָּדוֹשׁ בָּרוּךְ הוּא מַצִּילֵנוּ מִיָּדָם

AND THIS IS WHAT HAS STOOD BY OUR ANCESTORS AND US

When Our Enemies Choose Genocide

"For it was not only one man who rose up to destroy us – but the Holy One saves us from their hands." Remarkably enough, when enemies of the Jewish people decide upon our total annihilation there is a comforting prophecy which comes into play. Isolated attacks against some Jews may at times succeed. However, God committed Himself to redeem us from anyone whose efforts are directed against Jewish survival:

> Yet in spite of this, when they are in the land of their enemies, I will not cast them away, neither will I abhor them, to destroy them utterly and to break My covenant with them, for I am the Lord their God. But I will for their sakes remember the covenant of their ancestors, whom I brought forth out of Egypt in the sight of the heathen, that I might be their God: I am the Lord. (Lev. 26:44–45)

This is why those who came to totally destroy us failed so utterly – because God must be true to His commitment to our ancestors.

The wine cup is put down and the matzot are uncovered.

צֵא וּלְמַד

GO [to the verse]

AND LEARN

what Laban the Aramean
sought to do to our father Jacob:
Pharaoh condemned only the boys to death,
but Laban sought to uproot everything,

as it is written:

"AN ARAMEAN SOUGHT MY FATHER'S DEATH,   *Deut. 26*
AND HE WENT DOWN TO EGYPT
AND RESIDED THERE,
JUST A HANDFUL OF SOULS;
AND THERE HE BECAME A NATION –
LARGE, MIGHTY, AND GREAT."

(Num. 10:35). With regard to those false-friend enemies, Moses entreated God
to intervene and scatter them. After all, they may have been unknown to him.
Only the Lord can be counted on to see through the false pieties of human beings and to know their inner thoughts. However, with regard to the open haters,
those we can identify, we can readily pursue them and cause them to flee. The
biblical verse is almost an exact echo of the pithy prayer attributed to Voltaire:
"Lord, protect me from my friends; I can take care of my enemies myself."

In the course of history, Jews have had both kinds of enemies. In the Torah
there is a paradigm for each one – and it is in the Haggada that we are reminded
which one it is who represents a greater threat to our survival. *Paro*, Pharaoh in
Hebrew, is spelled *peh, resh, ayin, heh*. The two letters central to his name, clear
and unhidden, are *resh, ayin*, pronounced *ra* – he was quintessentially evil. We
had no difficulty in recognizing his wickedness or his desire to harm us. Laban
however was different. His name is identical to the Hebrew for the word "white,"
a symbol of purity. All of his actions reeked with deceit. His promises could
never be trusted, his friendship never could be counted upon.

The wine cup is put down and the מצות are uncovered.

צֵא וּלְמַד

מַה בִּקֵּשׁ לָבָן הָאֲרַמִּי
לַעֲשׂוֹת לְיַעֲקֹב אָבִינוּ
שֶׁפַּרְעֹה לֹא גָזַר
אֶלָּא עַל הַזְּכָרִים
וְלָבָן בִּקֵּשׁ לַעֲקֹר אֶת הַכֹּל

שֶׁנֶּאֱמַר

דברים כו

אֲרַמִּי אֹבֵד אָבִי
וַיֵּרֶד מִצְרַיְמָה, וַיָּגָר שָׁם בִּמְתֵי מְעָט
וַיְהִי־שָׁם לְגוֹי גָּדוֹל עָצוּם וָרָב

AN ARAMEAN SOUGHT MY FATHER'S DEATH

Laban vs. Pharaoh

There are two words in Hebrew to describe an enemy. One is *oyev*, the other is *soneh*. There is a fine distinction between them. The word *soneh* means an enemy who is clear and open about his hostility. It has a hissing sound in it, an onomatopoeic indication of hostility. A *soneh* does not try to conceal his unfriendliness and antagonism. On the other hand, the word *oyev* sounds very much like the word *ohev*, a friend and a lover. This is a foe who stabs you in the back, while to your face he offers a pleasant smile. He is an adversary who masks his enmity with the disguise of amity.

Long ago, Moses already acknowledged this important distinction: "So it was, whenever the Ark set out, Moses would say, 'Arise, O Lord, may Your enemies [*oiyvekha*] be scattered and may those who hate You [*sanekha*] flee from You'"

"AND HE WENT DOWN TO EGYPT" –
Compelled by what had been spoken.

"AND RESIDED THERE" –
From this, learn that our father Jacob went down
not to be absorbed into Egypt,
but only to reside there for a time.
As it is said:
"They said to Pharaoh,   *Gen. 47*
'We have come to *reside* in this land,
for there is no pasture for your servants' flocks,
for the famine is heavy in the land of Canaan;
and now, if you please,
let your servants dwell in the land of Goshen.'"

"JUST A HANDFUL OF SOULS" –
As it is said:
"Your ancestors were but seventy souls   *Deut. 10*
when they went down to Egypt –
and now the LORD has made you
as many as the sky has stars."

---

subterfuges, threatened the spiritual sanctity as well as the continuity of the
Jewish people. Laban's smile is always more dangerous than Pharaoh's sword.
It is a lesson we have sadly had to learn throughout the many years of our exile
and Diaspora.

וַיֵּרֶד מִצְרַיְמָה
אָנוּס עַל פִּי הַדִּבּוּר

וַיָּגָר שָׁם
מְלַמֵּד שֶׁלֹּא יָרַד יַעֲקֹב אָבִינוּ
לְהִשְׁתַּקֵּעַ בְּמִצְרַיִם, אֶלָּא לָגוּר שָׁם
שֶׁנֶּאֱמַר

בראשית מז

וַיֹּאמְרוּ אֶל־פַּרְעֹה
לָגוּר בָּאָרֶץ בָּאנוּ
כִּי־אֵין מִרְעֶה לַצֹּאן אֲשֶׁר לַעֲבָדֶיךָ
כִּי־כָבֵד הָרָעָב בְּאֶרֶץ כְּנָעַן
וְעַתָּה יֵשְׁבוּ־נָא עֲבָדֶיךָ בְּאֶרֶץ גֹּשֶׁן:

בִּמְתֵי מְעָט
כְּמָה שֶׁנֶּאֱמַר

דברים י

בְּשִׁבְעִים נֶפֶשׁ יָרְדוּ אֲבֹתֶיךָ מִצְרָיְמָה
וְעַתָּה שָׂמְךָ יהוה אֱלֹהֶיךָ
כְּכוֹכְבֵי הַשָּׁמַיִם לָרֹב:

"Go and learn" are the opening words of the paragraph, which goes on to contrast the two kinds of enemies. It is not by way of a superficial look that we can make a proper determination of their true character or of the ultimate danger they represent to us. As harsh as Pharaoh's decree was, it would have been responsible only for the death of Jewish males. Laban however, with his

"AND THERE HE BECAME A NATION" –
From this, learn that Israel was distinct there.

"LARGE, MIGHTY" –
As it is said:
"And the children of Israel were fertile,   *Ex. 1*
and they swarmed,
and grew *more and more numerous*
and strong, and the land was filled with them."

---

the merit of three things the Jews were redeemed from Egypt. Three crucial choices for the preservation of their unique identity and their divine mission insured their survival. The children of Israel did not change their names, they did not change their language, and they did not change their garments.

Biblical commentators point out the seemingly strange fact that the Book of Exodus begins by telling us, "And these are the names of the children of Israel who came to Egypt with Jacob" (Ex. 1:1). The Torah then proceeds to list them – as if this were new information, as if we were unfamiliar with the names of Jacob's sons – all of whom played such significant roles in the Book of Genesis and all of whose names we learned at the times of their birth. Why does the Torah repeat the names of the children of Israel upon their entry to Egypt? The answer is alluded to in one letter, the very first letter of the opening verse describing the first Diaspora of Jewish history.

"*And* these are the names," not "These are the names." These continued to be their names even though they now entered a foreign land. The Torah is teaching us that no matter what challenges they would face in a foreign culture and in alien surroundings, the one thing they would never forsake was their identity given at birth, the Hebrew name which linked them to their forebears and which mystically defined their life mission and purpose. The first step in destroying a connection with your past is renunciation of the identity by which you were known. And this – unlike Jews of a century ago who came to American shores with the desire to sever all ties with the shtetl of their birth and the religious restrictions of their faith and immediately "re-christianed" themselves with Anglo-Saxon surnames – the children of Jacob refused to do. They bore their Hebrew names as badges of honor, and in that way took the first step toward achieving the miracle of Jewish survival.

וַיְהִי־שָׁם לְגוֹי
מְלַמֵּד שֶׁהָיוּ יִשְׂרָאֵל מְצֻיָּנִים שָׁם

גָּדוֹל עָצוּם

כְּמָה שֶׁנֶּאֱמַר
וּבְנֵי יִשְׂרָאֵל פָּרוּ וַיִּשְׁרְצוּ וַיִּרְבּוּ
וַיַּעַצְמוּ בִּמְאֹד מְאֹד
וַתִּמָּלֵא הָאָרֶץ אֹתָם:

שמות א

THAT ISRAEL WAS DISTINCT THERE

How "Israel Was Distinct There"

It remains to this day almost certainly the most remarkable miracle of the Jewish people. In the famous words of Mark Twain:

> The Egyptian, the Babylonian, and the Persian rose, filled the planet with sound and splendor, then faded to dream stuff and passed away; the Greek and the Roman followed, and made a vast noise, and they are gone; other peoples have sprung up and held their torch high for a time, but it burned out, and they sit in twilight now, or have vanished. The Jew saw them all, beat them all and is now what he always was, exhibiting no decadence, no infirmities of age, no weakening of his parts, no slowing of his energies, no dulling of his alert and aggressive mind. All things are mortal but the Jew; all other forces pass but he remains. What is the secret of his immortality?

The Haggada here gives us a cryptic answer which takes us back to our very infancy as a nation. It was in Egypt, where a family of seventy immigrants found themselves subjugated as slaves and seemingly doomed to extinction, that the children of Israel discovered the secret for survival. "'And there he became a nation' (Deut. 26:5) – from this, learn that *Israel was distinct there*."

The descendants of Abraham, Isaac, and Jacob knew that they possessed a unique relationship with God. They understood that they were the bearers of a legacy of their ancestors that had the potential to be a light to all the nations and a source of blessing for mankind. They refused to accept suicide by assimilation. Instead they chose to "be distinct there." The Midrash clarifies that in

"AND GREAT" –

As it is said:
"I let you *grow wild* like meadow plants,   *Ezek. 16*
and you grew and matured and came forth in all your glory,
your breasts full and your hair grown,
and you were naked and exposed."

Some add:

"And I passed by you   *Ibid.*
and saw you wallowing in your own blood –
and I said to you, 'In your blood, live!'
and I said, 'In your blood, live!'"

---

connote a sentence. Yet in Hebrew it is not difficult to see the titles of the books in sequence conveying a message – a message suggesting which one of the three keys to Jewish survival is the most essential. Recite the five names in order and you have the following: *Bereshit, Shemot, Vayikra, Bemidbar, Devarim.* Now read them as a sentence imagining a comma after the second word: In the beginning [first and foremost] are names [remembering your name, your identity], [as a result of which] He [God] called out in the desert the words [of the Decalogue and the Torah].

The Torah makes many demands upon us. However, first and foremost, and implicit in the meaning of the words formed by the Hebrew titles of the five books of the Torah is to remember who you are, to recall the name you were given at birth. Your name is your heritage, your mission in life, your blessing, as well as your link to your past and your responsibility to the future. That is why the awesome privilege of being called to the Torah is announced by the public proclamation of a Hebrew name. To respond to our name is what makes us worthy of being a source of blessing to God and to Torah.

"IN YOUR BLOOD, LIVE!"

The Two Mitzvot of Blood

Before the Jews could leave Egypt they were commanded two mitzvot. Both shared something striking: they revolved around blood. But unlike the pagan world in which the shedding of blood was associated with death, the world of the Jewish slaves in Egypt was one in which the blood of these two ritual commandments emphasized life. The prophet Ezekiel depicted God proclaiming, "And

וָרָב

כְּמָה שֶׁנֶּאֱמַר

יחזקאל טז

רְבָבָה כְּצֶמַח הַשָּׂדֶה נְתַתִּיךְ

וַתִּרְבִּי וַתִּגְדְּלִי, וַתָּבֹאִי בַּעֲדִי עֲדָיִים

שָׁדַיִם נָכֹנוּ וּשְׂעָרֵךְ צִמֵּחַ, וְאַתְּ עֵרֹם וְעֶרְיָה:

Some add:

שם

וָאֶעֱבֹר עָלַיִךְ וָאֶרְאֵךְ מִתְבּוֹסֶסֶת בְּדָמָיִךְ

וָאֹמַר לָךְ בְּדָמַיִךְ חֲיִי   וָאֹמַר לָךְ בְּדָמַיִךְ חֲיִי:

Two other aspects of our lifestyles play a similar role in defining us. Our language and our clothing are the garments of our minds and our bodies. They shape how we think and the way in which we choose to appear to the world. To their eternal credit, Jacob's children in Egypt did not forget the Hebrew language, the only language sanctified with the descriptive of the holy tongue, *lashon hakodesh,* nor the manner of dress bespeaking the ideals of Jewish modesty and reserve. In Hebrew, these three crucial illustrations of Jewish identity – name, language, and garment – are termed *shem, lashon,* and *malbush.* Remarkably, the first letters of these three words form the word *shalem,* whole or complete.

The Midrash makes clear that the biblical Jews who were slaves in Egypt were far from perfect. Their sins may well have contributed to the tragedy of their oppression. Yet in spite of all their transgressions, God saw fit to redeem them because they were still "distinctive." The Exodus was made possible by Israel's unflagging commitment to these three keys to Jewish survival; Passover can be celebrated by us today because our ancestors in Egypt never forsook their Hebrew names, their attachment to the Hebrew language, and their pride in a manner of dress which identified them as the children of Israel.

Shem, lashon, and *malbush* are a triad of supreme values. All three were essential components for the Exodus. Yet it may be possible to assert that of these three, one is preeminent. Name, language, and garment share a category of distinctiveness which made us worthy of redemption – but one of them perhaps deserves top billing. Indeed, it may even be the hidden message implicit in the sequence of the names of the five books of the Torah.

In English, the names of the five books of the Torah have no meaning beyond the particular designation for each of the volumes. Genesis, Exodus, Leviticus, Numbers, and Deuteronomy are no more than a series of names; they do not

"AND THE EGYPTIANS DEALT CRUELLY WITH US
AND OPPRESSED US,
AND IMPOSED HARD LABOR ON US."

Deut. 26

"THE EGYPTIANS DEALT CRUELLY WITH US" –
As it is said:
"We must act wisely against [this people],
in case it grows great,
and when we are called to war
they may join our enemies,
fight against us,
and rise up to leave the land."

Ex. 1

---

to be cut off from the Jewish people. It is biblically applied to only a limited number of most severe transgressions. Almost all of them are instances of violations of negative commandments, that is, sins of commission. There are only two positive commandments in all of the Torah for which noncompliance, the sin of omission, makes one deserving of *karet*. They are the very two mitzvot singled out for observance on the night of the first Passover of history – precisely because they and they alone would make the Jews worthy of deliverance. How should we understand their unique significance?

A beautiful insight into the verse which begins the story of our patriarch Abraham's journey as servant of God may prove instructive. No sooner did Abraham make his great discovery of monotheism than he was presented with the divine mission of forsaking his past and moving on to the Promised Land. In the very first divine communication of the Almighty to Abraham, God told him, *"Lekh lekha"* (Gen. 12:1). The expression could be translated simply as the command "go," but sensitivity to the Hebrew makes clear there must be a special reason for the double imperative. The commentary of Rashi deals with it beautifully: the double form implies, you go – to you, "for your own good and for your own benefit." It is a journey of self-fulfillment. It is not a test of Abraham's obedience to God but a gift from God to Abraham whose benefits will become apparent in the future. What divine gift was hidden in the words which commanded Abraham's mission?

וַיָּרֵעוּ אֹתָנוּ הַמִּצְרִים
וַיְעַנּוּנוּ
וַיִּתְּנוּ עָלֵינוּ עֲבֹדָה קָשָׁה:

וַיָּרֵעוּ אֹתָנוּ הַמִּצְרִים

כְּמָה שֶׁנֶּאֱמַר
הָבָה נִתְחַכְּמָה לוֹ פֶּן־יִרְבֶּה
וְהָיָה כִּי־תִקְרֶאנָה מִלְחָמָה
וְנוֹסַף גַּם־הוּא עַל־שֹׂנְאֵינוּ
וְנִלְחַם־בָּנוּ
וְעָלָה מִן־הָאָרֶץ:

I passed by you and saw you wallowing in your own blood – and I said to you, 'In your blood, live!' and I said, 'In your blood, live!'" (16:6).

The rabbis understood this to be God's response to the words immediately preceding: "and you were naked and exposed." In a striking explanation of the phrase as metaphor, R. Matya ben Ḥarash taught:

The Almighty said, "The time for the fulfillment of the oath I swore to Abraham has arrived but they [the children of Israel] had no commandments in their hands with which to occupy themselves in order that they deserve to be redeemed, as it is said, 'and you were naked and exposed.'"

So the Almighty gave them two mitzvot, the blood of the Passover and the blood of the circumcision. They circumcised themselves on that night as it is said, "wallowing in your own bloods" – not blood, but bloods in the plural, the blood of circumcision as well as the blood of the Paschal lamb (see Rashi on Ex. 12:6). It was only because of the presence of these two forms of blood that redemption took place.

Circumcision and the Paschal lamb share another connection. The punishment of *karet* is extremely severe. In its broadest and most literal sense, it means

"AND OPPRESSED US" –

As it is said:

"They placed taskmasters over [the people]   *Ex. 1*

to *oppress* them under their burdens;

they built store cities for Pharaoh:

Pithom and Raamses."

"AND IMPOSED HARD LABOR ON US" –

As it is said:

"The Egyptians enslaved the children of Israel   *Ex. 1*

with *heavy rigor.*"

---

virtue of residence in the Holy Land were 100. And that was the fulfillment of the numerical value of *lekh lekha*.

Which of these two commentaries is correct? Was Abraham's great blessing personal or national – the gift of child or homeland? We have no hesitation in responding that both explanations are equally valid. There was a dual blessing in God's words which encapsulated the dual visions required for posterity.

These two ideals became two mitzvot. Circumcision, welcoming a newborn into our covenant with God, is personal. The Paschal lamb is a mitzva of national import, merging the story of our own lives with the history as well as the destiny of our people. The negation of either one of these two is tantamount to cutting oneself off from our people – the very meaning of *karet*. On Passover night our focus is both on family and on peoplehood, on our homes as well as our homeland. We treasure them both with our blood and our lives – because of both of them "[with our] blood [we] shall live, [with our] blood [we] shall live." (Ezek. 16:16).

וַיְעַנּוּנוּ

כְּמָה שֶׁנֶּאֱמַר

שמות א

וַיָּשִׂימוּ עָלָיו שָׂרֵי מִסִּים
לְמַעַן עַנֹּתוֹ בְּסִבְלֹתָם
וַיִּבֶן עָרֵי מִסְכְּנוֹת לְפַרְעֹה
אֶת־פִּתֹם וְאֶת־רַעַמְסֵס:

וַיִּתְּנוּ עָלֵינוּ עֲבֹדָה קָשָׁה

כְּמָה שֶׁנֶּאֱמַר

שמות א

וַיַּעֲבִדוּ מִצְרַיִם אֶת־בְּנֵי יִשְׂרָאֵל בְּפָרֶךְ:

To understand the deeper meaning of a text, commentators often make use of *gematria. Lekh lekha* is spelled *lamed* (thirty), *kaf* (twenty); when doubled the total is one hundred. With that as a given, the authors of *Tosafot* make a surprisingly simple suggestion. Abraham suffered greatly for want of a child. God reassured him that his wish would eventually be fulfilled. Go to the Promised Land – he was told – here, outside of Canaan, you will not find that blessing but there, at the age of one hundred, you will find the fulfillment and the blessing you so anxiously seek. The *lekh lekha* to which its number alludes is the blessing of progeny, the blessing of child and of family.

The Midrash offers another interpretation. God spoke to Abraham when he was 75 years old. It was then that Abraham began his physical attachment to the land that would become the home of the Jewish people and the dream of our national aspirations. Abraham lived 175 years. The years of blessing by

"AND WE CRIED OUT TO THE LORD,   *Deut. 26*
GOD OF OUR ANCESTORS,
AND THE LORD HEARD OUR VOICE,
AND HE SAW OUR OPPRESSION
AND OUR LABOR AND SLAVERY."

"AND WE CRIED OUT TO THE LORD,
GOD OF OUR ANCESTORS" –
> As it is said:
> "It came to be, as a long time passed,   *Ex. 2*
> that the king of Egypt died,
> and the children of Israel
> groaned under the burden of work,
> and they *cried out,*
> and their plea rose to God
>   from amid the work."

"AND THE LORD
HEARD OUR VOICE" –
> As it is said:
> "And God *heard* their groans,   *Ex. 2*
> and God remembered His covenant
> with Abraham, Isaac, and Jacob."

"AND HE SAW
OUR OPPRESSION" –
> The separation of husband from wife,
> as it is said:
> "And God saw the children of Israel,   *Ex. 2*
> and God knew."

וַנִּצְעַק אֶל־יְהוָה אֱלֹהֵי אֲבֹתֵינוּ
וַיִּשְׁמַע יְהוָה אֶת־קֹלֵנוּ
וַיַּרְא אֶת־עָנְיֵנוּ וְאֶת־עֲמָלֵנוּ וְאֶת־לַחֲצֵנוּ:

וַנִּצְעַק אֶל־יְהוָה אֱלֹהֵי אֲבֹתֵינוּ

כְּמָה שֶׁנֶּאֱמַר

וַיְהִי בַיָּמִים הָרַבִּים הָהֵם
וַיָּמָת מֶלֶךְ מִצְרַיִם
וַיֵּאָנְחוּ בְנֵי־יִשְׂרָאֵל מִן־הָעֲבֹדָה
וַיִּזְעָקוּ
וַתַּעַל שַׁוְעָתָם אֶל־הָאֱלֹהִים מִן־הָעֲבֹדָה:

וַיִּשְׁמַע יְהוָה אֶת־קֹלֵנוּ

כְּמָה שֶׁנֶּאֱמַר

וַיִּשְׁמַע אֱלֹהִים אֶת־נַאֲקָתָם
וַיִּזְכֹּר אֱלֹהִים אֶת־בְּרִיתוֹ
אֶת־אַבְרָהָם אֶת־יִצְחָק וְאֶת־יַעֲקֹב:

וַיַּרְא אֶת־עָנְיֵנוּ

זוֹ פְּרִישׁוּת דֶּרֶךְ אֶרֶץ
כְּמָה שֶׁנֶּאֱמַר

וַיַּרְא אֱלֹהִים אֶת־בְּנֵי יִשְׂרָאֵל
וַיֵּדַע אֱלֹהִים:

"AND OUR LABOR" –

> [The killing of] the sons,
> as it is said:
> "Throw every boy who is born   *Ex. 1*
> into the river,
> and the girls let live."

"AND SLAVERY" –

> The forced labor that was pressed
> down on them,
> as it is said:
> "I have seen the *slavery*   *Ex. 3*
> that Egypt forced upon you."

"AND THE LORD BROUGHT US OUT OF EGYPT   *Deut. 26*
WITH A STRONG HAND
AND AN OUTSTRETCHED ARM,
IN AN AWESOME HAPPENING,
WITH SIGNS AND WITH WONDERS."

"AND THE LORD BROUGHT US
OUT OF EGYPT" –

> Not through an angel,
> not through a seraph,
> not through any emissary.
> No, it was the Holy One,
> His glory,
> His own presence.

וְאֶת־עֲמָלֵנוּ
אֵלוּ הַבָּנִים
כְּמָה שֶׁנֶּאֱמַר
שמות א
כָּל־הַבֵּן הַיִּלּוֹד, הַיְאֹרָה תַּשְׁלִיכֻהוּ
וְכָל־הַבַּת תְּחַיּוּן:

וְאֶת־לַחֲצֵנוּ
זֶה הַדְּחַק
כְּמָה שֶׁנֶּאֱמַר
שמות ג
וְגַם־רָאִיתִי אֶת־הַלַּחַץ
אֲשֶׁר מִצְרַיִם לֹחֲצִים אֹתָם:

דברים כו
וַיּוֹצִאֵנוּ יהוה מִמִּצְרַיִם
בְּיָד חֲזָקָה וּבִזְרֹעַ נְטוּיָה
וּבְמֹרָא גָּדֹל
וּבְאֹתוֹת וּבְמֹפְתִים:

וַיּוֹצִאֵנוּ יהוה מִמִּצְרַיִם
לֹא עַל יְדֵי מַלְאָךְ
וְלֹא עַל יְדֵי שָׂרָף
וְלֹא עַל יְדֵי שָׁלִיחַ
אֶלָּא הַקָּדוֹשׁ בָּרוּךְ הוּא
בִּכְבוֹדוֹ וּבְעַצְמוֹ

As it is said:

"I shall pass through the land of Egypt on that night;   *Ex. 12*
I shall kill every firstborn son
in the land of Egypt,
man and beast,
and I shall pass judgment
on all the gods of Egypt:
I am the Lord."
"I shall pass through
the land of Egypt on that night" –   I and no angel.
"I shall kill every firstborn son in
the land of Egypt" –   I and no seraph.
"And I shall pass judgment on all
the gods of Egypt" –   I and no emissary.
"I am the Lord" –   It is I and no other.

"WITH A STRONG HAND" –

This refers to the pestilence,
as it is said:
"You shall see the *hand* of the Lord   *Ex. 9*
among your cattle in the field,
among your horses and donkeys and camels,
in the herd and in the flock,
bringing harsh, heavy pestilence."

"AND AN OUTSTRETCHED ARM" –

This refers to the sword,
as it is said:
"And His sword was drawn in His hand,   *1 Chron. 21*
stretched out over Jerusalem."

שֶׁנֶּאֱמַר

שמות יב

וְעָבַרְתִּי בְאֶרֶץ־מִצְרַיִם בַּלַּיְלָה הַזֶּה

וְהִכֵּיתִי כָל־בְּכוֹר בְּאֶרֶץ מִצְרַיִם

מֵאָדָם וְעַד־בְּהֵמָה

וּבְכָל־אֱלֹהֵי מִצְרַיִם אֶעֱשֶׂה שְׁפָטִים

אֲנִי יהוה:

אֲנִי וְלֹא מַלְאָךְ	וְעָבַרְתִּי בְאֶרֶץ־מִצְרַיִם
אֲנִי וְלֹא שָׂרָף	וְהִכֵּיתִי כָל־בְּכוֹר
אֲנִי וְלֹא הַשָּׁלִיחַ	וּבְכָל־אֱלֹהֵי מִצְרַיִם אֶעֱשֶׂה שְׁפָטִים
אֲנִי הוּא וְלֹא אַחֵר	אֲנִי יהוה

בְּיָד חֲזָקָה

זוֹ הַדֶּבֶר

כְּמָה שֶׁנֶּאֱמַר

הִנֵּה יַד־יהוה

שמות ט

הוֹיָה בְּמִקְנְךָ אֲשֶׁר בַּשָּׂדֶה

בַּסּוּסִים בַּחֲמֹרִים בַּגְּמַלִּים

בַּבָּקָר וּבַצֹּאן

דֶּבֶר כָּבֵד מְאֹד:

וּבִזְרֹעַ נְטוּיָה

זוֹ הַחֶרֶב

כְּמָה שֶׁנֶּאֱמַר

דברי הימים א'
כא

וְחַרְבּוֹ שְׁלוּפָה בְּיָדוֹ

נְטוּיָה עַל־יְרוּשָׁלָ‍ִם:

"IN AN AWESOME HAPPENING" –

This refers to the revelation of His Presence,
as it is said:
"Has any god ever tried to come   *Deut. 4*
and take a nation out of the midst of another,
with trials
and with signs
and wonders,
in war
and with a strong hand,
with an outstretched arm,
inspiring *great awe,*
as the LORD your God has done all this
for you in Egypt,
before your eyes?"

"WITH SIGNS" –

This refers to the staff,
as it is said:
"Take this staff in your hand,   *Ex. 4*
and with it you shall perform the *signs.*"

"AND WITH WONDERS" –

This refers to the blood,
as it is said:
"I shall make *wonders*   *Joel 3*
in the sky and on the earth –

A drop of wine is spilled from the cup as each wonder is mentioned:

BLOOD, AND FIRE,
AND PILLARS OF SMOKE."

וּבְמֹרָא גָּדֹל

זֶה גִּלּוּי שְׁכִינָה

כְּמָה שֶׁנֶּאֱמַר

אוֹ הֲנִסָּה אֱלֹהִים לָבוֹא לָקַחַת לוֹ גוֹי מִקֶּרֶב גּוֹי

בְּמַסֹּת בְּאֹתֹת וּבְמוֹפְתִים וּבְמִלְחָמָה

וּבְיָד חֲזָקָה, וּבִזְרוֹעַ נְטוּיָה

וּבְמוֹרָאִים גְּדֹלִים

כְּכֹל אֲשֶׁר־עָשָׂה לָכֶם יהוה אֱלֹהֵיכֶם בְּמִצְרַיִם

לְעֵינֶיךָ:

וּבְאֹתוֹת

זֶה הַמַּטֶּה

כְּמָה שֶׁנֶּאֱמַר

וְאֶת־הַמַּטֶּה הַזֶּה תִּקַּח בְּיָדֶךָ

אֲשֶׁר תַּעֲשֶׂה־בּוֹ אֶת־הָאֹתֹת:

וּבְמוֹפְתִים

זֶה הַדָּם

כְּמָה שֶׁנֶּאֱמַר

וְנָתַתִּי מוֹפְתִים

בַּשָּׁמַיִם וּבָאָרֶץ

A drop of wine is spilled from the cup as each wonder is mentioned:

דָּם וָאֵשׁ וְתִימֲרוֹת עָשָׁן:

דָּבָר אַחֵר Another interpretation:

"With a strong hand" –	Two.
"And an outstretched arm" –	Two.
"In an awesome happening" –	Two.
"With signs" –	Two.
"And with wonders" –	Two.

THESE WERE THE TEN PLAGUES
that the Holy One brought
upon Egypt,
and these are they –

A drop of wine is spilled from the cup as each plague, and each of the acronyms,
Detzakh, Adash and Be'aḥav, is mentioned:

BLOOD	FROGS	LICE
WILD ANIMALS	PESTILENCE	BOILS
HAIL	LOCUSTS	DARKNESS

THE STRIKING DOWN OF THE FIRSTBORN.

---

of goodness and of light, the god of evil and of darkness. Dualism refused to accept the biblical truth that "there was evening and there was morning, one day" (Gen. 1:5), the faith of monotheism that night is the prelude to dawn and hardship the prologue to heavenly redemption – both aspects of one and the same divine power.

As part of the Exodus, the Jewish people witnessed God's might, His awesome power to bring plagues, death, and destruction upon His enemies. True, the Jews benefited. But what they saw was a God of violence and of vengeance, a God able to afflict the Egyptians with ten plagues, culminating in the death of their firstborn, as well as the drowning of their entire army in the Red Sea. One could be deluded into thinking that the God who made His appearance specialized in the kind of role illustrated by the first plague, turning water into blood and making needed water undrinkable.

דָּבָר אַחֵר

בְּיָד חֲזָקָה	שְׁתַּיִם
וּבִזְרֹעַ נְטוּיָה	שְׁתַּיִם
וּבְמֹרָא גָּדֹל	שְׁתַּיִם
וּבְאֹתוֹת	שְׁתַּיִם
וּבְמֹפְתִים	שְׁתַּיִם

אֵלּוּ עֶשֶׂר מַכּוֹת

שֶׁהֵבִיא הַקָּדוֹשׁ בָּרוּךְ הוּא
עַל הַמִּצְרִים בְּמִצְרַיִם
וְאֵלּוּ הֵן

A drop of wine is spilled from the cup as each plague, and each of the acronyms,
בְּאַחַ"ב and עֲדַ"שׁ, דְּצַ"ךְ, is mentioned:

דָּם	צְפַרְדֵּעַ	כִּנִּים
עָרוֹב	דֶּבֶר	שְׁחִין
בָּרָד	אַרְבֶּה	חֹשֶׁךְ

מַכַּת בְּכוֹרוֹת.

THE TEN PLAGUES

The Plague of Blood and Dualism

More than atheism (the belief in no God), dualism (the belief in two gods) was the heresy of the ancient world. Dualism was the pagan response to the problem of evil. How could a good God permit all the ills of this world? The only reason that made any sense was that power was shared by two deities. As Zoroastrianism explained, there is a god of day and a god of night – the god

Rabbi Yehuda grouped these under acronyms –
DETZAKH, ADASH, BE'AḤAV.

---

learn that faith in the Holy One, blessed be He, is also called "light." Hence, light and faith in God, the first commandment, correspond.

The second [commandment] states, "You shall have no other gods before Me" (Ex. 20:3; Deut. 5:7), and [the second utterance] states, "There shall be a firmament between the waters, and it shall divide between water and water" (Gen. 1:6). "There shall be a firmament" refers to the Jewish people who are part of God above (Job 31:2), for they are attached to that plane which is called *shamayim* [heaven, or firmament]. "Between the waters" – among the words of Torah, which is called water as our sages explain, "And it [the Jewish people] shall divide between water and water" – between God, who is called "the Source of living water," and false deities, which are called "broken wells" (Jer. 2:13) containing bitter, putrid, and stagnant water. Thus, the division between water and water is dependent on the Jewish people learning Torah.

The third [commandment] states, "Do not take the name of God in vain" (Ex. 20:7; Deut. 5:11), and [the third utterance] states, "The waters below the firmament shall be gathered into one place" (Gen. 1:9). Do not cause a separation in the unity of the waters [referring to the *Shekhina*, the indwelling Divine Presence] by uttering a false oath.

The fourth [commandment] states, "Remember the Shabbat to keep it holy" (Ex. 20:8), and [the fourth utterance] states, "The earth shall sprout vegetation" (Gen 1:11). When does the earth become fertile and become covered with vegetation? On the Shabbat, when the bride [the Shabbat] unites with the King [God]. This brings forth vegetation and blessing for the world. Every weekday is provided its food by virtue of the blessing it receives from the Shabbat, just as the manna which came down only during the week, was by virtue of the Shabbat.

The fifth [commandment] states, "Honor your father and mother," (Ex. 20:12; Deut. 5:16), and [the fifth utterance] states, "There shall be luminaries in the sky" (Gen. 1:14). This means that the luminaries are your father and mother – the sun is your father, and the moon your mother.

The sixth [commandment] states, "Do not murder" (Ex. 20:13; Deut. 5:17), and [the sixth utterance] states, "The waters shall teem with living creatures" (Gen. 1:20). Do not kill a man, who is also called "a living creature" (2:7). And do not be like fish, the larger of which swallows the smaller.

רַבִּי יְהוּדָה הָיָה נוֹתֵן בָּהֶם סִימָנִים
דְּצַ"ךְ עֲדַ"שׁ בְּאַחַ"ב

Jump forward to the last part of the story and note carefully the sequel. No sooner had the Jews safely crossed the sea and witnessed the death of their oppressors than, the Torah tells us, they went out into the desert of Shur and they found no water: "They came to Mara but they could not drink from Mara because the water was bitter; therefore it was named Mara" (Ex. 15:23). It was then that God performed a miracle. He instructed Moses to cast a piece of wood into the waters, and God turned the bitter waters to sweet. The same God who previously had shown Himself as the One who could make drinkable water undrinkable now made clear to the Jewish people that He is the same God who has the power to bless as well as to curse, to make the undrinkable serve as source for life-giving sustenance. Precisely because *dam* was the first plague, the story of Mara immediately followed redemption at the sea to proclaim the oneness of God, the same God who can punish as well as reward.

Ten Plagues – Ten Commandments – Ten Sayings of Creation
The story of the Exodus has two major moments – and each one of them is significantly highlighted by the same number, the number ten. There were ten plagues and there were ten commandments. The correspondence is intentional. The Ten Commandments set out our obligations; the ten plagues make clear that divine punishment is the consequence of moral disobedience.

Why precisely ten? Because there is another all-important "ten," which goes back to the very beginning of Creation. With ten sayings, the Mishna tells us, God created the world (Mishna Avot 5:1). Follow the story of Creation and note that there were ten times when God said, "Let there be" – and there was. For profound reasons, Creation was a process rather than an instantaneous event, a process consisting of ten stages of divinely ordained moments. The Ten Commandments are the spiritual corollaries of and are parallel to the ten divine utterances which allowed the world to come into existence. The Zohar, the masterwork of Jewish mysticism, makes clear the connection:

The first [commandment, instructing us to have faith in God] states, "I am the Lord your God" (Ex. 20:2; Deut. 5:6). Regarding Creation, [the first utterance] states, "There shall be light and there was light" (Gen. 1:3). From the verse "God is my light and salvation, whom shall I fear?" (Ps. 27:1), we

רַבִּי יוֹסֵי הַגְּלִילִי

RABBI Yossei HaGelili says: How can you know
that the Egyptians were struck with ten plagues in Egypt
and another fifty at the sea?
For in Egypt it is said,
"The astrologers said to Pharaoh, 'This is the *finger* of God,'" *Ex. 8*
while at the sea it is said,
"When Israel saw the great *hand* *Ex. 14*
the LORD raised against the Egyptians,
the people feared the LORD,
and they believed in the LORD and in His servant Moses."
If a finger struck them with ten plagues,
conclude from this that
THEY WERE STRUCK WITH TEN PLAGUES IN EGYPT
AND WITH FIFTY PLAGUES AT THE SEA.

---

man with Our image, of Our likeness" (Gen. 1:26). Do not testify falsely
against one who bears the divine image. And if one testifies falsely, it is as if
he blasphemed.

The tenth [commandment] states, "Do not be envious of your neighbor's
wife" (Ex. 20:14; Deut. 5:18), and [the tenth utterance] states, "It is not good
that man should be alone. I will make him a helper to match him" (Gen. 2:18).
This refers to each person's soul mate, who matches him perfectly. Hence,
"Do not be envious of your neighbor's wife."

What does all this tell us? That the world was created for the sake of Torah,
and as long as the Jewish people occupy themselves with Torah, the world will
continue to exist. But if the Jewish people abandon Torah, the verse declares,
"Were it not for My covenant [the Torah] with day and night, I would not have
established the laws of heaven and earth" (Jer. 33:25).

Creation requires commitment to the Ten Commandments for its survival.
Disobedience is punished by ten plagues. And so important is it to remember
that the choice between these two rests in our own hands that the Midrash offers this fascinating suggestion: "This is the reason we were created with exactly
ten fingers – so that we might always be reminded that we have the power to

רַבִּי יוֹסֵי הַגְּלִילִי אוֹמֵר

מִנַּיִן אַתָּה אוֹמֵר

שֶׁלָּקוּ הַמִּצְרִים בְּמִצְרַיִם עֶשֶׂר מַכּוֹת

וְעַל הַיָּם לָקוּ חֲמִשִּׁים מַכּוֹת

בְּמִצְרַיִם מַה הוּא אוֹמֵר

שמות ח

וַיֹּאמְרוּ הַחַרְטֻמִּם אֶל־פַּרְעֹה, אֶצְבַּע אֱלֹהִים הוּא:

וְעַל הַיָּם מַה הוּא אוֹמֵר

שמות יד

וַיַּרְא יִשְׂרָאֵל אֶת־הַיָּד הַגְּדֹלָה אֲשֶׁר עָשָׂה יְהוה בְּמִצְרַיִם

וַיִּירְאוּ הָעָם אֶת־יְהוה

וַיַּאֲמִינוּ בַּיהוה וּבְמשֶׁה עַבְדּוֹ:

כַּמָּה לָקוּ בָאֶצְבַּע עֶשֶׂר מַכּוֹת.

אֱמֹר מֵעַתָּה

בְּמִצְרַיִם לָקוּ עֶשֶׂר מַכּוֹת

וְעַל הַיָּם לָקוּ חֲמִשִּׁים מַכּוֹת.

The seventh [commandment] states, "Do not commit adultery" (Ex. 20:13; Deut. 5:17), and [the seventh utterance] states, "The earth shall bring forth living creatures...in their species" (Gen. 1:24). From this we learn that a man should not approach a woman who is not his soul mate. For this reason the verse [states], "in their species." A woman must not bear children from one who is not her "species," i.e., her soul mate.

The eighth [commandment] states, "Do not steal" (Ex. 20:13; Deut. 5:17), and [the eighth utterance] states, "I have given you every seed-bearing plant on the surface of the earth" (Gen. 1:11). That is, that which I have given you, and allowed you to use, is yours. Do not steal that which belongs to someone else.

The ninth [commandment] states, "Do not testify as a false witness" (Ex. 20:13; Deut. 5:17), and [the ninth utterance] states, "We shall make

Rabbi Eliezer says: How can you know
    that each and every plague
    the Holy One brought upon the Egyptians in Egypt
    was in fact made up of four plagues?
    For it is said,
    "His fury was sent down upon them,   *Ps. 78*
    great anger, rage, and distress,
    a company of messengers of destruction."
    "Great anger" –   one,
    "rage" –   two,
    "distress" –   three,
    "a company of messengers of destruction" –   four.
    Conclude from this that
    THEY WERE STRUCK WITH FORTY PLAGUES IN EGYPT
    AND WITH TWO HUNDRED PLAGUES AT THE SEA.

---

water, it will immediately jump out. But if you place the frog into cool water and slowly heat it to boiling, the frog will not notice and will slowly cook to death. The concept has a profound application for human behavior: It can well be used as a metaphor for the inability or unwillingness of people to react to or to be aware of threats that rise gradually, in slow but inexorably greater intensity.

When God first revealed to Abraham the events that would befall his descendants in Egypt, He spoke of three stages (Gen. 15:13). First the Jews would become strangers in a land not theirs. Then they would become enslaved. Finally they would be oppressed. Just as in Nazi Germany many millennia later, genocide does not begin with mass murder – it starts with small steps of racism and religious oppression which if ignored incrementally begin to reach unimagined dimensions. The frog in the oven serves as powerful warning to those incapable of perceiving danger to our survival in the early stages.

רַבִּי אֱלִיעֶזֶר אוֹמֵר מִנַּיִן שֶׁכָּל מַכָּה וּמַכָּה
שֶׁהֵבִיא הַקָּדוֹשׁ בָּרוּךְ הוּא עַל הַמִּצְרִים בְּמִצְרַיִם
הָיְתָה שֶׁל אַרְבַּע מַכּוֹת,

שֶׁנֶּאֱמַר: יְשַׁלַּח־בָּם חֲרוֹן אַפּוֹ
עֶבְרָה וָזַעַם וְצָרָה, מִשְׁלַחַת מַלְאֲכֵי רָעִים:

עֶבְרָה	אַחַת
וָזַעַם	שְׁתַּיִם
וְצָרָה	שָׁלוֹשׁ
מִשְׁלַחַת מַלְאֲכֵי רָעִים	אַרְבַּע

אֱמוֹר מֵעַתָּה
בְּמִצְרַיִם לָקוּ אַרְבָּעִים מַכּוֹת
וְעַל הַיָּם לָקוּ מָאתַיִם מַכּוֹת.

---

decide between the 'ten' of the plagues or the 'ten' of the Decalogue. The judgment between death or life literally and figuratively resides in our own hands."

The Special Message of Frogs

The second plague, the plague of frogs, included a fascinating feature. The Torah
tells us in its warning, "And the Nile will swarm with frogs, and they will go up
and come into your house and into your bedroom and upon your bed and into
the house of your servants and into your people, and into your ovens and into
your kneading troughs" (Ex. 7:28). In short they would be everywhere. Why
then the specific mention of ovens?

Perhaps here the Torah is alerting us to a truth noted many centuries later
about frogs. In a famous experiment performed in 1897 by a scientist with the
unlikely name of Scripture, it was found that if *you plunge a frog* into boiling

Rabbi Akiva says: How can you know
  that each and every plague
  the Holy One brought upon the Egyptians in Egypt
  was in fact made up of five plagues?
  For it is said,
  "His fury was sent down upon them,   *Ps. 78*
  great anger, rage, and distress,
  a company of messengers of destruction."
  "His fury" –   one,
  "great anger" –   two,
  "rage" –   three,
  "distress" –   four,
  "a company of messengers of destruction" –   five.
  Conclude from this that
  THEY WERE STRUCK WITH FIFTY PLAGUES IN EGYPT
  AND WITH TWO HUNDRED AND FIFTY PLAGUES
  AT THE SEA.

The mathematical shorthand for these two names is four and five. At the end of the Haggada – when we are taught the more profound symbolic meaning of numbers – the response to "Who knows four?" is "I know four: four mothers," the matriarchs Sarah, Rebecca, Rachel, and Leah. Four is the number identified with unquestioned and unlimited mother love. And that is the number identified with the Tetragrammaton, which concludes with the grammatical form and letter denoting the feminine form of a word. "Who knows five?" is answered with "I know five: five books of the Torah." The Torah is the book of law. The Torah makes demands upon us and holds us accountable for fulfilling its commandments. It corresponds to the name of God that identifies Him as sovereign Judge and Lawgiver. Mercy and love on the one hand, and justice and law on the other hand correspond respectively to the "four" and the "five" that together define our understanding of God. God in His infinite wisdom knows how to best balance these characteristics so that they are not in conflict with each other but rather in a harmonious relationship required for the world's survival.

What intrigued two of the greatest scholars of talmudic times was a question relating to a seminal moment of Jewish history. God redeemed our ancestors

תהלים עח

רַבִּי עֲקִיבָא אוֹמֵר מִנַּיִן שֶׁכָּל מַכָּה וּמַכָּה
שֶׁהֵבִיא הַקָּדוֹשׁ בָּרוּךְ הוּא עַל הַמִּצְרִים בְּמִצְרַיִם
הָיְתָה שֶׁל חָמֵשׁ מַכּוֹת, שֶׁנֶּאֱמַר: יְשַׁלַּח־בָּם
חֲרוֹן אַפּוֹ, עֶבְרָה וָזַעַם וְצָרָה, מִשְׁלַחַת מַלְאֲכֵי רָעִים:

אַחַת	חֲרוֹן אַפּוֹ
שְׁתַּיִם	עֶבְרָה
שָׁלוֹשׁ	וָזַעַם
אַרְבַּע	וְצָרָה
חָמֵשׁ	מִשְׁלַחַת מַלְאֲכֵי רָעִים

אֱמֹר מֵעַתָּה
בְּמִצְרַיִם לָקוּ חֲמִשִּׁים מַכּוֹת
וְעַל הַיָּם לָקוּ חֲמִשִּׁים וּמָאתַיִם מַכּוֹת.

────────────────────────────

HOW CAN YOU KNOW THAT EACH AND EVERY PLAGUE

Four or Five – What Is the Difference?

The dispute between R. Eliezer and R. Akiva seems on the surface both strange and irrelevant. Was each one of the ten plagues actually comprised of four as R. Eliezer would have it, or was it five in accordance with the view of R. Akiva? What were they really getting at? After all, the Torah in fact reckoned every plague as one and gave us a grand total of ten. What was the point of the disagreement between these two great rabbinic scholars?

The answer may well lie in a pointed and well-known difference between two of the names of God. In Hebrew, when we choose to emphasize God's kindness and compassion we use the four-letter name of God, the Tetragrammaton. In the language of the rabbis, that name corresponds to divine attribute of *middat haraḥamim*. On the other hand, when we speak of the Almighty in His role as Judge and Ruler, the God who holds everyone in the world accountable for their actions, we refer to Him as *Elokim*, the five-letter name of God, which corresponds to the divine attribute of *middat hadin*.

כַּמָּה מַעֲלוֹת טוֹבוֹת

HOW MUCH GOOD,
LAYER UPON LAYER,
THE OMNIPRESENT HAS DONE FOR US:

Had He brought us out of Egypt
without bringing judgment upon
[our oppressors],
that would have been enough.

Had He brought judgment upon them
but not upon their gods,
that would have been enough.

Had He brought judgment upon their gods
without killing their firstborn sons,
that would have been enough.

---

things for us alone without the favors and miracles that followed, it would have been enough? No, that is clearly not true. We would hardly have reason to rejoice if the entire series of events would not have played out as a direct result of God's intervention – nor would we probably be here today to celebrate. We mention fifteen things – again that very same number as the Hebrew date in Nisan for Passover and the number of parts of the Seder – because they, each and every one of them, has special significance.

This is a night when we need to say thank you to God. Gratitude must be part of our national response to the events of the Exodus. But the specific moments that we choose to single out share a very important attribute which make their expression particularly mandatory. To mention them is not simply to fulfill the mitzva of gratitude but rather *to correct the far more horrendous sin of ingratitude* – to rectify the egregious wrongs of our ancestors who responded to divine gifts not merely with silence but, far worse, with complaints and criticisms.

כַּמָּה מַעֲלוֹת טוֹבוֹת לַמָּקוֹם עָלֵינוּ

אִלּוּ הוֹצִיאָנוּ מִמִּצְרַיִם

דַּיֵּנוּ   וְלֹא עָשָׂה בָהֶם שְׁפָטִים

אִלּוּ עָשָׂה בָהֶם שְׁפָטִים

דַּיֵּנוּ   וְלֹא עָשָׂה בֵאלֹהֵיהֶם

אִלּוּ עָשָׂה בֵאלֹהֵיהֶם

דַּיֵּנוּ   וְלֹא הָרַג אֶת בְּכוֹרֵיהֶם

---

by way of ten plagues against their oppressors. How are we to best understand them? Should they be thought of primarily as acts of kindness for the sake of the righteous or demonstrations of divine punishment for the wicked? Was God acting in the modality of *raḥamim* or of *din*? Perhaps on the deepest level of all, the rabbis wanted to define the steps required as prelude to deliverance as rooted in one or the other of God's two major names by way of their dual major meanings.

And like all rabbinic controversies "for the sake of Heaven," we ought to conclude that "these and those are both the words of the living God" (Eiruvin 13b). Both opinions are correct – and that is what makes their dispute so fascinating and so relevant. Each plague was a "five" – a form of justice and punishment. But each plague was also a "four" – compassionate and kind – because God's punishment of the wicked is nothing less than an act of kindness for the righteous.

THAT WOULD HAVE BEEN ENOUGH

Why Do These Fifteen Most Deserve Our Gratitude?

The section of the Haggada known as "*Dayeinu*," "that would have been enough," hardly makes sense if we take it literally. Had You, God, done any one of these

Had He killed their firstborn sons
　　without giving us their wealth,
　　　　that would have been enough.

Had He given us their wealth
　　without splitting the sea for us,
　　　　that would have been enough.

Had He split the sea for us
　　but not brought us through it dry,
　　　　that would have been enough.

Had He brought us through [the sea] dry
　　without drowning our enemies in it,
　　　　that would have been enough.

Had He drowned our enemies in it
　　without providing for our needs
　　for forty years in the desert,
　　　　that would have been enough.

He drew flowing water from a rock and brought down water like rivers, but they continued further to sin against Him, to provoke the most High in the desert. (Ps. 78:13–18)

With unbounded kindness God fed us with the miracle food of manna in the desert. The response of the people? "Our souls loathe this bread" (Num. 21:5). God blessed us with the Shabbat and provided a double portion of manna on Friday so the Jews would lack nothing by observing their divinely ordained day of rest – but "it came about that on the seventh day some of the people went out to gather manna but they did not find any; the Lord then said to Moses, 'How long will you refuse to obey My commandments and My teachings?'" (Ex. 16:27–28). With providential care God led us to the Promised Land. The nation's reaction? "They spread an evil report about the land which they had scouted, telling the children of Israel, 'the land we passed through to explore is a land that consumes its inhabitants.'" (Num. 13:32).

אִלּוּ הָרַג אֶת בְּכוֹרֵיהֶם
וְלֹא נָתַן לָנוּ אֶת מָמוֹנָם   דַּיֵּנוּ

אִלּוּ נָתַן לָנוּ אֶת מָמוֹנָם
וְלֹא קָרַע לָנוּ אֶת הַיָּם   דַּיֵּנוּ

אִלּוּ קָרַע לָנוּ אֶת הַיָּם
וְלֹא הֶעֱבִירָנוּ בְּתוֹכוֹ בֶּחָרָבָה   דַּיֵּנוּ

אִלּוּ הֶעֱבִירָנוּ בְּתוֹכוֹ בֶּחָרָבָה
וְלֹא שִׁקַּע צָרֵינוּ בְּתוֹכוֹ   דַּיֵּנוּ

אִלּוּ שִׁקַּע צָרֵינוּ בְּתוֹכוֹ
וְלֹא סִפֵּק צָרְכֵּנוּ בַּמִּדְבָּר
אַרְבָּעִים שָׁנָה   דַּיֵּנוּ

With infinite goodness, God took us out of Egypt. The Jew's response? "Because God hates us, He has brought us out of the land of Egypt to deliver us into the hands of the Amorites to destroy us" (Deut. 1:27). The Jews witnessed the judgments upon the Egyptians and the slaying of their firstborn – and "our forefathers in Egypt did not understand Your wonders; they did not remember Your manifold deeds of kindness; and they were rebellious by the sea, the Sea of Reeds" (Ps. 106:7). God gave us the wealth of the Egyptians, and the prophet Hosea pictures the Almighty weeping with the realization that "I gave her [My people] much silver and gold and they made it for *baal* [the Golden Calf]" (2:10).

God split the sea, brought us through it dry, and drowned our enemies in it. But although He split the sea and took them across, He made the water stand as a heap, He led them with a cloud by day and all night with the light of fire, He split rocks in the desert and gave them to drink from great deeps,

Had He provided for our needs
  for forty years in the desert,
    without feeding us with manna,
      that would have been enough.

Had He fed us with manna
  without giving us Shabbat,
    that would have been enough.

Had He given us Shabbat
  without drawing us close
  around Mount Sinai,
    that would have been enough.

Had He drawn us close around Mount Sinai
  without giving us the Torah,
    that would have been enough.

Had He given us the Torah
  without bringing us to the land of Israel,
    that would have been enough.

Had He brought us to the land of Israel
  without building for us
  the House He chose
    that would have been enough.

Dayeinu is not an attempt to sum up God's gifts in the past; it is a sincere effort to atone for all the moments when we responded to God's beneficence with the disparagement and belittling of ungrateful children. We stand ashamed for not having appreciated every part of the story, from the Exodus to Sinai as well as to the Holy Land. *Dayeinu* is telling God we regret beyond words having been ingrates in the past so that on Passover night we may pledge eternal gratitude for all of His gifts in the future.

אִלּוּ סִפֵּק צָרְכֵּנוּ בַּמִּדְבָּר אַרְבָּעִים שָׁנָה
וְלֹא הֶאֱכִילָנוּ אֶת הַמָּן   דַּיֵּנוּ

אִלּוּ הֶאֱכִילָנוּ אֶת הַמָּן
וְלֹא נָתַן לָנוּ אֶת הַשַּׁבָּת   דַּיֵּנוּ

אִלּוּ נָתַן לָנוּ אֶת הַשַּׁבָּת
וְלֹא קֵרְבָנוּ לִפְנֵי הַר סִינַי   דַּיֵּנוּ

אִלּוּ קֵרְבָנוּ לִפְנֵי הַר סִינַי
וְלֹא נָתַן לָנוּ אֶת הַתּוֹרה   דַּיֵּנוּ

אִלּוּ נָתַן לָנוּ אֶת הַתּוֹרה
וְלֹא הִכְנִיסָנוּ לְאֶרֶץ יִשְׂרָאֵל   דַּיֵּנוּ

אִלּוּ הִכְנִיסָנוּ לְאֶרֶץ יִשְׂרָאֵל
וְלֹא בָנָה לָנוּ אֶת
בֵּית הַבְּחִירָה   דַּיֵּנוּ

There are far more than fifteen things which would warrant our saying to God "for this alone You deserve thanks." In fact:

If our mouths were as full of song as the sea, and our tongues with jubilation as its myriad waves, if our lips were full of praise like the spacious heavens, and our eyes shone like the sun and moon, if our hands were outstretched like eagles of the sky, and our feet as swift as hinds, still we could not thank You enough Lord our God and God of our ancestors or bless Your name for even one of the thousand thousands and myriad myriads of favors You did for our ancestors and for us. (Shabbat morning service)

עַל אַחַת כַּמָּה וְכַמָּה

HOW MANY
AND MANIFOLD THEN,
THE OMNIPRESENT'S KINDNESSES
ARE TO US –

for He brought us out of Egypt
and brought judgment upon
[our oppressors]
and upon their gods,
and He killed their firstborn sons
and gave us their wealth,
and He split the sea for us
and brought us through it on dry land
and drowned our enemies there,
and He provided for our needs
for forty years in the desert
and fed us manna,
and He gave us Shabbat,
and He drew us close
around Mount Sinai
and gave us the Torah,
and He brought us
to the land of Israel
and built for us the House He chose,

SO WE
COULD FIND
ATONEMENT [THERE]
FOR ALL OUR SINS.

עַל אַחַת

כַּמָּה וְכַמָּה

טוֹבָה כְּפוּלָה וּמְכֻפֶּלֶת

לַמָּקוֹם עָלֵינוּ

שֶׁהוֹצִיאָנוּ מִמִּצְרַיִם

וְעָשָׂה בָהֶם שְׁפָטִים

וְעָשָׂה בֵאלֹהֵיהֶם

וְהָרַג בְּכוֹרֵיהֶם

וְנָתַן לָנוּ אֶת מָמוֹנָם

וְקָרַע לָנוּ אֶת הַיָּם

וְהֶעֱבִירָנוּ בְתוֹכוֹ בֶּחָרָבָה

וְשִׁקַּע צָרֵינוּ בְּתוֹכוֹ

וְסִפֵּק צָרְכֵּנוּ בַּמִּדְבָּר אַרְבָּעִים שָׁנָה

וְהֶאֱכִילָנוּ אֶת הַמָּן

וְנָתַן לָנוּ אֶת הַשַּׁבָּת

וְקֵרְבָנוּ לִפְנֵי הַר סִינַי

וְנָתַן לָנוּ אֶת הַתּוֹרָה

וְהִכְנִיסָנוּ לְאֶרֶץ יִשְׂרָאֵל

וּבָנָה לָנוּ אֶת בֵּית הַבְּחִירָה

לְכַפֵּר עַל כָּל עֲוֹנוֹתֵינוּ.

רַבָּן גַּמְלִיאֵל **Rabban Gamliel** would say:
Anyone who does not say
these three things on Pesaḥ
has not fulfilled his obligation,
and these are they:

PESAH, MATZA, AND BITTER HERBS.

The
PESAH

is what our ancestors would eat
while the Temple stood:
and what does it recall?
It recalls the Holy One's
passing over (*Pasaḥ*) the houses
of our ancestors in Egypt,
as it is said:
"You shall say: *Ex. 12*
'It is a Pesaḥ offering for the LORD,
for He passed
over the houses of the children of Israel in Egypt
while He struck the Egyptians,
but saved those in our homes' –
and the people bowed
and prostrated themselves."

רַבָּן גַּמְלִיאֵל הָיָה אוֹמֵר
כָּל שֶׁלֹּא אָמַר שְׁלוֹשָׁה דְבָרִים אֵלּוּ בַּפֶּסַח
לֹא יָצָא יְדֵי חוֹבָתוֹ
וְאֵלּוּ הֵן

פֶּסַח מַצָּה וּמָרוֹר

פֶּסַח

שֶׁהָיוּ אֲבוֹתֵינוּ אוֹכְלִים
בִּזְמַן שֶׁבֵּית הַמִּקְדָּשׁ הָיָה קַיָּם
עַל שׁוּם מָה
עַל שׁוּם שֶׁפָּסַח הַקָּדוֹשׁ בָּרוּךְ הוּא
עַל בָּתֵּי אֲבוֹתֵינוּ בְּמִצְרַיִם
שֶׁנֶּאֱמַר

שמות יב

וַאֲמַרְתֶּם זֶבַח־פֶּסַח הוּא לַיהוה
אֲשֶׁר פָּסַח עַל־בָּתֵּי בְנֵי־יִשְׂרָאֵל בְּמִצְרַיִם
בְּנָגְפּוֹ אֶת־מִצְרַיִם
וְאֶת־בָּתֵּינוּ הִצִּיל
וַיִּקֹּד הָעָם וַיִּשְׁתַּחֲווּ:

The matzot are now lifted:

THIS MATZA

that we eat:
what does it recall?
It recalls the dough of our ancestors,
which did not have time to rise
before the King, King of kings,
the Holy One, blessed be He,
revealed Himself and redeemed them,
as it is said:
"They baked the dough   *Ex. 12*
that they had brought out of Egypt
into unleavened cakes, for it had not risen,
for they were cast out of Egypt
and could not delay,
and they made no provision for the way."

The bitter herbs are now lifted:

THESE BITTER HERBS

that we eat:
what do they recall?
They recall the bitterness
that the Egyptians imposed
on the lives of our ancestors in Egypt,
as it is said:
"They embittered their lives with hard labor,   *Ex. 1*
with clay and with bricks
and with all field labors, with all the work
with which they enslaved them – hard labor."

The מצות *are now lifted:*

מַצָּה זוֹ

שֶׁאָנוּ אוֹכְלִים, עַל שׁוּם מָה

עַל שׁוּם שֶׁלֹּא הִסְפִּיק בְּצֵקָם שֶׁל אֲבוֹתֵינוּ לְהַחֲמִיץ

עַד שֶׁנִּגְלָה עֲלֵיהֶם מֶלֶךְ מַלְכֵי הַמְּלָכִים

הַקָּדוֹשׁ בָּרוּךְ הוּא, וּגְאָלָם

שֶׁנֶּאֱמַר

וַיֹּאפוּ אֶת־הַבָּצֵק אֲשֶׁר הוֹצִיאוּ מִמִּצְרַיִם

עֻגֹת מַצּוֹת, כִּי לֹא חָמֵץ

כִּי־גֹרְשׁוּ מִמִּצְרַיִם, וְלֹא יָכְלוּ לְהִתְמַהְמֵהַּ

וְגַם־צֵדָה לֹא־עָשׂוּ לָהֶם:

שמות יב

The bitter herbs are now lifted:

מָרוֹר זֶה

שֶׁאָנוּ אוֹכְלִים עַל שׁוּם מָה

עַל שׁוּם שֶׁמֵּרְרוּ הַמִּצְרִים אֶת חַיֵּי אֲבוֹתֵינוּ בְּמִצְרָיִם

שֶׁנֶּאֱמַר

וַיְמָרְרוּ אֶת־חַיֵּיהֶם בַּעֲבֹדָה קָשָׁה,

בְּחֹמֶר וּבִלְבֵנִים

וּבְכָל־עֲבֹדָה בַּשָּׂדֶה

אֵת כָּל־עֲבֹדָתָם אֲשֶׁר־עָבְדוּ בָהֶם בְּפָרֶךְ:

שמות א

בְּכָל דּוֹר וָדוֹר

GENERATION BY GENERATION,

each person must see himself
as if he himself had come out of Egypt,

Pesaḥim 119b

as it is said:

> "And you shall tell your child on that day,

Ex. 13

> 'Because of this the LORD acted for me
> when I came out of Egypt.'"
> It was not only our ancestors
> whom the Holy One redeemed;
> He redeemed us too along with them,

as it is said:

> "He took us out of there,

Deut. 6

> to bring us to the land
> He promised our ancestors
> and to give it to us."

The matzot are covered and the cup is raised.

לְפִיכָךְ Therefore it is our duty
to thank, praise, laud,
glorify, exalt, honor,
bless, raise high, and acclaim
the One who has performed all these miracles
for our ancestors and for us;
who has brought us out from slavery to freedom,
from sorrow to joy, from grief to celebration;
from darkness to great light
and from enslavement to redemption;
and so we shall sing a new song before Him.

HALLELUYA!

בְּכָל דּוֹר וָדוֹר

פסחים קטז:

חַיָּב אָדָם לִרְאוֹת אֶת עַצְמוֹ כְּאִלּוּ הוּא יָצָא מִמִּצְרַיִם

שֶׁנֶּאֱמַר

שמות יג

וְהִגַּדְתָּ לְבִנְךָ בַּיּוֹם הַהוּא

לֵאמֹר

בַּעֲבוּר זֶה

עָשָׂה יהוה לִי בְּצֵאתִי מִמִּצְרָיִם:

לֹא אֶת אֲבוֹתֵינוּ בִּלְבָד

גָּאַל הַקָּדוֹשׁ בָּרוּךְ הוּא

אֶלָּא אַף אוֹתָנוּ גָּאַל עִמָּהֶם

שֶׁנֶּאֱמַר

דברים ו

וְאוֹתָנוּ הוֹצִיא מִשָּׁם

לְמַעַן הָבִיא אֹתָנוּ לָתֶת לָנוּ אֶת־הָאָרֶץ

אֲשֶׁר נִשְׁבַּע לַאֲבֹתֵינוּ:

The מצות are covered and the cup is raised.

לְפִיכָךְ אֲנַחְנוּ חַיָּבִים

לְהוֹדוֹת, לְהַלֵּל, לְשַׁבֵּחַ, לְפָאֵר

לְרוֹמֵם, לְהַדֵּר, לְבָרֵךְ, לְעַלֵּה וּלְקַלֵּס

לְמִי שֶׁעָשָׂה לַאֲבוֹתֵינוּ וְלָנוּ אֶת כָּל הַנִּסִּים הָאֵלֶּה

הוֹצִיאָנוּ מֵעַבְדוּת לְחֵרוּת, מִיָּגוֹן לְשִׂמְחָה

מֵאֵבֶל לְיוֹם טוֹב וּמֵאֲפֵלָה לְאוֹר גָּדוֹל

וּמִשִּׁעְבּוּד לִגְאֻלָּה וְנֹאמַר לְפָנָיו שִׁירָה חֲדָשָׁה

הַלְלוּיָהּ.

The cup is put down.

הַלְלוּיָהּ **HALLELUYA!**   Ps. 113

Servants of the LORD, give praise;
praise the name of the LORD.
Blessed be the name of the LORD, now and for evermore.
From the rising of the sun to its setting,
may the LORD's name be praised.
High is the LORD above all nations;
His glory is above the heavens.
Who is like the LORD our God, who sits enthroned so high,
yet turns so low to see the heavens and the earth?
He raises the poor from the dust
and the needy from the refuse heap,
giving them a place alongside princes,
the princes of His people.
He makes the woman in a childless house
a happy mother of children.

HALLELUYA!

בְּצֵאת When Israel came out of Egypt,   Ps. 114
the house of Jacob from a people of foreign tongue,
Judah became His sanctuary, Israel His dominion.
The sea saw and fled; the Jordan turned back.
The mountains skipped like rams, the hills like lambs.
Why was it, sea, that you fled? Jordan, why did you turn back?
Why, mountains, did you skip like rams,
and you, hills, like lambs?
It was at the presence of the LORD, Creator of the earth,
at the presence of the God of Jacob,
who turned the rock into a pool of water,
flint into a flowing spring.

The cup is put down.

הַלְלוּיָהּ

הַלְלוּ עַבְדֵי יהוה, הַלְלוּ אֶת־שֵׁם יהוה:

יְהִי שֵׁם יהוה מְבֹרָךְ, מֵעַתָּה וְעַד־עוֹלָם:

מִמִּזְרַח־שֶׁמֶשׁ עַד־מְבוֹאוֹ, מְהֻלָּל שֵׁם יהוה:

רָם עַל־כָּל־גּוֹיִם יהוה, עַל הַשָּׁמַיִם כְּבוֹדוֹ:

מִי כַּיהוה אֱלֹהֵינוּ, הַמַּגְבִּיהִי לָשָׁבֶת:

הַמַּשְׁפִּילִי לִרְאוֹת, בַּשָּׁמַיִם וּבָאָרֶץ:

מְקִימִי מֵעָפָר דָּל, מֵאַשְׁפֹּת יָרִים אֶבְיוֹן:

לְהוֹשִׁיבִי עִם־נְדִיבִים, עִם נְדִיבֵי עַמּוֹ:

מוֹשִׁיבִי עֲקֶרֶת הַבַּיִת, אֵם־הַבָּנִים שְׂמֵחָה

הַלְלוּיָהּ:

בְּצֵאת יִשְׂרָאֵל מִמִּצְרָיִם, בֵּית יַעֲקֹב מֵעַם לֹעֵז:

הָיְתָה יְהוּדָה לְקָדְשׁוֹ, יִשְׂרָאֵל מַמְשְׁלוֹתָיו:

הַיָּם רָאָה וַיָּנֹס, הַיַּרְדֵּן יִסֹּב לְאָחוֹר:

הֶהָרִים רָקְדוּ כְאֵילִים, גְּבָעוֹת כִּבְנֵי־צֹאן:

מַה־לְּךָ הַיָּם כִּי תָנוּס, הַיַּרְדֵּן תִּסֹּב לְאָחוֹר:

הֶהָרִים תִּרְקְדוּ כְאֵילִים, גְּבָעוֹת כִּבְנֵי־צֹאן:

מִלִּפְנֵי אָדוֹן חוּלִי אָרֶץ, מִלִּפְנֵי אֱלוֹהַּ יַעֲקֹב:

הַהֹפְכִי הַצּוּר אֲגַם־מָיִם, חַלָּמִישׁ לְמַעְיְנוֹ־מָיִם:

The cup is raised.

בָּרוּךְ Blessed are You, LORD our God,
King of the Universe,
who has redeemed us
and redeemed our ancestors from Egypt,
and brought us to this night
to eat matza and bitter herbs.
So may the LORD our God bring us in peace
to other seasons and festivals
that are coming to us,
happy in the building of Your city
and rejoicing in Your service;
and there we shall eat of sacrifices
and Pesah offerings
[*On Motza'ei Shabbat:* of Pesah offerings and sacrifices],
of which the blood will reach
the side of Your altar to be accepted.
And we shall thank You in a new song
for our redemption
and for our lives' salvation.
Blessed are You, LORD, Redeemer of Israel.

Blessed are You, LORD our God, King of the Universe,
who creates the fruit of the vine.

Drink while reclining to the left.

RAHTZA / WASHING

In preparation for the meal,
all participants wash their hands and recite the blessing:

בָּרוּךְ Blessed are You, LORD our God,
King of the Universe,
who has made us holy through His commandments,
and has commanded us about washing hands.

The cup is raised.

בָּרוּךְ אַתָּה יהוה אֱלֹהֵינוּ מֶלֶךְ הָעוֹלָם
אֲשֶׁר גְּאָלָנוּ, וְגָאַל אֶת אֲבוֹתֵינוּ מִמִּצְרַיִם
וְהִגִּיעָנוּ הַלַּיְלָה הַזֶּה, לֶאֱכָל בּוֹ מַצָּה וּמָרוֹר.
כֵּן יהוה אֱלֹהֵינוּ וֵאלֹהֵי אֲבוֹתֵינוּ
יַגִּיעֵנוּ לְמוֹעֲדִים וְלִרְגָלִים אֲחֵרִים
הַבָּאִים לִקְרָאתֵנוּ לְשָׁלוֹם
שְׂמֵחִים בְּבִנְיַן עִירֶךָ וְשָׂשִׂים בַּעֲבוֹדָתֶךָ
וְנֹאכַל שָׁם
מִן הַזְּבָחִים וּמִן הַפְּסָחִים
‏/מוצאי שבת ‎*On:* מִן הַפְּסָחִים וּמִן הַזְּבָחִים/
אֲשֶׁר יַגִּיעַ דָּמָם עַל קִיר מִזְבַּחֲךָ לְרָצוֹן
וְנוֹדֶה לְךָ שִׁיר חָדָשׁ
עַל גְּאֻלָּתֵנוּ וְעַל פְּדוּת נַפְשֵׁנוּ
בָּרוּךְ אַתָּה יהוה, גָּאַל יִשְׂרָאֵל.

בָּרוּךְ אַתָּה יהוה אֱלֹהֵינוּ מֶלֶךְ הָעוֹלָם, בּוֹרֵא פְּרִי הַגָּפֶן.

Drink while reclining to the left.

רחצה

In preparation for the meal,
all participants wash their hands and recite the blessing:

בָּרוּךְ אַתָּה יהוה אֱלֹהֵינוּ מֶלֶךְ הָעוֹלָם
אֲשֶׁר קִדְּשָׁנוּ בְּמִצְוֹתָיו
וְצִוָּנוּ עַל נְטִילַת יָדָיִם.

MOTZI MATZA

The leader holds all three matzot and recites:

בָּרוּךְ Blessed are You, LORD our God,
King of the Universe,
who brings forth bread from the earth.

The lowermost matza is replaced.

*The leader recites the following blessing while holding
the uppermost and middle matzot:*

בָּרוּךְ Blessed are You, LORD our God,
King of the Universe, who has made us holy
through His commandments,
and has commanded us to eat matza.

*A piece of the uppermost matza, together with a piece of the middle matza,
is given to each member of the company.
Eat while reclining to the left.*

MAROR / BITTER HERBS

The maror is dipped in the ḥaroset before it is eaten.

בָּרוּךְ Blessed are You, LORD our God,
King of the Universe,
who has made us holy through His commandments,
and has commanded us to eat bitter herbs.

KOREKH / WRAPPING

*Bitter herbs are sandwiched between two pieces of matza
taken from the lowermost matza.*

זֵכֶר In memory of the Temple, in the tradition of Hillel.
This is what Hillel would do when the Temple still
stood:
he would wrap [the Pesaḥ offering] up
with matza and bitter herbs, and eat them together,
to fulfill what is said:
"You shall eat it with matza and bitter herbs."   *Num. 9*

Eat while reclining to the left.

מוציא מצה

The leader holds all three מצות *and recites:*

בָּרוּךְ אַתָּה יהוה אֱלֹהֵינוּ מֶלֶךְ הָעוֹלָם
הַמּוֹצִיא לֶחֶם מִן הָאָרֶץ.

The lowermost מצה *is replaced.*

The leader recites the following blessing
while holding the uppermost and middle מצות:

בָּרוּךְ אַתָּה יהוה אֱלֹהֵינוּ מֶלֶךְ הָעוֹלָם
אֲשֶׁר קִדְּשָׁנוּ בְּמִצְוֹתָיו
וְצִוָּנוּ עַל אֲכִילַת מַצָּה.

A piece of the uppermost מצה, *together with a piece of the middle* מצה,
is given to each member of the company.
Eat while reclining to the left.

מרור

The מרור *is dipped in the* חרוסת *before it is eaten.*

בָּרוּךְ אַתָּה יהוה אֱלֹהֵינוּ מֶלֶךְ הָעוֹלָם
אֲשֶׁר קִדְּשָׁנוּ בְּמִצְוֹתָיו
וְצִוָּנוּ עַל אֲכִילַת מָרוֹר.

כורך

Bitter herbs are sandwiched between two pieces of מצה
taken from the lowermost מצה.

זֵכֶר לַמִּקְדָּשׁ כְּהִלֵּל.
כֵּן עָשָׂה הִלֵּל בִּזְמַן שֶׁבֵּית הַמִּקְדָּשׁ הָיָה קַיָּם
הָיָה כּוֹרֵךְ פֶּסַח, מַצָּה וּמָרוֹר, וְאוֹכֵל בְּיַחַד
לְקַיֵּם מַה שֶּׁנֶּאֱמַר: עַל־מַצּוֹת וּמְרֹרִים יֹאכְלֻהוּ:

במדבר ט

Eat while reclining to the left.

SHULḤAN OREKH / TABLE SETTING

The festive meal is now eaten.

TZAFUN / HIDDEN

At the end of the meal, the remaining piece
of the middle matza which had been hidden earlier (the afikoman),
is eaten.

BAREKH / BLESSING

The third cup of wine is poured.

שִׁיר הַמַּעֲלוֹת A song of ascents.   *Ps. 126*
When the LORD brought back the exiles of Zion
we were like people who dream.
Then were our mouths filled with laughter,
and our tongues with songs of joy.
Then was it said among the nations,
"The LORD has done great things for them."
The LORD did do great things for us and we rejoiced.
Bring back our exiles, LORD,
like streams in a dry land.
May those who sowed in tears, reap in joy.
May one who goes out weeping,
carrying a bag of seed,
come back with songs of joy,
carrying his sheaves.

Some say:

תְּהִלַּת My mouth shall speak the praise of God, and all *Ps. 145*
creatures shall bless His holy name for ever and all time. We *Ps. 115*
will bless God now and for ever. Halleluya! Thank the LORD *Ps. 136*
for He is good: His loving-kindness is for ever. Who can tell *Ps. 106*
of the LORD's mighty acts and make all His praise be heard?

שלחן עורך

The festive meal is now eaten.

צפון

At the end of the meal, the remaining piece
of the middle מצה which had been hidden earlier (the אפיקומן),
is eaten.

ברך

The third cup of wine is poured.

תהלים קכו

שִׁיר הַמַּעֲלוֹת

בְּשׁוּב יהוה אֶת־שִׁיבַת צִיּוֹן,

הָיִינוּ כְּחֹלְמִים:

אָז יִמָּלֵא שְׂחוֹק פִּינוּ וּלְשׁוֹנֵנוּ רִנָּה

אָז יֹאמְרוּ בַגּוֹיִם

הִגְדִּיל יהוה לַעֲשׂוֹת עִם־אֵלֶּה:

הִגְדִּיל יהוה לַעֲשׂוֹת עִמָּנוּ, הָיִינוּ שְׂמֵחִים:

שׁוּבָה יהוה אֶת־שְׁבִיתֵנוּ, כַּאֲפִיקִים בַּנֶּגֶב:

הַזֹּרְעִים בְּדִמְעָה, בְּרִנָּה יִקְצֹרוּ:

הָלוֹךְ יֵלֵךְ וּבָכֹה נֹשֵׂא מֶשֶׁךְ־הַזָּרַע

בֹּא־יָבֹא בְרִנָּה נֹשֵׂא אֲלֻמֹּתָיו:

Some say:

תהלים קמה

תְּהִלַּת יהוה יְדַבֶּר פִּי, וִיבָרֵךְ כָּל־בָּשָׂר שֵׁם קָדְשׁוֹ לְעוֹלָם

תהלים קטו

וָעֶד: וַאֲנַחְנוּ נְבָרֵךְ יָהּ מֵעַתָּה וְעַד־עוֹלָם, הַלְלוּיָהּ:

תהלים קלז
תהלים קו

הוֹדוּ לַיהוה כִּי־טוֹב, כִּי לְעוֹלָם חַסְדּוֹ: מִי יְמַלֵּל גְּבוּרוֹת

יהוה, יַשְׁמִיעַ כָּל־תְּהִלָּתוֹ:

ZIMMUN / INVITATION

When three or more men say Birkat haMazon together, the following zimmun is said.
When three or more women say Birkat haMazon, substitute "Friends" for "Gentlemen."
The leader should ask permission from those with precedence to lead the Birkat haMazon.

Leader Gentlemen, let us say grace.

Others May the name of the LORD be blessed from now and for ever. *Ps. 113*

Leader May the name of the LORD be blessed from now and for ever.
With your permission, (my father and teacher / my mother and
teacher / the Kohanim present / our teacher the Rabbi /
the master of this house / the mistress of this house)
my masters and teachers, let us bless (*in a minyan:* our God,)
the One from whose food we have eaten.

Others Blessed be (*in a minyan:* our God,) the One
from whose food we have eaten,
and by whose goodness we live.

> *People present who have not taken part in the meal say:*
> *Blessed be (*in a minyan:* our God,) the One
> whose name is continually blessed for ever and all time.

Leader Blessed be (*in a minyan:* our God,) the One
from whose food we have eaten,
and by whose goodness we live.
Blessed be He, and blessed be His name.

BLESSING OF NOURISHMENT

בָּרוּךְ Blessed are You, LORD our God, King of the Universe,
who in His goodness feeds the whole world
with grace, kindness and compassion.
He gives food to all living things, for His kindness is for ever.
Because of His continual great goodness,
we have never lacked food,
nor may we ever lack it for the sake of His great name.
For He is God who feeds and sustains all, does good to all,
and prepares food for all creatures He has created.
Blessed are You, LORD, who feeds all.

סדר הזימון

When three or more men say ברכת המזון *together, the following* זימון *is said.*
When three or more women say ברכת המזון, *substitute* חֲבֵרוֹתַי *for* רַבּוֹתַי.
The leader should ask permission from those with precedence to lead the ברכת המזון.

Leader רַבּוֹתַי, נְבָרֵךְ.

תהלים קיג

Others יְהִי שֵׁם יהוה מְבֹרָךְ מֵעַתָּה וְעַד־עוֹלָם:

Leader יְהִי שֵׁם יהוה מְבֹרָךְ מֵעַתָּה וְעַד־עוֹלָם:

בִּרְשׁוּת (אָבִי מוֹרִי / אִמִּי מוֹרָתִי / כֹּהֲנִים / מוֹרֵנוּ הָרַב /
בַּעַל הַבַּיִת הַזֶּה / בַּעֲלַת הַבַּיִת הַזֶּה)

מָרָנָן וְרַבָּנָן וְרַבּוֹתַי
נְבָרֵךְ (במניין: אֱלֹהֵינוּ) שֶׁאָכַלְנוּ מִשֶּׁלּוֹ.

Others בָּרוּךְ (במניין: אֱלֹהֵינוּ) שֶׁאָכַלְנוּ מִשֶּׁלּוֹ וּבְטוּבוֹ חָיִינוּ.

People present who have not taken part in the meal say:
*בָּרוּךְ (במניין: אֱלֹהֵינוּ) וּמְבֹרָךְ שְׁמוֹ תָּמִיד לְעוֹלָם וָעֶד.

Leader בָּרוּךְ (במניין: אֱלֹהֵינוּ) שֶׁאָכַלְנוּ מִשֶּׁלּוֹ וּבְטוּבוֹ חָיִינוּ.

בָּרוּךְ הוּא וּבָרוּךְ שְׁמוֹ.

ברכת הזן

בָּרוּךְ אַתָּה יהוה אֱלֹהֵינוּ מֶלֶךְ הָעוֹלָם
הַזָּן אֶת הָעוֹלָם כֻּלּוֹ בְּטוּבוֹ בְּחֵן בְּחֶסֶד וּבְרַחֲמִים
הוּא נוֹתֵן לֶחֶם לְכָל בָּשָׂר כִּי לְעוֹלָם חַסְדּוֹ.
וּבְטוּבוֹ הַגָּדוֹל, תָּמִיד לֹא חָסַר לָנוּ
וְאַל יֶחְסַר לָנוּ מָזוֹן לְעוֹלָם וָעֶד בַּעֲבוּר שְׁמוֹ הַגָּדוֹל.
כִּי הוּא אֵל זָן וּמְפַרְנֵס לַכֹּל וּמֵטִיב לַכֹּל
וּמֵכִין מָזוֹן לְכָל בְּרִיּוֹתָיו אֲשֶׁר בָּרָא.
בָּרוּךְ אַתָּה יהוה, הַזָּן אֶת הַכֹּל.

BLESSING OF LAND

נוֹדֶה We thank You,
Lord our God,
for having granted as a heritage to our ancestors
a desirable, good and spacious land;
for bringing us out, Lord our God
from the land of Egypt,
freeing us from the house of slavery;
for Your covenant which You sealed in our flesh;
for Your Torah which You taught us;
for Your laws which You made known to us;
for the life, grace and kindness
You have bestowed on us;
and for the food
by which You continually feed and sustain us,
every day,
every season,
every hour.

For all this, Lord our God,
we thank and bless You.
May Your name be blessed continually
by the mouth of all that lives,
for ever and all time –
for so it is written:
"You will eat and be satisfied,   *Deut. 8*
then you shall bless the Lord your God
for the good land He has given you."
Blessed are You, Lord,
for the land and for the food.

נוֹדֶה לְךָ יהוה אֱלֹהֵינוּ
עַל שֶׁהִנְחַלְתָּ לַאֲבוֹתֵינוּ

אֶרֶץ חֶמְדָּה טוֹבָה וּרְחָבָה
וְעַל שֶׁהוֹצֵאתָנוּ יהוה אֱלֹהֵינוּ
מֵאֶרֶץ מִצְרַיִם
וּפְדִיתָנוּ מִבֵּית עֲבָדִים
וְעַל בְּרִיתְךָ שֶׁחָתַמְתָּ בִּבְשָׂרֵנוּ
וְעַל תּוֹרָתְךָ שֶׁלִּמַּדְתָּנוּ
וְעַל חֻקֶּיךָ שֶׁהוֹדַעְתָּנוּ
וְעַל חַיִּים חֵן וָחֶסֶד שֶׁחוֹנַנְתָּנוּ
וְעַל אֲכִילַת מָזוֹן
שָׁאַתָּה זָן וּמְפַרְנֵס אוֹתָנוּ תָּמִיד
בְּכָל יוֹם וּבְכָל עֵת וּבְכָל שָׁעָה.

וְעַל הַכֹּל, יהוה אֱלֹהֵינוּ
אֲנַחְנוּ מוֹדִים לָךְ וּמְבָרְכִים אוֹתָךְ
יִתְבָּרַךְ שִׁמְךָ בְּפִי כָּל חַי
תָּמִיד לְעוֹלָם וָעֶד
כַּכָּתוּב:
וְאָכַלְתָּ וְשָׂבָעְתָּ,
וּבֵרַכְתָּ אֶת־יהוה אֱלֹהֶיךָ
עַל־הָאָרֶץ הַטֹּבָה אֲשֶׁר נָתַן־לָךְ:
בָּרוּךְ אַתָּה יהוה, עַל הָאָרֶץ וְעַל הַמָּזוֹן.

דברים ח

BLESSING FOR JERUSALEM

רַחֵם נָא Have compassion,
please, LORD our God,
on Israel Your people,
on Jerusalem Your city,
on Zion the dwelling place of Your glory,
on the royal house of David Your anointed,
and on the great and holy House
that bears Your name.
Our God, our Father,
tend us, feed us, sustain us and support us,
relieve us and send us relief,
LORD our God, swiftly from all our troubles.
Please, LORD our God, do not make us dependent
on the gifts or loans of other people,
but only on Your full, open,
holy and generous hand
so that we may suffer neither shame nor humiliation
for ever and all time.

On Shabbat, say:
רְצֵה Favor and strengthen us, LORD our God,
through Your commandments,
especially through the commandment of the seventh day,
this great and holy Sabbath.
For it is, for You, a great and holy day.
On it we cease work and rest in love
in accord with Your will's commandment.
May it be Your will, LORD our God,
to grant us rest without distress,
grief, or lament on our day of rest.
May You show us the consolation of Zion Your city,
and the rebuilding of Jerusalem Your holy city,
for You are the Master of salvation
and consolation.

בִּרְכַּת יְרוּשָׁלַיִם

רַחֶם נָא יהוה אֱלֹהֵינוּ
עַל יִשְׂרָאֵל עַמֶּךָ

וְעַל יְרוּשָׁלַיִם עִירֶךָ

וְעַל צִיּוֹן מִשְׁכַּן כְּבוֹדֶךָ

וְעַל מַלְכוּת בֵּית דָּוִד מְשִׁיחֶךָ

וְעַל הַבַּיִת הַגָּדוֹל וְהַקָּדוֹשׁ שֶׁנִּקְרָא שִׁמְךָ עָלָיו.

אֱלֹהֵינוּ, אָבִינוּ

רְעֵנוּ, זוּנֵנוּ, פַּרְנְסֵנוּ וְכַלְכְּלֵנוּ

וְהַרְוִיחֵנוּ, וְהַרְוַח לָנוּ יהוה אֱלֹהֵינוּ מְהֵרָה מִכָּל צָרוֹתֵינוּ.

וְנָא אַל תַּצְרִיכֵנוּ, יהוה אֱלֹהֵינוּ

לֹא לִידֵי מַתְּנַת בָּשָׂר וָדָם וְלֹא לִידֵי הַלְוָאָתָם

כִּי אִם לְיָדְךָ הַמְּלֵאָה, הַפְּתוּחָה,

הַקְּדוֹשָׁה וְהָרְחָבָה

שֶׁלֹּא נֵבוֹשׁ וְלֹא נִכָּלֵם לְעוֹלָם וָעֶד.

On שבת, say:

רְצֵה וְהַחֲלִיצֵנוּ, יהוה אֱלֹהֵינוּ, בְּמִצְוֺתֶיךָ
וּבְמִצְוַת יוֹם הַשְּׁבִיעִי

הַשַּׁבָּת הַגָּדוֹל וְהַקָּדוֹשׁ הַזֶּה

כִּי יוֹם זֶה גָּדוֹל וְקָדוֹשׁ הוּא לְפָנֶיךָ

לִשְׁבָּת בּוֹ, וְלָנוּחַ בּוֹ בְּאַהֲבָה כְּמִצְוַת רְצוֹנֶךָ

וּבִרְצוֹנְךָ הָנִיחַ לָנוּ, יהוה אֱלֹהֵינוּ

שֶׁלֹּא תְהֵא צָרָה וְיָגוֹן וַאֲנָחָה בְּיוֹם מְנוּחָתֵנוּ

וְהַרְאֵנוּ, יהוה אֱלֹהֵינוּ, בְּנֶחָמַת צִיּוֹן עִירֶךָ

וּבְבִנְיַן יְרוּשָׁלַיִם עִיר קָדְשֶׁךָ

כִּי אַתָּה הוּא בַּעַל הַיְשׁוּעוֹת וּבַעַל הַנֶּחָמוֹת.

אֱלֹהֵינוּ Our God and God of our ancestors,
may there rise, come, reach, appear, be favored, heard, regarded
and remembered before You, our recollection and remembrance,
as well as the remembrance of our ancestors,
and of the Messiah son of David Your servant,
and of Jerusalem Your holy city,
and of all Your people the house of Israel –
for deliverance and well-being, grace, loving-kindness and
compassion, life and peace, on this day of the festival of Matzot.
On it remember us, LORD our God, for good;
recollect us for blessing, and deliver us for life.
In accord with Your promise of salvation and compassion,
spare us and be gracious to us;
have compassion on us and deliver us,
for our eyes are turned to You because You are God,
gracious and compassionate.

And may Jerusalem the holy city be rebuilt soon, in our time.
Blessed are You, LORD, who in His compassion
will rebuild Jerusalem. Amen.

BLESSING OF GOD'S GOODNESS
בָּרוּךְ Blessed are You, LORD our God, King of the Universe –
God our Father, our King, our Sovereign,
our Creator our Redeemer, our Maker,
our Holy One, the Holy One of Jacob.
He is our Shepherd, Israel's Shepherd,
the good King who does good to all.
Every day He has done, is doing, and will do good to us.
He has acted, is acting,
and will always act kindly toward us for ever,
granting us grace, kindness and compassion, relief and rescue,
prosperity, blessing, redemption and comfort,
sustenance and support, compassion, life,
peace and all good things,
and of all good things may He never let us lack.

אֱלֹהֵינוּ וֵאלֹהֵי אֲבוֹתֵינוּ

יַעֲלֶה וְיָבוֹא וְיַגִּיעַ, וְיֵרָאֶה וְיֵרָצֶה וְיִשָּׁמַע, וְיִפָּקֵד
וְיִזָּכֵר זִכְרוֹנֵנוּ וּפִקְדוֹנֵנוּ, וְזִכְרוֹן אֲבוֹתֵינוּ

וְזִכְרוֹן מָשִׁיחַ בֶּן דָּוִד עַבְדֶּךָ, וְזִכְרוֹן יְרוּשָׁלַיִם עִיר קָדְשֶׁךָ
וְזִכְרוֹן כָּל עַמְּךָ בֵּית יִשְׂרָאֵל
לְפָנֶיךָ, לִפְלֵיטָה לְטוֹבָה, לְחֵן וּלְחֶסֶד וּלְרַחֲמִים
לְחַיִּים וּלְשָׁלוֹם בְּיוֹם חַג הַמַּצּוֹת הַזֶּה.
זָכְרֵנוּ יהוה אֱלֹהֵינוּ בּוֹ לְטוֹבָה וּפָקְדֵנוּ בוֹ לִבְרָכָה
וְהוֹשִׁיעֵנוּ בוֹ לְחַיִּים.
וּבִדְבַר יְשׁוּעָה וְרַחֲמִים, חוּס וְחָנֵּנוּ וְרַחֵם עָלֵינוּ, וְהוֹשִׁיעֵנוּ
כִּי אֵלֶיךָ עֵינֵינוּ, כִּי אֵל חַנּוּן וְרַחוּם אָתָּה.

וּבְנֵה יְרוּשָׁלַיִם עִיר הַקֹּדֶשׁ בִּמְהֵרָה בְיָמֵינוּ.
בָּרוּךְ אַתָּה יהוה, בּוֹנֵה בְרַחֲמָיו יְרוּשָׁלָיִם, אָמֵן.

ברכת הטוב והמטיב

בָּרוּךְ אַתָּה יהוה אֱלֹהֵינוּ מֶלֶךְ הָעוֹלָם
הָאֵל אָבִינוּ, מַלְכֵּנוּ, אַדִּירֵנוּ
בּוֹרְאֵנוּ, גּוֹאֲלֵנוּ, יוֹצְרֵנוּ, קְדוֹשֵׁנוּ, קְדוֹשׁ יַעֲקֹב
רוֹעֵנוּ, רוֹעֵה יִשְׂרָאֵל, הַמֶּלֶךְ הַטּוֹב וְהַמֵּטִיב לַכֹּל
שֶׁבְּכָל יוֹם וָיוֹם הוּא הֵיטִיב, הוּא מֵיטִיב, הוּא יֵיטִיב לָנוּ
הוּא גְמָלָנוּ, הוּא גוֹמְלֵנוּ, הוּא יִגְמְלֵנוּ לָעַד
לְחֵן וּלְחֶסֶד וּלְרַחֲמִים, וּלְרֶוַח, הַצָּלָה וְהַצְלָחָה
בְּרָכָה וִישׁוּעָה, נֶחָמָה, פַּרְנָסָה וְכַלְכָּלָה
וְרַחֲמִים וְחַיִּים וְשָׁלוֹם וְכָל טוֹב
וּמִכָּל טוּב לְעוֹלָם אַל יְחַסְּרֵנוּ.

ADDITIONAL REQUESTS

הָרַחֲמָן May the Compassionate One reign over us
for ever and all time.

May the Compassionate One be blessed in heaven and on earth.

May the Compassionate One be praised
from generation to generation,
be glorified by us to all eternity,
and honored among us for ever and all time.

May the Compassionate One
grant us an honorable livelihood.

May the Compassionate One
break the yoke from our neck
and lead us upright to our land.

May the Compassionate One
send us many blessings to this house
and this table at which we have eaten.

May the Compassionate One
send us Elijah the prophet –
may he be remembered for good –
to bring us good tidings of salvation and consolation.

May the Compassionate One
bless the State of Israel, first flowering of our redemption.

May the Compassionate One
bless the members of Israel's Defense Forces,
who stand guard over our land.

A guest says:

יְהִי רָצוֹן May it be Your will that the master of this house shall not suffer
shame in this world, nor humiliation in the World to Come. May all he
owns prosper greatly, and may his and our possessions be successful and
close to hand. Let not the Accuser hold sway over his deeds or ours, and
may no thought of sin, iniquity or transgression enter him or us from
now and for evermore.

בקשות נוספות

הָרַחֲמָן הוּא יִמְלֹךְ עָלֵינוּ לְעוֹלָם וָעֶד.

הָרַחֲמָן הוּא יִתְבָּרַךְ בַּשָּׁמַיִם וּבָאָרֶץ.

הָרַחֲמָן הוּא יִשְׁתַּבַּח לְדוֹר דּוֹרִים

וְיִתְפָּאַר בָּנוּ לָעַד וּלְנֵצַח נְצָחִים

וְיִתְהַדַּר בָּנוּ לָעַד וּלְעוֹלְמֵי עוֹלָמִים.

הָרַחֲמָן הוּא יְפַרְנְסֵנוּ בְּכָבוֹד.

הָרַחֲמָן הוּא יִשְׁבֹּר עֻלֵנוּ מֵעַל צַוָּארֵנוּ

וְהוּא יוֹלִיכֵנוּ קוֹמְמִיּוּת לְאַרְצֵנוּ.

הָרַחֲמָן הוּא יִשְׁלַח לָנוּ

בְּרָכָה מְרֻבָּה בַּבַּיִת הַזֶּה וְעַל שֻׁלְחָן זֶה שֶׁאָכַלְנוּ עָלָיו.

הָרַחֲמָן הוּא יִשְׁלַח לָנוּ

אֶת אֵלִיָּהוּ הַנָּבִיא זָכוּר לַטּוֹב

וִיבַשֶּׂר לָנוּ בְּשׂוֹרוֹת טוֹבוֹת יְשׁוּעוֹת וְנֶחָמוֹת.

הָרַחֲמָן הוּא יְבָרֵךְ

אֶת מְדִינַת יִשְׂרָאֵל רֵאשִׁית צְמִיחַת גְּאֻלָּתֵנוּ.

הָרַחֲמָן הוּא יְבָרֵךְ

אֶת חַיָּלֵי צְבָא הַהֲגַנָּה לְיִשְׂרָאֵל

הָעוֹמְדִים עַל מִשְׁמַר אַרְצֵנוּ.

A guest says:

יְהִי רָצוֹן שֶׁלֹּא יֵבוֹשׁ בַּעַל הַבַּיִת בָּעוֹלָם הַזֶּה, וְלֹא יִכָּלֵם לָעוֹלָם הַבָּא, וְיִצְלַח מְאֹד בְּכָל נְכָסָיו, וְיִהְיוּ נְכָסָיו וּנְכָסֵינוּ מֻצְלָחִים וּקְרוֹבִים לָעִיר, וְאַל יִשְׁלֹט שָׂטָן לֹא בְּמַעֲשֵׂה יָדָיו וְלֹא בְּמַעֲשֵׂה יָדֵינוּ. וְאַל יִזְדַּקֵּר לֹא לְפָנָיו וְלֹא לְפָנֵינוּ שׁוּם דְּבַר הִרְהוּר חֵטְא, עֲבֵירָה וְעָוֹן, מֵעַתָּה וְעַד עוֹלָם.

הָרַחֲמָן May the Compassionate One bless –

When eating at one's own table, say (include the words in parentheses that apply):
me, (my wife / husband / my father, my teacher / my mother,
my teacher / my children) and all that is mine,

A guest at someone else's table says (include the words in parentheses that apply):
the master of this house, him (and his wife, the mistress of
this house / and his children) and all that is his,

Children at their parents' table say (include the words in parentheses that apply):
my father, my teacher (master of this house), and my mother,
my teacher (mistress of this house), them, their household,
their children, and all that is theirs.

For all other guests, add:
and all the diners here,

אוֹתָנוּ – together with us and all that is ours. Just as our forefathers
Abraham, Isaac and Jacob were blessed in all, from all, with all,
so may He bless all of us together with a complete blessing,
and let us say: Amen.

בַּמָּרוֹם On high, may grace be invoked for them and for us,
as a safeguard of peace.
May we receive a blessing from the LORD
and a just reward from the God of our salvation,
and may we find grace and good favor in the eyes of God and man.

On Shabbat: May the Compassionate One let us inherit
the time, that will be entirely Shabbat
and rest for life everlasting.

May the Compassionate One let us inherit the day, that is all good.

הָרַחֲמָן May the Compassionate One make us worthy
of the Messianic Age and life in the World to Come.
He is a tower of salvation to His king,   *II Sam. 22*
showing kindness to His anointed,
to David and his descendants for ever.
He who makes peace in His high places,
may He make peace for us and all Israel, and let us say: Amen.

הָרַחֲמָן הוּא יְבָרֵךְ

When eating at one's own table, say (include the words in parentheses that apply):

אוֹתִי (וְאֶת אִשְׁתִּי / וְאֶת בַּעְלִי / וְאֶת אָבִי מוֹרִי / וְאֶת אִמִּי מוֹרָתִי / וְאֶת זַרְעִי) וְאֶת כָּל אֲשֶׁר לִי.

A guest at someone else's table says (include the words in parentheses that apply):

אֶת בַּעַל הַבַּיִת הַזֶּה, אוֹתוֹ (וְאֶת אִשְׁתּוֹ בַּעֲלַת הַבַּיִת הַזֶּה / וְאֶת זַרְעוֹ) וְאֶת כָּל אֲשֶׁר לוֹ.

Children at their parents' table say (include the words in parentheses that apply):

אֶת אָבִי מוֹרִי (בַּעַל הַבַּיִת הַזֶּה), וְאֶת אִמִּי מוֹרָתִי (בַּעֲלַת הַבַּיִת הַזֶּה), אוֹתָם וְאֶת בֵּיתָם וְאֶת זַרְעָם וְאֶת כָּל אֲשֶׁר לָהֶם

For all other guests, add:

וְאֶת כָּל הַמְּסֻבִּין כָּאן

אוֹתָנוּ וְאֶת כָּל אֲשֶׁר לָנוּ כְּמוֹ שֶׁנִּתְבָּרְכוּ אֲבוֹתֵינוּ אַבְרָהָם יִצְחָק וְיַעֲקֹב, בַּכֹּל, מִכֹּל, כֹּל כֵּן יְבָרֵךְ אוֹתָנוּ כֻּלָּנוּ יַחַד בִּבְרָכָה שְׁלֵמָה, וְנֹאמַר אָמֵן.

בַּמָּרוֹם יְלַמְּדוּ עֲלֵיהֶם וְעָלֵינוּ זְכוּת שֶׁתְּהֵא לְמִשְׁמֶרֶת שָׁלוֹם וְנִשָּׂא בְרָכָה מֵאֵת יהוה וּצְדָקָה מֵאֱלֹהֵי יִשְׁעֵנוּ וְנִמְצָא חֵן וְשֵׂכֶל טוֹב בְּעֵינֵי אֱלֹהִים וְאָדָם.

בשבת: הָרַחֲמָן הוּא יַנְחִילֵנוּ יוֹם שֶׁכֻּלּוֹ שַׁבָּת וּמְנוּחָה לְחַיֵּי הָעוֹלָמִים.

הָרַחֲמָן הוּא יַנְחִילֵנוּ יוֹם שֶׁכֻּלּוֹ טוֹב.

הָרַחֲמָן הוּא יְזַכֵּנוּ לִימוֹת הַמָּשִׁיחַ וּלְחַיֵּי הָעוֹלָם הַבָּא מִגְדּוֹל יְשׁוּעוֹת מַלְכּוֹ וְעֹשֶׂה־חֶסֶד לִמְשִׁיחוֹ לְדָוִד וּלְזַרְעוֹ עַד־עוֹלָם:

עֹשֶׂה שָׁלוֹם בִּמְרוֹמָיו הוּא יַעֲשֶׂה שָׁלוֹם עָלֵינוּ וְעַל כָּל יִשְׂרָאֵל וְאִמְרוּ אָמֵן.

יִרְאוּ Fear the LORD, you His holy ones;   *Ps. 34*
those who fear Him lack nothing.
Young lions may grow weak and hungry,
but those who seek the LORD lack no good thing.
Thank the LORD for He is good: *Ps. 118*
His loving-kindness is for ever.
You open Your hand and satisfy the desire of every living thing.   *Ps. 145*
Blessed is the person who trusts in the LORD,   *Jer. 17*
whose trust is in the LORD alone.
Once I was young, and now I am old,   *Ps. 37*
yet I have never watched a righteous man forsaken
or his children begging for bread.
The LORD will give His people strength.   *Ps. 29*
The LORD will bless His people with peace.

Blessed are You, LORD our God, King of the Universe,
who creates the fruit of the vine.

Drink while reclining to the left.

A cup of wine is now poured in honor of Elijah, and the door opened.

שְׁפֹךְ POUR OUT Your rage   *Ps. 79*
   upon the nations that do not know You,
   and on regimes that have not called upon Your name.
   For Jacob is devoured;
   they have laid his places waste.
   Pour out Your great anger upon them,   *Ps. 69*
   and let Your blazing fury overtake them.
   Pursue them in Your fury and destroy them   *Lam. 3*
   from under the heavens of the LORD.

תהילים לד

יְראוּ אֶת־יהוה קְדֹשָׁיו
כִּי־אֵין מַחְסוֹר לִירֵאָיו:
כְּפִירִים רָשׁוּ וְרָעֵבוּ
וְדֹרְשֵׁי יהוה לֹא־יַחְסְרוּ כָל־טוֹב:

תהילים קיח

הוֹדוּ לַיהוה כִּי־טוֹב כִּי לְעוֹלָם חַסְדּוֹ:

תהילים קמה

פּוֹתֵחַ אֶת־יָדֶךָ וּמַשְׂבִּיעַ לְכָל־חַי רָצוֹן:

ירמיה יז

בָּרוּךְ הַגֶּבֶר אֲשֶׁר יִבְטַח בַּיהוה
וְהָיָה יהוה מִבְטַחוֹ:

תהילים לז

נַעַר הָיִיתִי גַּם־זָקַנְתִּי
וְלֹא־רָאִיתִי צַדִּיק נֶעֱזָב וְזַרְעוֹ מְבַקֶּשׁ־לָחֶם:

תהילים כט

יהוה עֹז לְעַמּוֹ יִתֵּן
יהוה יְבָרֵךְ אֶת־עַמּוֹ בַשָּׁלוֹם:

בָּרוּךְ אַתָּה יהוה אֱלֹהֵינוּ מֶלֶךְ הָעוֹלָם
בּוֹרֵא פְּרִי הַגָּפֶן.

Drink while reclining to the left.

A cup of wine is now poured in honor of Elijah, and the door opened.

תהילים עט

שְׁפֹךְ חֲמָתְךָ אֶל־הַגּוֹיִם אֲשֶׁר לֹא־יְדָעוּךָ
וְעַל מַמְלָכוֹת אֲשֶׁר בְּשִׁמְךָ לֹא קָרָאוּ:
כִּי אָכַל אֶת־יַעֲקֹב, וְאֶת־נָוֵהוּ הֵשַׁמּוּ:

תהילים סט

שְׁפָךְ־עֲלֵיהֶם זַעְמֶךָ וַחֲרוֹן אַפְּךָ יַשִּׂיגֵם:

איכה ג

תִּרְדֹּף בְּאַף וְתַשְׁמִידֵם מִתַּחַת שְׁמֵי יהוה:

HALLEL / PRAISING

The fourth cup of wine is poured, and Hallel is completed.

לֹא לָנוּ Not to us, LORD, not to us,   *Ps. 115*
but to Your name give glory,
for Your love, for Your faithfulness.
Why should the nations say, "Where now is their God?"
Our God is in heaven; whatever He wills He does.
Their idols are silver and gold, made by human hands.
They have mouths but cannot speak; eyes but cannot see.
They have ears but cannot hear; noses but cannot smell.
They have hands but cannot feel; feet but cannot walk.
No sound comes from their throat.
Those who make them become like them;
so will all who trust in them.
Israel, trust in the LORD –
He is their Help and their Shield.
House of Aaron, trust in the LORD –
He is their Help and their Shield.
You who fear the LORD, trust in the LORD –
He is their Help and their Shield.

יהוה זְכָרָנוּ The LORD remembers us and will bless us.
He will bless the house of Israel.
He will bless the house of Aaron.
He will bless those who fear the LORD, small and great alike.
May the LORD give you increase: you and your children.
May you be blessed by the LORD, Maker of heaven and earth.
The heavens are the LORD's,
but the earth He has given over to mankind.
It is not the dead who praise the LORD,
nor those who go down to the silent grave.
But we will bless the LORD, now and for ever.

HALLELUYA!

הלל

The fourth cup of wine is poured, and הלל *is completed.*

לֹא לָנוּ יהוה לֹא לָנוּ

כִּי־לְשִׁמְךָ תֵּן כָּבוֹד

עַל־חַסְדְּךָ עַל־אֲמִתֶּךָ:

לָמָּה יֹאמְרוּ הַגּוֹיִם אַיֵּה־נָא אֱלֹהֵיהֶם:

וֵאלֹהֵינוּ בַשָּׁמָיִם, כֹּל אֲשֶׁר־חָפֵץ עָשָׂה:

עֲצַבֵּיהֶם כֶּסֶף וְזָהָב, מַעֲשֵׂה יְדֵי אָדָם:

פֶּה־לָהֶם וְלֹא יְדַבֵּרוּ, עֵינַיִם לָהֶם וְלֹא יִרְאוּ:

אָזְנַיִם לָהֶם וְלֹא יִשְׁמָעוּ, אַף לָהֶם וְלֹא יְרִיחוּן:

יְדֵיהֶם וְלֹא יְמִישׁוּן, רַגְלֵיהֶם וְלֹא יְהַלֵּכוּ, לֹא־יֶהְגּוּ בִּגְרוֹנָם:

כְּמוֹהֶם יִהְיוּ עֹשֵׂיהֶם, כֹּל אֲשֶׁר־בֹּטֵחַ בָּהֶם:

יִשְׂרָאֵל בְּטַח בַּיהוה, עֶזְרָם וּמָגִנָּם הוּא:

בֵּית אַהֲרֹן בִּטְחוּ בַיהוה, עֶזְרָם וּמָגִנָּם הוּא:

יִרְאֵי יהוה בִּטְחוּ בַיהוה, עֶזְרָם וּמָגִנָּם הוּא:

יהוה זְכָרָנוּ יְבָרֵךְ

יְבָרֵךְ אֶת־בֵּית יִשְׂרָאֵל, יְבָרֵךְ אֶת־בֵּית אַהֲרֹן:

יְבָרֵךְ יִרְאֵי יהוה, הַקְּטַנִּים עִם־הַגְּדֹלִים:

יֹסֵף יהוה עֲלֵיכֶם, עֲלֵיכֶם וְעַל־בְּנֵיכֶם:

בְּרוּכִים אַתֶּם לַיהוה, עֹשֵׂה שָׁמַיִם וָאָרֶץ:

הַשָּׁמַיִם שָׁמַיִם לַיהוה, וְהָאָרֶץ נָתַן לִבְנֵי־אָדָם:

לֹא הַמֵּתִים יְהַלְלוּ־יָהּ, וְלֹא כָּל־יֹרְדֵי דוּמָה:

וַאֲנַחְנוּ נְבָרֵךְ יָהּ, מֵעַתָּה וְעַד־עוֹלָם

הַלְלוּיָהּ:

אָהַבְתִּי I love the Lord, *Ps. 116*
for He hears my voice, my pleas.
He turns His ear to me whenever I call.
The bonds of death encompassed me,
the anguish of the grave came upon me,
I was overcome by trouble and sorrow.
Then I called on the name of the Lord:
"Lord, I pray, save my life."
Gracious is the Lord, and righteous;
our God is full of compassion.
The Lord protects the simple hearted.
When I was brought low, He saved me.
My soul, be at peace once more,
for the Lord has been good to you.
For You have rescued me from death,
my eyes from weeping, my feet from stumbling.
I shall walk in the presence of the Lord
in the land of the living.
I had faith, even when I said, "I am greatly afflicted,"
even when I said rashly, "All men are liars."

מָה־אָשִׁיב How can I repay the Lord for all His goodness to me?
I will lift the cup of salvation and call on the name of the Lord.
I will fulfill my vows to the Lord
in the presence of all His people.
Grievous in the Lord's sight is the death of His devoted ones.
Truly, Lord, I am Your servant;
I am Your servant, the son of Your maidservant.
You set me free from my chains.
To You I shall bring a thanksgiving-offering
and call on the Lord by name.
I will fulfill my vows to the Lord in the presence of all His people,
in the courts of the House of the Lord,
in your midst, Jerusalem.
HALLELUYA!

תהלים קטז

אָהַבְתִּי

כִּי־יִשְׁמַע יְהוָה, אֶת־קוֹלִי תַּחֲנוּנָי:

כִּי־הִטָּה אָזְנוֹ לִי, וּבְיָמַי אֶקְרָא:

אֲפָפוּנִי חֶבְלֵי־מָוֶת וּמְצָרֵי שְׁאוֹל מְצָאוּנִי

צָרָה וְיָגוֹן אֶמְצָא:

וּבְשֵׁם־יְהוָה אֶקְרָא, אָנָּה יְהוָה מַלְּטָה נַפְשִׁי:

חַנּוּן יְהוָה וְצַדִּיק, וֵאלֹהֵינוּ מְרַחֵם:

שֹׁמֵר פְּתָאיִם יְהוָה, דַּלּוֹתִי וְלִי יְהוֹשִׁיעַ:

שׁוּבִי נַפְשִׁי לִמְנוּחָיְכִי, כִּי־יְהוָה גָּמַל עָלָיְכִי:

כִּי חִלַּצְתָּ נַפְשִׁי מִמָּוֶת, אֶת־עֵינִי מִן־דִּמְעָה, אֶת־רַגְלִי מִדֶּחִי:

אֶתְהַלֵּךְ לִפְנֵי יְהוָה, בְּאַרְצוֹת הַחַיִּים:

הֶאֱמַנְתִּי כִּי אֲדַבֵּר, אֲנִי עָנִיתִי מְאֹד:

אֲנִי אָמַרְתִּי בְחָפְזִי, כָּל־הָאָדָם כֹּזֵב:

מָה־אָשִׁיב לַיהוָה, כָּל־תַּגְמוּלוֹהִי עָלָי:

כּוֹס־יְשׁוּעוֹת אֶשָּׂא, וּבְשֵׁם יְהוָה אֶקְרָא:

נְדָרַי לַיהוָה אֲשַׁלֵּם, נֶגְדָה־נָּא לְכָל־עַמּוֹ:

יָקָר בְּעֵינֵי יְהוָה, הַמָּוְתָה לַחֲסִידָיו:

אָנָּה יְהוָה כִּי־אֲנִי עַבְדֶּךָ, אֲנִי־עַבְדְּךָ בֶּן־אֲמָתֶךָ

פִּתַּחְתָּ לְמוֹסֵרָי:

לְךָ־אֶזְבַּח זֶבַח תּוֹדָה, וּבְשֵׁם יְהוָה אֶקְרָא:

נְדָרַי לַיהוָה אֲשַׁלֵּם, נֶגְדָה־נָּא לְכָל־עַמּוֹ:

בְּחַצְרוֹת בֵּית יְהוָה, בְּתוֹכֵכִי יְרוּשָׁלָיִם

הַלְלוּיָהּ:

הַלְלוּ Praise the LORD, all nations; acclaim Him, all you peoples; *Ps. 117*
        for His loving-kindness to us is strong,
        and the LORD's faithfulness is everlasting.

HALLELUYA!

הוֹדוּ Thank the LORD for He is good, *Ps. 118*
        His loving-kindness is for ever.
Let Israel say   His loving-kindness is for ever.
Let the house of Aaron say   His loving-kindness is for ever.
Let those who fear the LORD say   His loving-kindness is for ever.

מִן־הַמֵּצַר In my distress I called on the LORD.
        The LORD answered me and set me free.
        The LORD is with me; I will not be afraid.
    What can man do to me? The LORD is with me.
    He is my Helper. I will see the downfall of my enemies.
    It is better to take refuge in the LORD than to trust in man.
    It is better to take refuge in the LORD than to trust in princes.
            The nations all surrounded me,
            but in the LORD's name I drove them off.
            They surrounded me on every side,
            but in the LORD's name I drove them off.
    They surrounded me like bees, they attacked me as fire attacks
    brushwood, but in the LORD's name I drove them off.
        They thrust so hard against me, I nearly fell,
            but the LORD came to my help.
        The LORD is my strength and my song;
            He has become my salvation.
Sounds of song and salvation resound in the tents of the righteous:
        "The LORD's right hand has done mighty deeds.
        The LORD's right hand is lifted high.
    The LORD's right hand has done mighty deeds."

תהלים קיז

הַלְלוּ אֶת־יהוה כָּל־גּוֹיִם, שַׁבְּחוּהוּ כָּל־הָאֻמִּים:

כִּי גָבַר עָלֵינוּ חַסְדּוֹ, וֶאֱמֶת־יהוה לְעוֹלָם

הַלְלוּיָהּ:

תהלים קיח

כִּי לְעוֹלָם חַסְדּוֹ:	הוֹדוּ לַיהוה כִּי־טוֹב
כִּי לְעוֹלָם חַסְדּוֹ:	יֹאמַר־נָא יִשְׂרָאֵל
כִּי לְעוֹלָם חַסְדּוֹ:	יֹאמְרוּ־נָא בֵית־אַהֲרֹן
כִּי לְעוֹלָם חַסְדּוֹ:	יֹאמְרוּ־נָא יִרְאֵי יהוה

מִן־הַמֵּצַר קָרָאתִי יָּהּ, עָנָנִי בַמֶּרְחָב יָהּ:

יהוה לִי לֹא אִירָא, מַה־יַּעֲשֶׂה לִי אָדָם:

יהוה לִי בְּעֹזְרָי, וַאֲנִי אֶרְאֶה בְשֹׂנְאָי:

טוֹב לַחֲסוֹת בַּיהוה, מִבְּטֹחַ בָּאָדָם:

טוֹב לַחֲסוֹת בַּיהוה, מִבְּטֹחַ בִּנְדִיבִים:

כָּל־גּוֹיִם סְבָבוּנִי, בְּשֵׁם יהוה כִּי אֲמִילַם:

סַבּוּנִי גַם־סְבָבוּנִי, בְּשֵׁם יהוה כִּי אֲמִילַם:

סַבּוּנִי כִדְבֹרִים, דֹּעֲכוּ כְּאֵשׁ קוֹצִים

בְּשֵׁם יהוה כִּי אֲמִילַם:

דָּחֹה דְחִיתַנִי לִנְפֹּל, וַיהוה עֲזָרָנִי:

עָזִּי וְזִמְרָת יָהּ, וַיְהִי־לִי לִישׁוּעָה:

קוֹל רִנָּה וִישׁוּעָה בְּאָהֳלֵי צַדִּיקִים, יְמִין יהוה עֹשָׂה חָיִל:

יְמִין יהוה רוֹמֵמָה, יְמִין יהוה עֹשָׂה חָיִל:

I will not die but live, and tell what the Lord has done.
The Lord has chastened me severely,
but He has not given me over to death.
Open for me the gates of righteousness
that I may enter them and thank the Lord.
This is the gateway to the Lord; through it,
the righteous shall enter.

אוֹדְךָ I will thank You,
for You answered me, and became my salvation.
I will thank You, for You answered me, and became my salvation.

The stone the builders rejected has become the main cornerstone.
The stone the builders rejected has become the main cornerstone.

This is the Lord's doing. It is wondrous in our eyes.
This is the Lord's doing. It is wondrous in our eyes.

This is the day the Lord has made. Let us rejoice and be glad in it.
This is the day the Lord has made. Let us rejoice and be glad in it.

אָנָּא LORD, PLEASE, SAVE US.

LORD, PLEASE, SAVE US.

LORD, PLEASE, GRANT US SUCCESS.

LORD, PLEASE, GRANT US SUCCESS.

בָּרוּךְ Blessed is one who comes in the name of the Lord;
we bless you from the House of the Lord.
Blessed is one who comes in the name of the Lord;
we bless you from the House of the Lord.

The Lord is God; He has given us light. Bind the festival
offering with thick cords [and bring it] to the horns of the altar.
The Lord is God; He has given us light. Bind the festival offering
with thick cords [and bring it] to the horns of the altar.

לֹא־אָמוּת כִּי־אֶחְיֶה, וַאֲסַפֵּר מַעֲשֵׂי יָהּ:

יַסֹּר יִסְּרַנִּי יָּהּ, וְלַמָּוֶת לֹא נְתָנָנִי:

פִּתְחוּ־לִי שַׁעֲרֵי־צֶדֶק, אָבֹא־בָם אוֹדֶה יָהּ:

זֶה־הַשַּׁעַר לַיהוה, צַדִּיקִים יָבֹאוּ בוֹ:

אוֹדְךָ כִּי עֲנִיתָנִי, וַתְּהִי־לִי לִישׁוּעָה:

אוֹדְךָ כִּי עֲנִיתָנִי, וַתְּהִי־לִי לִישׁוּעָה:

אֶבֶן מָאֲסוּ הַבּוֹנִים, הָיְתָה לְרֹאשׁ פִּנָּה:

אֶבֶן מָאֲסוּ הַבּוֹנִים, הָיְתָה לְרֹאשׁ פִּנָּה:

מֵאֵת יהוה הָיְתָה זֹּאת, הִיא נִפְלָאת בְּעֵינֵינוּ:

מֵאֵת יהוה הָיְתָה זֹּאת, הִיא נִפְלָאת בְּעֵינֵינוּ:

זֶה־הַיּוֹם עָשָׂה יהוה, נָגִילָה וְנִשְׂמְחָה בוֹ:

זֶה־הַיּוֹם עָשָׂה יהוה, נָגִילָה וְנִשְׂמְחָה בוֹ:

אָנָּא יהוה הוֹשִׁיעָה נָּא:

אָנָּא יהוה הוֹשִׁיעָה נָּא:

אָנָּא יהוה הַצְלִיחָה נָּא:

אָנָּא יהוה הַצְלִיחָה נָּא:

בָּרוּךְ הַבָּא בְּשֵׁם יהוה, בֵּרַכְנוּכֶם מִבֵּית יהוה:

בָּרוּךְ הַבָּא בְּשֵׁם יהוה, בֵּרַכְנוּכֶם מִבֵּית יהוה:

אֵל יהוה וַיָּאֶר לָנוּ, אִסְרוּ־חַג בַּעֲבֹתִים עַד־קַרְנוֹת הַמִּזְבֵּחַ:

אֵל יהוה וַיָּאֶר לָנוּ, אִסְרוּ־חַג בַּעֲבֹתִים עַד־קַרְנוֹת הַמִּזְבֵּחַ:

You are my God and I will thank You;
You are my God, I will exalt You.

You are my God and I will thank You; You are my God, I will exalt You.

Thank the LORD for He is good, His loving-kindness is for
ever.

Thank the LORD for He is good, His loving-kindness is for ever.

יְהַלְלוּךָ ALL YOUR WORKS WILL PRAISE YOU,
LORD our God, and Your devoted ones –
the righteous who do Your will,
together with all Your people
the house of Israel –
will joyously thank, bless, praise,
glorify, exalt, revere, sanctify,
and proclaim the sovereignty of Your name, our King.
For it is good to thank You
and fitting to sing psalms to Your name,
for from eternity to eternity You are God.

הודו Thank the LORD, for He is good,	His loving-kindness is for ever.	*Ps. 136*
Thank the God of gods,	His loving-kindness is for ever.	
Thank the LORD of lords,	His loving-kindness is for ever.	
To the One who alone works great wonders,	His loving-kindness is for ever.	
Who made the heavens with wisdom,	His loving-kindness is for ever.	
Who spread the earth upon the waters,	His loving-kindness is for ever.	
Who made the great lights,	His loving-kindness is for ever.	
The sun to rule by day,	His loving-kindness is for ever.	
The moon and the stars to rule by night;	His loving-kindness is for ever.	

אֵלִי אַתָּה וְאוֹדֶךָּ, אֱלֹהַי אֲרוֹמְמֶךָּ:
אֵלִי אַתָּה וְאוֹדֶךָּ, אֱלֹהַי אֲרוֹמְמֶךָּ:

הוֹדוּ לַיהוה כִּי־טוֹב, כִּי לְעוֹלָם חַסְדּוֹ:
הוֹדוּ לַיהוה כִּי־טוֹב, כִּי לְעוֹלָם חַסְדּוֹ:

יְהַלְלוּךָ

יהוה אֱלֹהֵינוּ כָּל מַעֲשֶׂיךָ
וַחֲסִידֶיךָ צַדִּיקִים עוֹשֵׂי רְצוֹנֶךָ
וְכָל עַמְּךָ בֵּית יִשְׂרָאֵל
בְּרִנָּה יוֹדוּ וִיבָרְכוּ וִישַׁבְּחוּ
וִיפָאֲרוּ וִירוֹמְמוּ וְיַעֲרִיצוּ
וְיַקְדִּישׁוּ וְיַמְלִיכוּ אֶת שִׁמְךָ מַלְכֵּנוּ
כִּי לְךָ טוֹב לְהוֹדוֹת וּלְשִׁמְךָ נָאֶה לְזַמֵּר
כִּי מֵעוֹלָם וְעַד עוֹלָם אַתָּה אֵל.

כִּי לְעוֹלָם חַסְדּוֹ:	הוֹדוּ לַיהוה כִּי־טוֹב
כִּי לְעוֹלָם חַסְדּוֹ:	הוֹדוּ לֵאלֹהֵי הָאֱלֹהִים
כִּי לְעוֹלָם חַסְדּוֹ:	הוֹדוּ לַאֲדֹנֵי הָאֲדֹנִים
כִּי לְעוֹלָם חַסְדּוֹ:	לְעֹשֵׂה נִפְלָאוֹת גְּדֹלוֹת לְבַדּוֹ
כִּי לְעוֹלָם חַסְדּוֹ:	לְעֹשֵׂה הַשָּׁמַיִם בִּתְבוּנָה
כִּי לְעוֹלָם חַסְדּוֹ:	לְרֹקַע הָאָרֶץ עַל־הַמָּיִם
כִּי לְעוֹלָם חַסְדּוֹ:	לְעֹשֵׂה אוֹרִים גְּדֹלִים
כִּי לְעוֹלָם חַסְדּוֹ:	אֶת־הַשֶּׁמֶשׁ לְמֶמְשֶׁלֶת בַּיּוֹם
כִּי לְעוֹלָם חַסְדּוֹ:	אֶת־הַיָּרֵחַ וְכוֹכָבִים לְמֶמְשְׁלוֹת בַּלַּיְלָה

תהלים קלו

Who struck Egypt
through their firstborn,   His loving-kindness is for ever.
And brought out Israel
from their midst,   His loving-kindness is for ever.
With a strong hand
and outstretched arm,   His loving-kindness is for ever.
Who split the Reed Sea into parts,   His loving-kindness is for ever.
And made Israel pass through it,   His loving-kindness is for ever.
Casting Pharaoh and his army
into the Reed Sea;   His loving-kindness is for ever.
Who led His people
through the wilderness;   His loving-kindness is for ever.
Who struck down great kings,   His loving-kindness is for ever.
And slew mighty kings,   His loving-kindness is for ever.
Siḥon, king of the Amorites,   His loving-kindness is for ever.
And Og, king of Bashan,   His loving-kindness is for ever.
And gave their land as a heritage,   His loving-kindness is for ever.
A heritage for His servant Israel;   His loving-kindness is for ever.
Who remembered us
in our lowly state,   His loving-kindness is for ever.
And rescued us from our tormentors,   His loving-kindness is for ever.
Who gives food to all flesh,   His loving-kindness is for ever.
Give thanks to the God of heaven.   His loving-kindness is for ever.

THE SOUL

of all that lives shall bless Your name,
LORD our God,
and the spirit of all flesh shall always glorify
and exalt Your remembrance, our King.
From eternity to eternity You are God.
Without You, we have no King, Redeemer or Savior,
who liberates, rescues, sustains
and shows compassion in every time of trouble and distress.
We have no King but You,

לְמַכֵּה מִצְרַיִם בִּבְכוֹרֵיהֶם	כִּי לְעוֹלָם חַסְדּוֹ:
וַיּוֹצֵא יִשְׂרָאֵל מִתּוֹכָם	כִּי לְעוֹלָם חַסְדּוֹ:
בְּיָד חֲזָקָה וּבִזְרוֹעַ נְטוּיָה	כִּי לְעוֹלָם חַסְדּוֹ:
לְגֹזֵר יַם־סוּף לִגְזָרִים	כִּי לְעוֹלָם חַסְדּוֹ:
וְהֶעֱבִיר יִשְׂרָאֵל בְּתוֹכוֹ	כִּי לְעוֹלָם חַסְדּוֹ:
וְנִעֵר פַּרְעֹה וְחֵילוֹ בְיַם־סוּף	כִּי לְעוֹלָם חַסְדּוֹ:
לְמוֹלִיךְ עַמּוֹ בַּמִּדְבָּר	כִּי לְעוֹלָם חַסְדּוֹ:
לְמַכֵּה מְלָכִים גְּדֹלִים	כִּי לְעוֹלָם חַסְדּוֹ:
וַיַּהֲרֹג מְלָכִים אַדִּירִים	כִּי לְעוֹלָם חַסְדּוֹ:
לְסִיחוֹן מֶלֶךְ הָאֱמֹרִי	כִּי לְעוֹלָם חַסְדּוֹ:
וּלְעוֹג מֶלֶךְ הַבָּשָׁן	כִּי לְעוֹלָם חַסְדּוֹ:
וְנָתַן אַרְצָם לְנַחֲלָה	כִּי לְעוֹלָם חַסְדּוֹ:
נַחֲלָה לְיִשְׂרָאֵל עַבְדּוֹ	כִּי לְעוֹלָם חַסְדּוֹ:
שֶׁבְּשִׁפְלֵנוּ זָכַר לָנוּ	כִּי לְעוֹלָם חַסְדּוֹ:
וַיִּפְרְקֵנוּ מִצָּרֵינוּ	כִּי לְעוֹלָם חַסְדּוֹ:
נֹתֵן לֶחֶם לְכָל־בָּשָׂר	כִּי לְעוֹלָם חַסְדּוֹ:
הוֹדוּ לְאֵל הַשָּׁמָיִם	כִּי לְעוֹלָם חַסְדּוֹ:

נִשְׁמַת

כָּל חַי תְּבָרֵךְ אֶת שִׁמְךָ, יהוה אֱלֹהֵינוּ
וְרוּחַ כָּל בָּשָׂר תְּפָאֵר וּתְרוֹמֵם זִכְרְךָ מַלְכֵּנוּ תָּמִיד.
מִן הָעוֹלָם וְעַד הָעוֹלָם אַתָּה אֵל
וּמִבַּלְעָדֶיךָ אֵין לָנוּ מֶלֶךְ
גּוֹאֵל וּמוֹשִׁיעַ פּוֹדֶה וּמַצִּיל וּמְפַרְנֵס וּמְרַחֵם
בְּכָל עֵת צָרָה וְצוּקָה אֵין לָנוּ מֶלֶךְ אֶלָּא אָתָּה.

God of the first and last,
God of all creatures,
Master of all ages,
extolled by a multitude of praises,
who guides His world with loving-kindness
and His creatures with compassion.
The LORD neither slumbers nor sleeps.
He rouses the sleepers and wakens the slumberers.
He makes the dumb speak, sets the bound free,
supports the fallen,
and raises those bowed down.
To You alone we give thanks:
If our mouths were as full of song as the sea,
and our tongue with jubilation as its myriad waves,
if our lips were full of praise like the spacious heavens,
and our eyes shone like the sun and moon,
if our hands were outstretched like eagles of the sky,
and our feet as swift as hinds –
still we could not thank You enough,
LORD our God and God of our ancestors,
or bless Your name
for even one of the thousand thousands
and myriad myriads of favors
You did for our ancestors and for us.
You redeemed us from Egypt, LORD our God,
and freed us from the house of bondage.
In famine You nourished us;
in times of plenty You sustained us.
You delivered us from the sword,
saved us from the plague,
and spared us from serious and lasting illness.
Until now Your mercies have helped us.
Your love has not forsaken us.

אֱלֹהֵי הָרִאשׁוֹנִים וְהָאַחֲרוֹנִים, אֱלֹוַהּ כָּל בְּרִיּוֹת

אֲדוֹן כָּל תּוֹלָדוֹת, הַמְהֻלָּל בְּרֹב הַתִּשְׁבָּחוֹת

הַמְנַהֵג עוֹלָמוֹ בְּחֶסֶד וּבְרִיּוֹתָיו בְּרַחֲמִים.

וַיהוה לֹא יָנוּם וְלֹא יִישָׁן

הַמְעוֹרֵר יְשֵׁנִים וְהַמֵּקִיץ נִרְדָּמִים

וְהַמֵּשִׂיחַ אִלְּמִים וְהַמַּתִּיר אֲסוּרִים

וְהַסּוֹמֵךְ נוֹפְלִים וְהַזּוֹקֵף כְּפוּפִים.

לְךָ לְבַדְּךָ אֲנַחְנוּ מוֹדִים.

אִלּוּ פִינוּ מָלֵא שִׁירָה כַּיָּם

וּלְשׁוֹנֵנוּ רִנָּה כַּהֲמוֹן גַּלָּיו

וְשִׂפְתוֹתֵינוּ שֶׁבַח כְּמֶרְחֲבֵי רָקִיעַ

וְעֵינֵינוּ מְאִירוֹת כַּשֶּׁמֶשׁ וְכַיָּרֵחַ

וְיָדֵינוּ פְרוּשׂוֹת כְּנִשְׁרֵי שָׁמָיִם

וְרַגְלֵינוּ קַלּוֹת כָּאַיָּלוֹת

אֵין אֲנַחְנוּ מַסְפִּיקִים לְהוֹדוֹת לְךָ, יהוה אֱלֹהֵינוּ וֵאלֹהֵי אֲבוֹתֵינוּ

וּלְבָרֵךְ אֶת שְׁמֶךָ

עַל אַחַת מֵאֶלֶף אֶלֶף אַלְפֵי אֲלָפִים וְרִבֵּי רְבָבוֹת פְּעָמִים הַטּוֹבוֹת

שֶׁעָשִׂיתָ עִם אֲבוֹתֵינוּ וְעִמָּנוּ.

מִמִּצְרַיִם גְּאַלְתָּנוּ, יהוה אֱלֹהֵינוּ,

וּמִבֵּית עֲבָדִים פְּדִיתָנוּ

בְּרָעָב זַנְתָּנוּ וּבְשָׂבָע כִּלְכַּלְתָּנוּ,

מֵחֶרֶב הִצַּלְתָּנוּ וּמִדֶּבֶר מִלַּטְתָּנוּ

וּמֵחֳלָיִים רָעִים וְנֶאֱמָנִים דִּלִּיתָנוּ.

עַד הֵנָּה עֲזָרוּנוּ רַחֲמֶיךָ, וְלֹא עֲזָבוּנוּ חֲסָדֶיךָ

וְאַל תִּטְּשֵׁנוּ, יהוה אֱלֹהֵינוּ, לָנֶצַח.

May You, Lord our God, never abandon us.
Therefore the limbs You formed within us,
the spirit and soul You breathed into our nostrils,
and the tongue You placed in our mouth –
they will thank and bless, praise and glorify, exalt and esteem,
hallow and do homage to Your name, O our King.
For every mouth shall give thanks to You,
every tongue vow allegiance to You,
every knee shall bend to You,
every upright body shall bow to You,
all hearts shall fear You,
and our innermost being sing praises to Your name,
as is written:

> "All my bones shall say: Lord, who is like You?   *Ps. 35*
> You save the poor from one stronger than him,
> the poor and needy from one who would rob him."

Who is like You? Who is equal to You?
Who can be compared to You?
O great, mighty and awesome God, God Most High,
Maker of heaven and earth.
We will laud, praise and glorify You and bless Your holy name,
as it is said:

> "Of David. Bless the Lord, O my soul,   *Ps. 103*
> and all that is within me bless His holy name."

God – in Your absolute power,
Great – in the glory of Your name,
Mighty – for ever,
Awesome – in Your awe-inspiring deeds,
The King – who sits on a throne.
High and lofty
He inhabits eternity; exalted and holy is His name.
And it is written:

> Sing joyfully to the Lord,   *Ps. 33*
> you righteous, for praise from the upright is seemly

עַל כֵּן אֵבָרִים שֶׁפִּלַּגְתָּ בָּנוּ

וְרוּחַ וּנְשָׁמָה שֶׁנָּפַחְתָּ בְּאַפֵּנוּ,

וְלָשׁוֹן אֲשֶׁר שַׂמְתָּ בְּפִינוּ

הֵן הֵם יוֹדוּ וִיבָרְכוּ וִישַׁבְּחוּ וִיפָאֲרוּ

וִירוֹמְמוּ וְיַעֲרִיצוּ וְיַקְדִּישׁוּ וְיַמְלִיכוּ אֶת שִׁמְךָ מַלְכֵּנוּ

כִּי כָל פֶּה לְךָ יוֹדֶה וְכָל לָשׁוֹן לְךָ תִשָּׁבַע

וְכָל בֶּרֶךְ לְךָ תִכְרַע וְכָל קוֹמָה לְפָנֶיךָ תִשְׁתַּחֲוֶה

וְכָל לְבָבוֹת יִירָאוּךָ וְכָל קֶרֶב וּכְלָיוֹת יְזַמְּרוּ לִשְׁמֶךָ

כַּדָּבָר שֶׁכָּתוּב

תהלים לה

כָּל עַצְמֹתַי תֹּאמַרְנָה יהוה מִי כָמוֹךָ

מַצִּיל עָנִי מֵחָזָק מִמֶּנּוּ, וְעָנִי וְאֶבְיוֹן מִגֹּזְלוֹ:

מִי יִדְמֶה לָּךְ וּמִי יִשְׁוֶה לָּךְ וּמִי יַעֲרָךְ לָךְ

הָאֵל הַגָּדוֹל, הַגִּבּוֹר וְהַנּוֹרָא

אֵל עֶלְיוֹן, קוֹנֵה שָׁמַיִם וָאָרֶץ.

נְהַלֶּלְךָ וּנְשַׁבֵּחֲךָ וּנְפָאֶרְךָ וּנְבָרֵךְ אֶת שֵׁם קָדְשֶׁךָ

כָּאָמוּר

תהלים קג

לְדָוִד, בָּרְכִי נַפְשִׁי אֶת־יהוה,

וְכָל־קְרָבַי אֶת־שֵׁם קָדְשׁוֹ:

הָאֵל בְּתַעֲצֻמוֹת עֻזֶּךָ

הַגָּדוֹל בִּכְבוֹד שְׁמֶךָ

הַגִּבּוֹר לָנֶצַח וְהַנּוֹרָא בְּנוֹרְאוֹתֶיךָ

הַמֶּלֶךְ הַיּוֹשֵׁב עַל כִּסֵּא.

רָם וְנִשָּׂא

שׁוֹכֵן עַד מָרוֹם וְקָדוֹשׁ שְׁמוֹ

וְכָתוּב

תהלים לג

רַנְּנוּ צַדִּיקִים בַּיהוה, לַיְשָׁרִים נָאוָה תְהִלָּה:

By the mouth	of the upright	You shall be praised.
By the words	of the righteous	You shall be blessed.
By the tongue	of the devout	You shall be extolled,
And in the midst	of the holy	You shall be sanctified.

וּבְמַקְהֲלוֹת **And in the assemblies**
of tens of thousands of Your people, the house of Israel,
with joyous song shall Your name, our King,
be glorified in every generation.
For this is the duty of all creatures before You,
Lord our God and God of our ancestors:
to thank, praise, laud, glorify, exalt,
honor, bless, raise high and acclaim –
even beyond all the words of song and praise
of David, son of Jesse, Your servant, Your anointed.

יִשְׁתַּבַּח **May Your name be praised** for ever, our King,
the great and holy God, King in heaven and on earth.
For to You, Lord our God and God of our ancestors,
it is right to offer song and praise,
hymn and psalm, strength and dominion,
eternity, greatness and power,
song of praise and glory,
holiness and kingship,
blessings and thanks, from now and for ever.
Blessed are You, Lord,
God and King, exalted in praises,
God of thanksgivings,
Master of wonders,
who delights in hymns of song,
King, God, Giver of life to the worlds.

בְּפִי   יְשָׁרִים   תִּתְהַלָּל
וּבְדִבְרֵי   צַדִּיקִים   תִּתְבָּרֵךְ
וּבִלְשׁוֹן   חֲסִידִים   תִּתְרוֹמָם
וּבְקֶרֶב   קְדוֹשִׁים   תִּתְקַדָּשׁ

וּבְמַקְהֲלוֹת רִבְבוֹת עַמְּךָ בֵּית יִשְׂרָאֵל
בְּרִנָּה יִתְפָּאַר שִׁמְךָ מַלְכֵּנוּ בְּכָל דּוֹר וָדוֹר
שֶׁכֵּן חוֹבַת כָּל הַיְצוּרִים
לְפָנֶיךָ יהוה אֱלֹהֵינוּ וֵאלֹהֵי אֲבוֹתֵינוּ
לְהוֹדוֹת, לְהַלֵּל, לְשַׁבֵּחַ, לְפָאֵר, לְרוֹמֵם
לְהַדֵּר, לְבָרֵךְ, לְעַלֵּה וּלְקַלֵּס
עַל כָּל דִּבְרֵי שִׁירוֹת וְתִשְׁבְּחוֹת
דָּוִד בֶּן יִשַׁי, עַבְדְּךָ מְשִׁיחֶךָ.

יִשְׁתַּבַּח שִׁמְךָ לָעַד מַלְכֵּנוּ
הָאֵל הַמֶּלֶךְ הַגָּדוֹל וְהַקָּדוֹשׁ בַּשָּׁמַיִם וּבָאָרֶץ
כִּי לְךָ נָאֶה, יהוה אֱלֹהֵינוּ וֵאלֹהֵי אֲבוֹתֵינוּ
שִׁיר וּשְׁבָחָה, הַלֵּל וְזִמְרָה
עֹז וּמֶמְשָׁלָה, נֶצַח, גְּדֻלָּה וּגְבוּרָה
תְּהִלָּה וְתִפְאֶרֶת, קְדֻשָּׁה וּמַלְכוּת
בְּרָכוֹת וְהוֹדָאוֹת, מֵעַתָּה וְעַד עוֹלָם.
בָּרוּךְ אַתָּה יהוה, אֵל מֶלֶךְ גָּדוֹל בַּתִּשְׁבָּחוֹת
אֵל הַהוֹדָאוֹת אֲדוֹן הַנִּפְלָאוֹת
הַבּוֹחֵר בְּשִׁירֵי זִמְרָה,
מֶלֶךְ, אֵל, חֵי הָעוֹלָמִים.

Blessed are You, LORD our God, King of the Universe,
who creates the fruit of the vine.

Drink the fourth cup while reclining to the left.

בָּרוּךְ Blessed are You, LORD our God,
King of the Universe,
for the vine and the fruit of the vine,
and for the produce of the field;
for the desirable, good
and spacious land that You willingly gave as heritage to
our ancestors, that they might eat of its fruit
and be satisfied with its goodness.
Have compassion, LORD our God,
on Israel Your people, on Jerusalem,
Your city, on Zion the home of Your glory,
on Your altar and Your Temple.
May You rebuild Jerusalem,
the holy city swiftly in our time,
and may You bring us back there,
rejoicing in its rebuilding,
eating from its fruit,
satisfied by its goodness,
and blessing You for it in holiness and purity.
(*On Shabbat:* Be pleased to refresh us on this Sabbath Day.)
Grant us joy on this festival of Matzot.
For You, God, are good and do good to all
and we thank You for the land
and for the fruit of the vine.
Blessed are You, LORD,
for the land and for the fruit of the vine.

Outside Israel, this poem is recited on the first night of the festival only.

בָּרוּךְ אַתָּה יהוה אֱלֹהֵינוּ מֶלֶךְ הָעוֹלָם
בּוֹרֵא פְּרִי הַגָּפֶן.

Drink the fourth cup while reclining to the left.

בָּרוּךְ אַתָּה יהוה אֱלֹהֵינוּ מֶלֶךְ הָעוֹלָם
עַל הַגֶּפֶן וְעַל פְּרִי הַגֶּפֶן
וְעַל תְּנוּבַת הַשָּׂדֶה וְעַל אֶרֶץ חֶמְדָּה טוֹבָה וּרְחָבָה
שֶׁרָצִיתָ וְהִנְחַלְתָּ לַאֲבוֹתֵינוּ
לֶאֱכֹל מִפִּרְיָהּ וְלִשְׂבֹּעַ מִטּוּבָהּ.
רַחֶם נָא יהוה אֱלֹהֵינוּ עַל יִשְׂרָאֵל עַמֶּךָ
וְעַל יְרוּשָׁלַיִם עִירֶךָ
וְעַל צִיּוֹן מִשְׁכַּן כְּבוֹדֶךָ
וְעַל מִזְבְּחֲךָ וְעַל הֵיכָלֶךָ.
וּבְנֵה יְרוּשָׁלַיִם עִיר הַקֹּדֶשׁ בִּמְהֵרָה בְיָמֵינוּ
וְהַעֲלֵנוּ לְתוֹכָהּ וְשַׂמְּחֵנוּ בְּבִנְיָנָהּ
וְנֹאכַל מִפִּרְיָהּ וְנִשְׂבַּע מִטּוּבָהּ
וּנְבָרֶכְךָ עָלֶיהָ בִּקְדֻשָּׁה וּבְטָהֳרָה.
(בשבת: וּרְצֵה וְהַחֲלִיצֵנוּ בְּיוֹם הַשַּׁבָּת הַזֶּה)
וְשַׂמְּחֵנוּ בְּיוֹם חַג הַמַּצּוֹת הַזֶּה
כִּי אַתָּה יהוה טוֹב וּמֵטִיב לַכֹּל
וְנוֹדֶה לְךָ
עַל הָאָרֶץ וְעַל פְּרִי הַגֶּפֶן/ ארץ ישראל *If from*: גַּפְנָהּ./

בָּרוּךְ אַתָּה יהוה
עַל הָאָרֶץ וְעַל פְּרִי הַגֶּפֶן/ ארץ ישראל *If from*: גַּפְנָהּ./

Outside ארץ ישראל, *this poem is recited on the first night of the festival only.*

וּבְכֵן וַיְהִי בַּחֲצִי הַלַּיְלָה AND SO – IT HAPPENED AT MIDNIGHT. *Ex. 12*

Many were the miracles You performed long ago,	at night.
At the beginning of the watch,	on this night,
You won [Abraham]'s battle, when [his men were] split,	and the night

IT HAPPENED AT MIDNIGHT.

You judged the king of Gerar in his dream	at night.
You put dread into [Laban] the Aramean's heart	that night.
And Israel struggled with an angel and overcame him	at night

IT HAPPENED AT MIDNIGHT.

You crushed the firstborns of Patros [Egypt] in the middle   of the night.
They could not find their strength, when they rose up
[against Israel]   at night.
You flung [Sisera] the commander of Haroshet
off course with the stars   of night

IT HAPPENED AT MIDNIGHT.

[Sennacherib] the blasphemer thought to raise his hand
against the beloved [city]; but You dried up the bodies
of his fallen   in the night.
You overthrew Bel, idol and pedestal together, in the dead   of night.
To [Daniel] the beloved man were revealed
the secrets of that vision   of the night

IT HAPPENED AT MIDNIGHT.

[Belshazzar], who drank himself merry
from the holy vessels, was killed on that same   night.
[Daniel] was brought out unharmed from the
lions' den; he who had explained those terrors   of the night.
[Haman] the Agagite bore his hatred and wrote his orders   at night

IT HAPPENED AT MIDNIGHT.

You awakened Your might against him, disturbing
[King Ahashverosh's] sleep   at night.
You shall tread the winepress of [Se'ir],
who asks anxiously, "What   of the night?"
You will cry out like the watchman, calling,
"Morning is come,   and also night"

IT HAPPENED AT MIDNIGHT.

שמות יב

וּבְכֵן וַיְהִי בַּחֲצִי הַלַּיְלָה

בַּלַּיְלָה	אָז רֹב נִסִּים הִפְלֵאתָ
הַלַּיְלָה	בְּרֹאשׁ אַשְׁמוּרוֹת זֶה
לַיְלָה	גֵּר צֶדֶק נִצַּחְתּוֹ, כְּנֶחֱלַק לוֹ
וַיְהִי בַּחֲצִי הַלַּיְלָה	

הַלַּיְלָה	דַּנְתָּ מֶלֶךְ גְּרָר בַּחֲלוֹם
לַיְלָה	הִפְחַדְתָּ אֲרַמִּי בְּאֶמֶשׁ
לַיְלָה	וְיִשְׂרָאֵל יָשַׂר לָאֵל, וַיּוּכַל לוֹ
וַיְהִי בַּחֲצִי הַלַּיְלָה	

הַלַּיְלָה	זֶרַע בְּכוֹרֵי פַתְרוֹס מָחַצְתָּ בַּחֲצִי
בַּלַּיְלָה	חֵילָם לֹא מָצְאוּ בְּקוּמָם
לַיְלָה	טִיסַת נְגִיד חֲרֹשֶׁת סִלִּיתָ בְּכוֹכְבֵי
וַיְהִי בַּחֲצִי הַלַּיְלָה	

בַּלַּיְלָה	יָעַץ מְחָרֵף לְנוֹפֵף אִוּוּי, הוֹבַשְׁתָּ פְגָרָיו
לַיְלָה	כָּרַע בֵּל וּמַצָּבוֹ בְּאִישׁוֹן
לַיְלָה	לְאִישׁ חֲמוּדוֹת נִגְלָה רָז חֲזוֹת
וַיְהִי בַּחֲצִי הַלַּיְלָה	

בַּלַּיְלָה	מִשְׁתַּכֵּר בִּכְלֵי קֹדֶשׁ נֶהֱרַג בּוֹ
לַיְלָה	נוֹשַׁע מִבּוֹר אֲרָיוֹת, פּוֹתֵר בִּעֲתוּתֵי
בַּלַּיְלָה	שִׂנְאָה נָטַר אֲגָגִי, וְכָתַב סְפָרִים
וַיְהִי בַּחֲצִי הַלַּיְלָה	

לַיְלָה	עוֹרַרְתָּ נִצְחֲךָ עָלָיו בְּנֶדֶד שְׁנַת
מִלַּיְלָה	פּוּרָה תִדְרֹךְ לְשׁוֹמֵר מַה
לַיְלָה	צָרַח כַּשֹּׁמֵר, וְשָׂח אָתָא בֹקֶר וְגַם
וַיְהִי בַּחֲצִי הַלַּיְלָה	

Draw near the day that will be neither day	nor night.
Highest One, make known that day is Yours	and also night.
Appoint watchmen [to guard] Your city all day long	and all night,
Light up like daylight the darkness	of night

IT HAPPENED AT MIDNIGHT.

Outside Israel, this poem is recited on the second night of the festival only.

וּבְכֵן וַאֲמַרְתֶּם זֶבַח פֶּסַח TELL [your children]: "THIS IS THE PESAH." *Ex. 12*

You showed Your immense power in wonders	on Pesah;
to the head of all seasons You have raised up	Pesah.
You revealed to [Abraham] the Ezrahi what would come	
at midnight	on Pesah.

TELL [your children]: "THIS IS THE PESAH."

You knocked at his doors in the heat of the day	on Pesah;
he gave Your shining [messengers] unleavened cakes to eat	on Pesah;
and he ran to the herd, hinting at the ox in the Torah reading	of Pesah.

TELL [your children]: "THIS IS THE PESAH."

The men of Sodom raged and burned in fire	on Pesah.
Lot was saved; he baked matzot at the end	of Pesah.
You swept bare the land of Mof and Nof [Egypt]	
in Your great rage	on Pesah.

TELL [your children]: "THIS IS THE PESAH."

The firstborns of [Egypt's] vigor You crushed, LORD,	
on the night of guarding,	on Pesah.
[But,] Mighty One, You passed over Your firstborn son	
when You saw the blood	of the Pesah,
allowing no destruction through my doors	on Pesah.

TELL [your children]: "THIS IS THE PESAH."

קָרֵב יוֹם אֲשֶׁר הוּא לֹא יוֹם וְלֹא   לַיְלָה

רָם הוֹדַע כִּי לְךָ הַיּוֹם אַף לְךָ   הַלַּיְלָה

שׁוֹמְרִים הַפְקֵד לְעִירְךָ כָּל הַיּוֹם וְכָל   הַלַּיְלָה

תָּאִיר כְּאוֹר יוֹם חֶשְׁכַּת   לַיְלָה

וַיְהִי בַּחֲצִי הַלַּיְלָה

Outside ארץ ישראל, *this poem is recited on the second night of the festival only.*

שמות יב

וּבְכֵן וַאֲמַרְתֶּם זֶבַח פֶּסַח

אֹמֶץ גְּבוּרוֹתֶיךָ הִפְלֵאתָ   בַּפֶּסַח

בְּרֹאשׁ כָּל מוֹעֲדוֹת נִשֵּׂאתָ   פֶּסַח

גִּלִּיתָ לְאֶזְרָחִי חֲצוֹת לֵיל   פֶּסַח

וַאֲמַרְתֶּם זֶבַח פֶּסַח

דְּלָתָיו דָּפַקְתָּ כְּחֹם הַיּוֹם   בַּפֶּסַח

הִסְעִיד נוֹצְצִים עֻגוֹת מַצּוֹת   בַּפֶּסַח

וְאֶל הַבָּקָר, רָץ זֵכֶר לְשׁוֹר עֵרֶךְ   פֶּסַח

וַאֲמַרְתֶּם זֶבַח פֶּסַח

זֹעֲמוּ סְדוֹמִים, וְלֹהֲטוּ בָּאֵשׁ   בַּפֶּסַח

חֻלַּץ לוֹט מֵהֶם, וּמַצּוֹת אָפָה בְּקֵץ   פֶּסַח

טֵאטֵאתָ אַדְמַת מֹף וְנֹף בְּעָבְרְךָ   בַּפֶּסַח

וַאֲמַרְתֶּם זֶבַח פֶּסַח

יָהּ, רֹאשׁ כָּל אוֹן מָחַצְתָּ בְּלֵיל שִׁמּוּר   פֶּסַח

כַּבִּיר, עַל בֵּן בְּכוֹר פָּסַחְתָּ בְּדַם   פֶּסַח

לְבִלְתִּי תֵּת מַשְׁחִית לָבֹא בִּפְתָחַי   בַּפֶּסַח

וַאֲמַרְתֶּם זֶבַח פֶּסַח

The walled city [of Jericho] was closed [for fear] when it was   Pesaḥ.
Midian was destroyed in the din, [after a dream of] Omer barley on Pesaḥ.
The fat ones of [Assyria; of] Pul and Lud were
                                    burned away in fires   on Pesaḥ.
                 TELL [your children]: "THIS IS THE PESAḤ."

This day [Sennacherib] halted at Nob [and laid siege]
                                  until the time   of Pesaḥ.
A hand wrote Babylonia's doom on the wall   at Pesaḥ:
the lamp was lit, the table was laid   on Pesaḥ.
               TELL [your children]: "THIS IS THE PESAḤ."

Hadassa gathered the people to fast three days   at Pesaḥ;
You crushed [Haman,] the head of that evil family,
                  on a gallows fifty cubits high   on Pesaḥ.
[Loss and widowhood –] You will bring these two
            in a moment to [Edom, which rules us now,]   on Pesaḥ.
Strengthen Your hand, raise Your right hand,
              as on the night first sanctified   as Pesaḥ.
              TELL [your children]: "THIS IS THE PESAḤ."

כִּי לוֹ יָאֶה FOR HIM IT IS FITTING
Majestic in Kingship, truly chosen: His legions say to Him:
"Yours and Yours; Yours, for it is Yours; Yours, only Yours;
Yours, LORD, is the Kingdom."   *1 Chron. 29*
FOR HIM IT IS FITTING, FOR HIM IT IS RIGHT.

Unmistakable in His Kingship, truly glorious: His venerable ones say to Him:
"Yours and Yours; Yours, for it is Yours; Yours, only Yours;
Yours, LORD, is the kingdom."
FOR HIM IT IS FITTING, FOR HIM IT IS RIGHT.

Worthy of Kingship, truly mighty: His officers say to Him:
"Yours and Yours; Yours, for it is Yours; Yours, only Yours;
Yours, LORD, is the kingdom."
FOR HIM IT IS FITTING, FOR HIM IT IS RIGHT.

מִסְגֶּרֶת סֻגָּרָה בְּעִתּוֹתֵי   פֶּסַח
נִשְׁמְדָה מִדְיָן בִּצְלִיל שְׂעוֹרֵי עֹמֶר   פֶּסַח
שֹׂרְפוּ מִשְׁמַנֵּי פּוּל וְלוּד, בִּיקַד יְקוֹד   פֶּסַח
וַאֲמַרְתֶּם זֶבַח פֶּסַח

עוֹד הַיּוֹם בְּנֹב לַעֲמֹד, עַד גָּעָה עוֹנַת   פֶּסַח
פַּס יָד כָּתְבָה לְקַעֲקַע צוּל   בְּפֶסַח
צָפֹה הַצָּפִית עָרוֹךְ הַשֻּׁלְחָן   בְּפֶסַח
וַאֲמַרְתֶּם זֶבַח פֶּסַח

קָהָל כִּנְּסָה הֲדַסָּה, צוֹם לְשַׁלֵּשׁ   בְּפֶסַח
רֹאשׁ מִבֵּית רָשָׁע מָחַצְתָּ בְּעֵץ חֲמִשִּׁים   בְּפֶסַח
שְׁתֵּי אֵלֶּה, רֶגַע תָּבִיא לְעוּצִית   בְּפֶסַח
תָּעֹז יָדְךָ, תָּרוּם יְמִינְךָ, כְּלֵיל הִתְקַדֶּשׁ חַג   פֶּסַח
וַאֲמַרְתֶּם זֶבַח פֶּסַח

כִּי לוֹ נָאֶה, כִּי לוֹ יָאֶה

אַדִּיר בִּמְלוּכָה   בָּחוּר כַּהֲלָכָה   גְּדוּדָיו יֹאמְרוּ לוֹ
דברי הימים א׳ כט
לְךָ וּלְךָ, לְךָ כִּי לְךָ, לְךָ אַף לְךָ, לְךָ יהוה הַמַּמְלָכָה
כִּי לוֹ נָאֶה, כִּי לוֹ יָאֶה

דָּגוּל בִּמְלוּכָה   הָדוּר כַּהֲלָכָה   וָתִיקָיו יֹאמְרוּ לוֹ
לְךָ וּלְךָ, לְךָ כִּי לְךָ, לְךָ אַף לְךָ, לְךָ יהוה הַמַּמְלָכָה
כִּי לוֹ נָאֶה, כִּי לוֹ יָאֶה

זַכַּאי בִּמְלוּכָה   חָסִין כַּהֲלָכָה   טַפְסְרָיו יֹאמְרוּ לוֹ
לְךָ וּלְךָ, לְךָ כִּי לְךָ, לְךָ אַף לְךָ, לְךָ יהוה הַמַּמְלָכָה
כִּי לוֹ נָאֶה, כִּי לוֹ יָאֶה

One in Kingship, truly omnipotent: His learned ones say to Him:
"Yours and Yours; Yours, for it is Yours; Yours, only Yours;
Yours, LORD, is the kingdom."
FOR HIM IT IS FITTING, FOR HIM IT IS RIGHT.

King in His Kingship, truly awesome: those surrounding Him say to Him:
"Yours and Yours; Yours, for it is Yours; Yours, only Yours;
Yours, LORD, is the kingdom."
FOR HIM IT IS FITTING, FOR HIM IT IS RIGHT.

Humble in Kingship, truly the Redeemer, His righteous ones say to Him:
"Yours and Yours; Yours, for it is Yours; Yours, only Yours;
Yours, LORD, is the kingdom."
FOR HIM IT IS FITTING, FOR HIM IT IS RIGHT.

Holy in Kingship, truly compassionate, His angels say to Him:
"Yours and Yours; Yours, for it is Yours; Yours, only Yours;
Yours, LORD, is the kingdom."
FOR HIM IT IS FITTING, FOR HIM IT IS RIGHT.

Powerful in Kingship, truly our Support, His perfect ones say to Him:
"Yours and Yours; Yours, for it is Yours; Yours, only Yours;
Yours, LORD, is the kingdom."
FOR HIM IT IS FITTING, FOR HIM IT IS RIGHT.

NIRTZA / PARTING

חֲסַל סִדּוּר פֶּסַח The Pesah service is finished,
as it was meant to be performed,
in accordance with all its rules and laws.
Just as we have been privileged to lay out its order,
so may we be privileged to perform it [in the Temple].
Pure One, dwelling in Your heaven,
raise up this people, too abundant to be counted.
Soon, lead the shoots of [Israel's] stock,
redeemed, into Zion with great joy.

NEXT YEAR IN JERUSALEM REBUILT!

יָחִיד בִּמְלוּכָה ⁣ כַּבִּיר כַּהֲלָכָה ⁣ לִמּוּדָיו יֹאמְרוּ לוֹ
לְךָ וּלְךָ, לְךָ כִּי לְךָ, לְךָ אַף לְךָ, לְךָ יהוה הַמַּמְלָכָה
כִּי לוֹ נָאֶה, כִּי לוֹ יָאֶה

מֶלֶךְ בִּמְלוּכָה ⁣ נוֹרָא כַּהֲלָכָה ⁣ סְבִיבָיו יֹאמְרוּ לוֹ
לְךָ וּלְךָ, לְךָ כִּי לְךָ, לְךָ אַף לְךָ, לְךָ יהוה הַמַּמְלָכָה
כִּי לוֹ נָאֶה, כִּי לוֹ יָאֶה

עָנָו בִּמְלוּכָה ⁣ פּוֹדֶה כַּהֲלָכָה ⁣ צַדִּיקָיו יֹאמְרוּ לוֹ
לְךָ וּלְךָ, לְךָ כִּי לְךָ, לְךָ אַף לְךָ, לְךָ יהוה הַמַּמְלָכָה
כִּי לוֹ נָאֶה, כִּי לוֹ יָאֶה

קָדוֹשׁ בִּמְלוּכָה ⁣ רַחוּם כַּהֲלָכָה ⁣ שִׁנְאַנָּיו יֹאמְרוּ לוֹ
לְךָ וּלְךָ, לְךָ כִּי לְךָ, לְךָ אַף לְךָ, לְךָ יהוה הַמַּמְלָכָה
כִּי לוֹ נָאֶה, כִּי לוֹ יָאֶה

תַּקִּיף בִּמְלוּכָה ⁣ תּוֹמֵךְ כַּהֲלָכָה ⁣ תְּמִימָיו יֹאמְרוּ לוֹ
לְךָ וּלְךָ, לְךָ כִּי לְךָ, לְךָ אַף לְךָ, לְךָ יהוה הַמַּמְלָכָה
כִּי לוֹ נָאֶה, כִּי לוֹ יָאֶה

נרצה

חֲסַל סִדּוּר פֶּסַח כְּהִלְכָתוֹ, כְּכָל מִשְׁפָּטוֹ וְחֻקָּתוֹ
כַּאֲשֶׁר זָכִינוּ לְסַדֵּר אוֹתוֹ, כֵּן נִזְכֶּה לַעֲשׂוֹתוֹ
זָךְ שׁוֹכֵן מְעוֹנָה, קוֹמֵם קְהַל עֲדַת מִי מָנָה
קָרֵב נַהֵל נִטְעֵי כַנָּה, פְּדוּיִים לְצִיּוֹן בְּרִנָּה.

לְשָׁנָה הַבָּאָה בִּירוּשָׁלַיִם הַבְּנוּיָה.

Outside Israel, the Omer is counted on the second night of the festival.

בָּרוּךְ Blessed are You, Lᴏʀᴅ our God
King of the Universe,
who has made us holy through His commandments,
and has commanded us about counting the Omer.

Hᴏday is the first day of the Omer.

אַדִּיר הוּא HE IS MAJESTIC
may He build His house soon,
soon,
speedily in our days.
Build, O God,
build, O God,
build Your house soon.

He is chosen,	He is great,	He is unmistakable
He is glorious,	He is venerable,	He is worthy
He is kind,	He is pure,	He is One
He is mighty,	He is learned,	He is King
He is awesome,	He is elevated,	He is strong
He is Savior,	He is righteous,	He is holy
He is compassionate,	He is Almighty,	He is powerful

may He build His house soon,
soon,
speedily in our days.
Build, O God,
build, O God,
BUILD YOUR HOUSE SOON.

Outside ארץ ישראל, *the* עומר *is counted on the second night of the festival.*

בָּרוּךְ אַתָּה יהוה אֱלֹהֵינוּ מֶלֶךְ הָעוֹלָם
אֲשֶׁר קִדְּשָׁנוּ בְּמִצְוֹתָיו, וְצִוָּנוּ עַל סְפִירַת הָעֹמֶר.

הַיּוֹם יוֹם אֶחָד בָּעֹמֶר.

אַדִּיר הוּא

יִבְנֶה בֵּיתוֹ בְּקָרוֹב
בִּמְהֵרָה בִּמְהֵרָה,
בְּיָמֵינוּ בְּקָרוֹב
אֵל בְּנֵה   אֵל בְּנֵה   בְּנֵה בֵּיתְךָ בְּקָרוֹב

דָּגוּל הוּא	גָּדוֹל הוּא	בָּחוּר הוּא
זַכַּאי הוּא	וָתִיק הוּא	הָדוּר הוּא
יָחִיד הוּא	טָהוֹר הוּא	חָסִיד הוּא
מֶלֶךְ הוּא	לָמוּד הוּא	כַּבִּיר הוּא
עִזּוּז הוּא	שַׂגִּיב הוּא	נוֹרָא הוּא
קָדוֹשׁ הוּא	צַדִּיק הוּא	פּוֹדֶה הוּא
תַּקִּיף הוּא	שַׁדַּי הוּא	רַחוּם הוּא

יִבְנֶה בֵּיתוֹ בְּקָרוֹב
בִּמְהֵרָה בִּמְהֵרָה,
בְּיָמֵינוּ בְּקָרוֹב
אֵל בְּנֵה   אֵל בְּנֵה

בְּנֵה בֵּיתְךָ בְּקָרוֹב

אֶחָד מִי יוֹדֵעַ WHO K.NOWS ONE?
Who knows one?
I know one:
our God is One, in heaven and on earth.

Who knows two?
I know two:
two Tablets of the Covenant;
but our God is One,
in heaven and on earth.

Who knows three?
I know three:
three fathers,
two Tablets of the Covenant;
but our God is One,
in heaven and on earth.

Who knows four?
I know four:
four mothers, three fathers,
two Tablets of the Covenant;
but our God is One,
in heaven and on earth.

Who knows five?
I know five:
five books of the Torah,
four mothers, three fathers,
two Tablets of the Covenant;
but our God is One,
in heaven and on earth.

אֶחָד מִי יוֹדֵעַ

אֶחָד אֲנִי יוֹדֵעַ
אֶחָד אֱלֹהֵינוּ שֶׁבַּשָּׁמַיִם וּבָאָרֶץ

שְׁנַיִם מִי יוֹדֵעַ
שְׁנַיִם אֲנִי יוֹדֵעַ
שְׁנֵי לוּחוֹת הַבְּרִית
אֶחָד אֱלֹהֵינוּ שֶׁבַּשָּׁמַיִם וּבָאָרֶץ

שְׁלוֹשָׁה מִי יוֹדֵעַ
שְׁלוֹשָׁה אֲנִי יוֹדֵעַ
שְׁלוֹשָׁה אָבוֹת
שְׁנֵי לוּחוֹת הַבְּרִית
אֶחָד אֱלֹהֵינוּ שֶׁבַּשָּׁמַיִם וּבָאָרֶץ

אַרְבַּע מִי יוֹדֵעַ
אַרְבַּע אֲנִי יוֹדֵעַ
אַרְבַּע אִמָּהוֹת
שְׁלוֹשָׁה אָבוֹת
שְׁנֵי לוּחוֹת הַבְּרִית
אֶחָד אֱלֹהֵינוּ שֶׁבַּשָּׁמַיִם וּבָאָרֶץ

חֲמִשָּׁה מִי יוֹדֵעַ
חֲמִשָּׁה אֲנִי יוֹדֵעַ
חֲמִשָּׁה חֻמְשֵׁי תוֹרָה
אַרְבַּע אִמָּהוֹת   שְׁלוֹשָׁה אָבוֹת   שְׁנֵי לוּחוֹת הַבְּרִית
אֶחָד אֱלֹהֵינוּ שֶׁבַּשָּׁמַיִם וּבָאָרֶץ

Who knows six?
I know six:
six divisions of the Mishna,
five books of the Torah,
four mothers, three fathers,
two Tablets of the Covenant;
but our God is One,
in heaven and on earth.

Who knows seven?
I know seven:
seven days from Sabbath to Sabbath,
six divisions of the Mishna,
five books of the Torah,
four mothers,
three fathers,
two Tablets of the Covenant;
but our God is One,
in heaven and on earth.

Who knows eight?
I know eight:
eight days to a *brit*,
seven days from Sabbath to Sabbath,
six divisions of the Mishna,
five books of the Torah,
four mothers,
three fathers,
two Tablets of the Covenant;
but our God is One,
in heaven and on earth.

שִׁשָּׁה מִי יוֹדֵעַ

שִׁשָּׁה אֲנִי יוֹדֵעַ

שִׁשָּׁה סִדְרֵי מִשְׁנָה

חֲמִשָּׁה חֻמְשֵׁי תוֹרָה   אַרְבַּע אִמָּהוֹת

שְׁלוֹשָׁה אָבוֹת

שְׁנֵי לוּחוֹת הַבְּרִית

אֶחָד אֱלֹהֵינוּ שֶׁבַּשָּׁמַיִם וּבָאָרֶץ

שִׁבְעָה מִי יוֹדֵעַ

שִׁבְעָה אֲנִי יוֹדֵעַ

שִׁבְעָה יְמֵי שַׁבַּתָּא

שִׁשָּׁה סִדְרֵי מִשְׁנָה   חֲמִשָּׁה חֻמְשֵׁי תוֹרָה

אַרְבַּע אִמָּהוֹת   שְׁלוֹשָׁה אָבוֹת

שְׁנֵי לוּחוֹת הַבְּרִית

אֶחָד אֱלֹהֵינוּ שֶׁבַּשָּׁמַיִם וּבָאָרֶץ

שְׁמוֹנָה מִי יוֹדֵעַ

שְׁמוֹנָה אֲנִי יוֹדֵעַ

שְׁמוֹנָה יְמֵי מִילָה

שִׁבְעָה יְמֵי שַׁבַּתָּא   שִׁשָּׁה סִדְרֵי מִשְׁנָה

חֲמִשָּׁה חֻמְשֵׁי תוֹרָה   אַרְבַּע אִמָּהוֹת

שְׁלוֹשָׁה אָבוֹת

שְׁנֵי לוּחוֹת הַבְּרִית

אֶחָד אֱלֹהֵינוּ שֶׁבַּשָּׁמַיִם וּבָאָרֶץ

Who knows nine?
I know nine:
nine months until birth,
eight days to a *brit*,
seven days from Sabbath to Sabbath,
six divisions of the Mishna, five books of the Torah,
four mothers, three fathers,
two Tablets of the Covenant;
but our God is One,
in heaven and on earth.

Who knows ten?
I know ten:
Ten Commandments,
nine months until birth,
eight days to a *brit*,
seven days from Sabbath to Sabbath,
six divisions of the Mishna, five books of the Torah,
four mothers, three fathers,
two Tablets of the Covenant;
but our God is One,
in heaven and on earth.

Who knows eleven?
I know eleven:
eleven stars [in Joseph's dream],
Ten Commandments,
nine months until birth,
eight days to a *brit*,
seven days from Sabbath to Sabbath,
six divisions of the Mishna, five books of the Torah,
four mothers, three fathers,
two Tablets of the Covenant;
but our God is One,
in heaven and on earth.

תִּשְׁעָה מִי יוֹדֵעַ

תִּשְׁעָה אֲנִי יוֹדֵעַ

תִּשְׁעָה יַרְחֵי לֵדָה

שְׁמוֹנָה יְמֵי מִילָה   שִׁבְעָה יְמֵי שַׁבַּתָּא

שִׁשָּׁה סִדְרֵי מִשְׁנָה   חֲמִשָּׁה חֻמְשֵׁי תוֹרָה

אַרְבַּע אִמָּהוֹת   שְׁלוֹשָׁה אָבוֹת   שְׁנֵי לוּחוֹת הַבְּרִית

אֶחָד אֱלֹהֵינוּ שֶׁבַּשָּׁמַיִם וּבָאָרֶץ

עֲשָׂרָה מִי יוֹדֵעַ

עֲשָׂרָה אֲנִי יוֹדֵעַ

עֲשָׂרָה דִבְּרַיָא

תִּשְׁעָה יַרְחֵי לֵדָה   שְׁמוֹנָה יְמֵי מִילָה

שִׁבְעָה יְמֵי שַׁבַּתָּא   שִׁשָּׁה סִדְרֵי מִשְׁנָה

חֲמִשָּׁה חֻמְשֵׁי תוֹרָה   אַרְבַּע אִמָּהוֹת   שְׁלוֹשָׁה אָבוֹת

שְׁנֵי לוּחוֹת הַבְּרִית

אֶחָד אֱלֹהֵינוּ שֶׁבַּשָּׁמַיִם וּבָאָרֶץ

אַחַד עָשָׂר מִי יוֹדֵעַ

אַחַד עָשָׂר אֲנִי יוֹדֵעַ

אַחַד עָשָׂר כּוֹכְבַיָא

עֲשָׂרָה דִבְּרַיָא   תִּשְׁעָה יַרְחֵי לֵדָה

שְׁמוֹנָה יְמֵי מִילָה   שִׁבְעָה יְמֵי שַׁבַּתָּא

שִׁשָּׁה סִדְרֵי מִשְׁנָה   חֲמִשָּׁה חֻמְשֵׁי תוֹרָה

אַרְבַּע אִמָּהוֹת   שְׁלוֹשָׁה אָבוֹת   שְׁנֵי לוּחוֹת הַבְּרִית

אֶחָד אֱלֹהֵינוּ שֶׁבַּשָּׁמַיִם וּבָאָרֶץ

Who knows twelve?
I know twelve:
twelve tribes, eleven stars,
Ten Commandments,
nine months until birth,
eight days to a *brit*,
seven days from Sabbath to Sabbath,
six divisions of the Mishna,
five books of the Torah,
four mothers, three fathers,
two Tablets of the Covenant;
but our God is One,
in heaven and on earth.

Who knows thirteen?
I know thirteen:
thirteen attributes [of God's compassion],
twelve tribes,
eleven stars,
Ten Commandments,
nine months until birth,
eight days to a *brit*,
seven days from Sabbath to Sabbath,
six divisions of the Mishna,
five books of the Torah,
four mothers,
three fathers,
two Tablets of the Covenant;
BUT OUR GOD IS ONE, IN HEAVEN AND ON EARTH.

שְׁנֵים עָשָׂר מִי יוֹדֵעַ

שְׁנֵים עָשָׂר אֲנִי יוֹדֵעַ

שְׁנֵים עָשָׂר שִׁבְטַיָּא

אַחַד עָשָׂר כּוֹכְבַיָּא   עֲשָׂרָה דִבְּרַיָּא

תִּשְׁעָה יַרְחֵי לֵדָה   שְׁמוֹנָה יְמֵי מִילָה

שִׁבְעָה יְמֵי שַׁבַּתָּא   שִׁשָּׁה סִדְרֵי מִשְׁנָה

חֲמִשָּׁה חֻמְשֵׁי תוֹרָה   אַרְבַּע אִמָּהוֹת

שְׁלוֹשָׁה אָבוֹת

שְׁנֵי לוּחוֹת הַבְּרִית

אֶחָד אֱלֹהֵינוּ שֶׁבַּשָּׁמַיִם וּבָאָרֶץ

שְׁלוֹשָׁה עָשָׂר מִי יוֹדֵעַ

שְׁלוֹשָׁה עָשָׂר אֲנִי יוֹדֵעַ

שְׁלוֹשָׁה עָשָׂר מִדַּיָּא

שְׁנֵים עָשָׂר שִׁבְטַיָּא   אַחַד עָשָׂר כּוֹכְבַיָּא

עֲשָׂרָה דִבְּרַיָּא   תִּשְׁעָה יַרְחֵי לֵדָה

שְׁמוֹנָה יְמֵי מִילָה   שִׁבְעָה יְמֵי שַׁבַּתָּא

שִׁשָּׁה סִדְרֵי מִשְׁנָה   חֲמִשָּׁה חֻמְשֵׁי תוֹרָה

אַרְבַּע אִמָּהוֹת

שְׁלוֹשָׁה אָבוֹת

שְׁנֵי לוּחוֹת הַבְּרִית

אֶחָד אֱלֹהֵינוּ שֶׁבַּשָּׁמַיִם וּבָאָרֶץ

חַד גַּדְיָא

ONE LITTLE GOAT
one little goat
my father bought for two zuzim;
one little goat, one little goat.

Along came a cat and ate the goat
my father bought for two zuzim;
one little goat, one little goat.

Then came a dog and bit the cat
who ate the goat
my father bought for two zuzim;
one little goat, one little goat.

Then came a stick and hit the dog
who bit the cat who ate the goat
my father bought for two zuzim;
one little goat, one little goat.

Then came a fire and burned the stick
that hit the dog who bit the cat
who ate the goat
my father bought for two zuzim;
one little goat, one little goat.

Then came water and put out the fire
that burned the stick that hit the dog
who bit the cat who ate the goat
my father bought for two zuzim;
one little goat, one little goat.

חַד גַּדְיָא   חַד גַּדְיָא

דְּזַבִּן אַבָּא בִּתְרֵי זוּזֵי

חַד גַּדְיָא   חַד גַּדְיָא

וַאֲתָא שׁוּנְרָא   וְאָכְלָה לְגַדְיָא

דְּזַבִּן אַבָּא בִּתְרֵי זוּזֵי

חַד גַּדְיָא   חַד גַּדְיָא

וַאֲתָא כַלְבָּא   וְנָשַׁךְ לְשׁוּנְרָא   דְּאָכְלָה לְגַדְיָא

דְּזַבִּן אַבָּא בִּתְרֵי זוּזֵי

חַד גַּדְיָא   חַד גַּדְיָא

וַאֲתָא חֻטְרָא   וְהִכָּה לְכַלְבָּא   דְּנָשַׁךְ לְשׁוּנְרָא

דְּאָכְלָה לְגַדְיָא

דְּזַבִּן אַבָּא בִּתְרֵי זוּזֵי

חַד גַּדְיָא   חַד גַּדְיָא

וַאֲתָא נוּרָא   וְשָׂרַף לְחֻטְרָא   דְּהִכָּה לְכַלְבָּא

דְּנָשַׁךְ לְשׁוּנְרָא   דְּאָכְלָה לְגַדְיָא

דְּזַבִּן אַבָּא בִּתְרֵי זוּזֵי

חַד גַּדְיָא   חַד גַּדְיָא

וַאֲתָא מַיָּא   וְכָבָה לְנוּרָא   דְּשָׂרַף לְחֻטְרָא   דְּהִכָּה לְכַלְבָּא

דְּנָשַׁךְ לְשׁוּנְרָא   דְּאָכְלָה לְגַדְיָא

דְּזַבִּן אַבָּא בִּתְרֵי זוּזֵי

חַד גַּדְיָא   חַד גַּדְיָא

Then came an ox
and drank the water that put out the fire
that burned the stick that hit the dog
who bit the cat
who ate the goat
my father bought for two zuzim;
one little goat, one little goat.

Then came a slaughterer and slew the ox
who drank the water that put out the fire
that burned the stick that hit the dog who
bit the cat who ate the goat
my father bought for two zuzim;
one little goat, one little goat.

Then came the Angel of Death
and slew the slaughterer
who slew the ox
who drank the water that put out the fire
that burned the stick that hit the dog who
bit the cat who ate the goat
my father bought for two zuzim;
one little goat, one little goat.

Then came the Holy One
and slew the Angel of Death,
who slew the slaughterer
who slew the ox
who drank the water that put out the fire
that burned the stick that hit the dog
who bit the cat who ate the goat
my father bought for two zuzim;
ONE LITTLE GOAT, ONE LITTLE GOAT.

וְאָתָא תוֹרָא   וְשָׁתָה לְמַיָּא   דְּכָבָה לְנוּרָא   דְּשָׂרַף לְחֻטְרָא
דְּהִכָּה לְכַלְבָּא   דְּנָשַׁךְ לְשׁוּנְרָא   דְּאָכְלָה לְגַדְיָא
דְּזַבִּן אַבָּא בִּתְרֵי זוּזֵי
חַד גַּדְיָא   חַד גַּדְיָא

וְאָתָא הַשּׁוֹחֵט   וְשָׁחַט לְתוֹרָא   דְּשָׁתָא לְמַיָּא
דְּכָבָה לְנוּרָא   דְּשָׂרַף לְחֻטְרָא   דְּהִכָּה לְכַלְבָּא
דְּנָשַׁךְ לְשׁוּנְרָא
דְּאָכְלָה לְגַדְיָא
דְּזַבִּן אַבָּא בִּתְרֵי זוּזֵי
חַד גַּדְיָא   חַד גַּדְיָא

וְאָתָא מַלְאַךְ הַמָּוֶת   וְשָׁחַט לְשׁוֹחֵט   דְּשָׁחַט לְתוֹרָא
דְּשָׁתָא לְמַיָּא   דְּכָבָה לְנוּרָא   דְּשָׂרַף לְחֻטְרָא
דְּהִכָּה לְכַלְבָּא   דְּנָשַׁךְ לְשׁוּנְרָא
דְּאָכְלָה לְגַדְיָא
דְּזַבִּן אַבָּא בִּתְרֵי זוּזֵי
חַד גַּדְיָא   חַד גַּדְיָא

וְאָתָא הַקָּדוֹשׁ בָּרוּךְ הוּא   וְשָׁחַט לְמַלְאַךְ הַמָּוֶת
דְּשָׁחַט לְשׁוֹחֵט   דְּשָׁחַט לְתוֹרָא   דְּשָׁתָא לְמַיָּא
דְּכָבָה לְנוּרָא   דְּשָׂרַף לְחֻטְרָא   דְּהִכָּה לְכַלְבָּא
דְּנָשַׁךְ לְשׁוּנְרָא
דְּאָכְלָה לְגַדְיָא
דְּזַבִּן אַבָּא בִּתְרֵי זוּזֵי
חַד גַּדְיָא   חַד גַּדְיָא